IMAGES
of Rail

Louisville & Nashville Railroad in South Central Kentucky

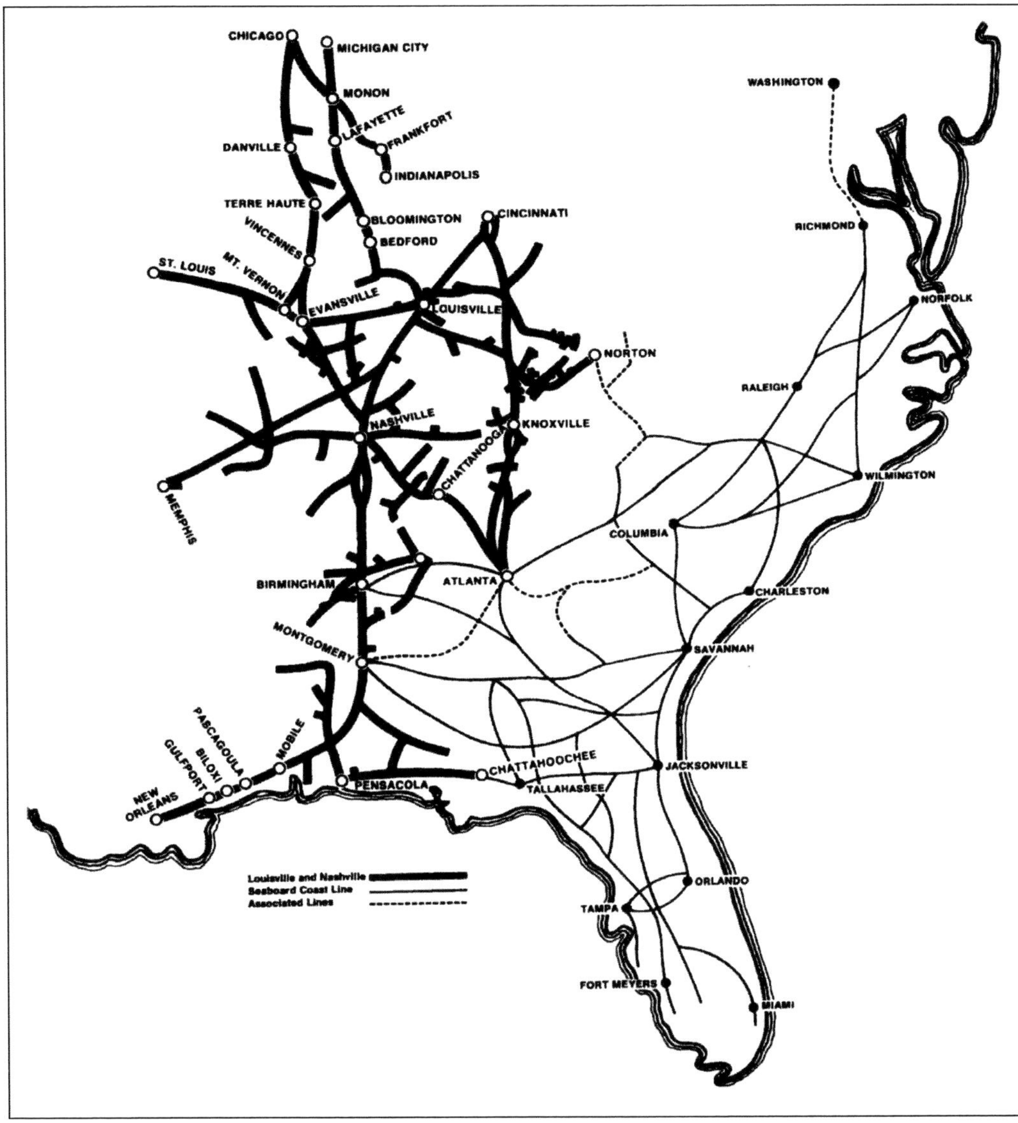

This map shows the Louisville & Nashville Railroad 6,500-mile system as Seaboard Coast Line Industries acquired control of the L&N in 1972. The L&N had acquired 287 miles of the Chicago & Eastern Illinois Railroad in 1969 and purchased the 541-mile Monon Railroad in 1971, providing access to Chicago. The portion of the map between Louisville, Kentucky and Nashville, Tennessee shows the area covered in this title. (L&N records, University of Louisville Archives.)

On the Cover: On May 18, 1942, a crowd gathered at Bowling Green for the arrival of the first road diesels on the Louisville & Nashville (L&N) Railroad. Twin E6 units 450A and 450B have brought train No. 99, the *Pan American*, from Louisville. The steam locomotive at right is on the Memphis section of the *Pan*, train No. 199. E6 450B, later numbered as L&N 770, lies in poor condition at Kentucky Railway Museum as the only surviving unit. (L&N records, University of Louisville Archives.)

IMAGES
of Rail

Louisville & Nashville Railroad in South Central Kentucky

Kevin Comer

ARCADIA
PUBLISHING

ISBN 978-0-7385-9214-5

Published by Arcadia Publishing
Charleston, South Carolina

Printed in the United States of America

Library of Congress Control Number: 2011940280

For all general information, please contact Arcadia Publishing:
Telephone 843-853-2070
Fax 843-853-0044
E-mail sales@arcadiapublishing.com
For customer service and orders:
Toll-Free 1-888-313-2665

Visit us on the Internet at www.arcadiapublishing.com

This book is dedicated to my wonderful family, along with the many people who also enjoy railroading and have become friends, and the employees of the Louisville and Nashville Railroad and its successor, CSX Transportation.

Contents

Acknowledgments 6

Introduction 7

1. Louisville & Nashville Railroad Main Line 11
2. Bowling Green 39
3. Memphis Line 75
4. Glasgow Railway and Mammoth Cave Railroad 87
5. Scottsville Branch 97
6. Family Lines, Seaboard, and CSX 105
7. Historic RailPark and Train Museum 115

ACKNOWLEDGMENTS

I would like to thank the many friends who helped this project come together. Ben Runner Jr. provided some of the images and assisted with scanning slides. Ben and I co-authored a previous Arcadia title, *Bowling Green*, in the Then & Now series. L&N experts Dennis Mize, Steven Johnson, and Lee Yoder provided slides from their collections as well as information about railroad operations. Friends Mike Dowell, Doyle Massey, Greg Lake, and Chris Gadbois provided requested photographs taken by them. Rick Williams contributed images from his collection of Rumsie Butler slides. L&N historian Charlie Castner assisted with finding images in the L&N Collection housed at the University of Louisville Archives as well as providing some of his own personal images and those from his collection from Dave Englert. Carrie Daniels at the University of Louisville was a tremendous help. Allen Haynes provided many images from his collection. Tres Seymour provided images from Mammoth Cave National Park archives. Still more images were provided by the Hart County Historical Society. The Allen County Historical Society and Logan County Public Library were very helpful with information. Leon Garrett allowed use of his wonderful color slides from the late 1940s. G. Marshall Love provided some Bowling Green–related images. Several images and much information came from the Kentucky Library and Museum at Western Kentucky University. A special thank you goes to WKU's Nancy Richey.

Others making photograph contributions were Greg Hughes, James Lee, Bryan Aldridge, Paul Hightower, Dick and Nancy Webber, Elijah C. Lee, J.R. Herron, Thomas Baker, Walter Durham, Floyd Brown, Bryan Snazelle, David Oroszi, James E. Carroll, Eloise Hadden, Auburn Historical Society, the National Park Service, Clifford Kuhl, Transit Authority of River City, Bobby Carter, Cliff Jacobsen, Alex Rose, and Leigh Lessenberry.

Dorian Walker, Brent Price, and Sharon Tabor assisted with items from the Historic RailPark Collection.

This work would not have been completed without the patience and guidance of editors Amy Perryman and Sandy Shalton of Arcadia Publishing.

Thanks also to my family for being supportive of the project and assisting in multiple ways.

Introduction

In southern Kentucky, shiny rails create a path of commerce between north and south, part of a behemoth of a railroad conglomerate that spreads all over the eastern and southern United States. It cuts through the center of small towns and larger cities, sometimes forgotten as it rolls through our daily lives. Today, that company—CSX Transportation—is a busy, profitable, freight-hauling railroad. However, not that long ago, another well-oiled railroad company plied the rails through southern Kentucky and into Tennessee. The Louisville & Nashville Railroad was a giant of a company, providing freight and passenger rail service to towns and cities far and wide, a huge influence on each town and community through which it passed. This is a story of accomplishment that started in the mid-19th century and, after significant changes, continues today.

In the 1830s, larger cities with ports on major navigable rivers were able to ship goods to other towns and cities, in turn receiving needed goods via the same method. This profitable endeavor created much competition between cities. Cities like Louisville, Kentucky, were in competition for this trade with cities like Cincinnati, Ohio, and Nashville, Tennessee. Roads at that time were little more than muddy trails, making transport in that method a tedious adventure. Droughts sometimes impacted the river trade, curtailing commerce. A stagecoach between Louisville & Nashville took 36 hours in the early days of this form of travel. The citizens of Louisville began to see railroads being constructed throughout the 1830s and began to push for a railroad of their own to help their commerce expand. Southern Kentucky towns Glasgow and Bowling Green also began to clamor for railroads. In December 1849, both these towns held meetings calling for railroad construction into Tennessee. In 1850, Louisville supporters met and elected a committee to secure a charter from the Kentucky legislature for a railroad to be built from Louisville south toward Nashville. The L&N received its charter on March 5, 1850. Communities lobbied for the line to pass through their counties, with both Bowling Green and Glasgow wanting the route. Bowling Green went so far as to gain a charter for the Bowling Green & Tennessee Railroad. The L&N amended its charter to build the road based on which communities raised the most subscription monies. Two routes were to be chosen from. The longer, upper route would pass through Bardstown, New Haven, Glasgow, and Scottsville in Kentucky and Gallatin in Tennessee. The shorter route would include Elizabethtown, Bowling Green, and Franklin, Kentucky, as well as Gallatin, Tennessee. By the summer of 1851, the L&N had made no decision. With a line to Memphis planned to join the main line, the lower route seemed to have a slight advantage, as it would be a closer connection. In February 1852, the Bowling Green & Tennessee was given a charter to extend tracks to Nashville or join with any railroad in Tennessee. Survey parties were sent out to plan the route from Bowling Green to Nashville. In May 1852, L&N president L.L. Shreve negotiated a consolidation of the two companies, picked the lower route through Bowling Green, and planned the Memphis Line to be built between Bowling Green and Memphis. The towns of Bardstown and Glasgow would push to connect their towns to the L&N Main Line with the Louisville & Bardstown Railroad (later purchased and known as the L&N Bardstown

Branch) and the Barren County Railroad (later becoming the current Glasgow Railway, owned privately but leased to the L&N and successors).

Work on the main line began in May 1853 but would not be completed until October 1859 due to some obstacles that had to be overcome, such as Muldraugh's Hill, Green River, and Tennessee Ridge. The plan was to build within 200 feet of Muldraugh's summit, then tunnel through. A massive bridge would be required over the Green River, and twin tunnels would cut through Tennessee Ridge. The Lebanon Branch was completed November 10, 1857, and the first trains ran on March 8, 1858, providing the L&N with completed revenue trackage between Louisville and Lebanon via Lebanon Junction. The last main line rail was laid near Glasgow Junction, and on October 27, 1859, the first Louisville-to-Nashville train operated. Temporary tracks bypassed the 2,000-foot-long Muldraugh's Hill Tunnel, which was not opened until January 1, 1860. The Memphis Line was completed on April 10, 1861, just two days prior to the start of the Civil War. Bowling Green, with that Memphis Line connection, became an important component of the L&N.

The L&N would play an important role for both armies during the war. This would be realized on September 18, 1861, when Gen. Simon Bolivar Buckner seized the Memphis Line and the main stem up to Lebanon Junction, before falling back and settling in at the Green River. Bowling Green soon became the headquarters for Gen. Albert Sidney Johnston, commander of the Confederate Army of the West. Bowling Green soon was named the Confederate capitol of Kentucky. To protect the city, river, and railroad, several forts were constructed on the hills surrounding Bowling Green. In October 1861, the Union had reconstructed the burned Bacon Creek Bridge only to have it destroyed again. The Confederates had also dropped two spans of the massive Green River Bridge, cutting the rail line. General Buckner, a native of Munfordville, had not wanted the bridge destroyed, but it came down, ironically by the hands of stonemason Alex Key and his sons, who had worked on the bridge for the L&N but later joined the ranks of the Confederacy.

Two companies of the 32nd Indiana, mostly German immigrants, settled in for the building of a pontoon bridge until the spans could be rebuilt. Before that could take place, Confederate sharpshooters from Gen. Thomas C. Hindman's forces at Cave City fired upon the 32nd, commanded by Col. August Willich. While Willich had been called back to headquarters, Prussian army veteran Col. Henry Von Treba was in command. Col. Benjamin F. Terry's Texas Cavalry ("Terry's Texas Rangers") charged the Yankee line. The skilled horsemen met the German infantry, and the two sides fought to a stalemate before Willich returned and ordered his Germans to fall back slowly. At this time, the 39th Indiana and 49th Ohio crossed the Green River outnumbering the rebels by two to one, and Hindman's forces retreated to Cave City. This 90-minute encounter became known as the Battle of Rowlett's Station, with Col. B.F. Terry being killed.

On February 6, 1862, Gen. Ulysses S. Grant took Fort Henry on the Tennessee River and set sights on Fort Donelson on the Cumberland River. Fearing being cut off, Johnston began evacuating Bowling Green on February 11, 1862, eventually destroying the L&N bridge over Barren River and burning the roundhouse, depot, several warehouses, and town buildings. The Union forces began shelling the town on February 14, hoping to run the confederates out before they could destroy supplies. Entering Bowling Green on February 15, Union soldiers found much destruction. The Union occupied the Confederate fortifications and remained in Bowling Green for the balance of the war.

During mid-September 1862, the Union army under Col. John T. Wilder held the Green River Bridge. The Union had constructed fortifications overlooking the bridge and expected to be able to hold the ground against Confederate assault. The assault came during the early morning hours on September 14, 1862, by Col. John Scott's cavalry. Scott had notified Brigadier General Chalmers at Cave City to join him and take the fortifications. Chalmers arrived and joined in the attack, but Wilder's forces held, handing an initial defeat to Chalmers. Wilder received reinforcements from Louisville, but his requests to Gen. Don Carlos Buell at Bowling Green were ignored. Gen. Braxton Bragg soon arrived with the balance of the Army of the Mississippi and demanded surrender. Wilder, unsure that he was surrounded, asked the advice of the enemy in the form of Gen. Simon Bolivar Buckner of Munfordville. Buckner gave Wilder a tour of the Confederate strength, and Wilder surrendered. Buell eventually moved north, as Bragg headed north, then east, to battle at Perryville, leaving the bridge back to the Union.

Col. John Hunt Morgan, a Confederate raider, did much harm to the L&N by destroying bridges, rail, depots, and storehouses. Morgan's men covertly wreaked havoc on the L&N lines during 1862 and 1863, which hampered operations and proved costly to the L&N Railroad coffers. Morgan's most effective raid resulted in the destruction of the southernmost tunnel of the twin tunnels through Tennessee Ridge north of Gallatin, Tennessee. This destruction closed the L&N line for 98 days.

Late in the war, bands of guerrillas also struck points on the railroad, robbing merchants and burning and destroying railroad property. The L&N battled with the Union army at times over the lengthy delays in moving supplies, while seemingly continuing commercial shipments. The threats of the railroad being taken over by the government never materialized, in part due to L&N president James Guthrie's politics. Despite the constant attacks and having to constantly rebuild track, depots, and bridges, the L&N survived the war, and actually profited over $6 million during the years 1861–1865. The L&N would use these profits to rebuild as well as grow and expand throughout the South after the war.

Albert Fink, the L&N's engineer and designer of the "Fink Truss" bridge at Green River, was instrumental in keeping the L&N repaired during the war. As the war came to an end, the L&N had 60 locomotives, 57 passenger cars, 321 boxcars, 114 flat cars, and 286 miles of track. The L&N began expanding to the north by constructing the Fourteenth Street Bridge over the Ohio River at Louisville, connecting with northern railroads. This eventually led to the L&N changing the gauge of the rails. Southern roads would change from the gauge of mostly 5 feet, to the standard gauge of 4 feet, 8.5 inches. This amazing feat was almost completely done on the L&N in one day, May 30, 1886.

The L&N also began to reach south of Nashville, to Montgomery, Alabama by leasing and, later, purchasing the Nashville & Decatur Railroad and the South & North Alabama Railroad. The Nashville, Chattanooga & St. Louis (NC&StL) Railroad had already linked the L&N to Atlanta, providing important rail transport for the later campaigns of the war. By 1885, the 444-mile trip from Chicago to Nashville could be made in 16 hours by train. By 1898, this time was down to 13.5 hours. Large shops had been constructed in south Louisville, and eventually, spectacular passenger stations were erected at Louisville and Nashville replacing the early stations. Both of these stations survive today in other uses.

In July 1926, a double-tracking project would replace the Muldraugh's Hill Tunnel with a 70-foot-deep, 4,600-foot long cut. The trestles there that were burned by John Hunt Morgan on December 28, 1862, were also replaced with fill from the cut. The L&N had been powered first by wood-burning locomotives and eventually switched to a coal-burning fleet during the 1870s. Many of the early locomotives were constructed by the L&N at its Louisville shops.

Later, many of those powered by steam were made by the railroad's own forces at Louisville. Dieselization on the railroad would begin in 1939 when a couple of diesel switchers were purchased for use in the Louisville yards. This was followed by 12 more switchers in 1941 and several during World War II. In the spring of 1942, about 16 passenger diesels were purchased, followed by both freight and passenger diesel purchases in the late 1940s. Dieselization was ultimately completed by November 3, 1956, and the L&N had 598 diesels in service and 4 on order. The 36 remaining steam locomotives would be scrapped. The final steam locomotive in revenue service was No. 1882 on the Carrollton Railroad making a run from Worthville, Kentucky, to Decoursey, Kentucky, on January 28, 1957. The lone surviving operating L&N steam locomotive, No. 152, pulls excursions at the Kentucky Railway Museum operating on the former Lebanon Branch out of New Haven, Kentucky.

The flagship of the L&N passenger trains was the *Pan American*. The *Pan* operated between Cincinnati and New Orleans with heavyweight coaches beginning in 1921. One of the amenities of the train was that passengers could listen to local radio stations during the trip by using headphones. Later, in 1933, WSM in Nashville began to broadcast the *Pan American* passing by their 878-foot tower just a few miles south of the city.

In the 1940s, the train was equipped with new lightweight streamlined sleepers, diners, lounges, and observation cars. Between 1921 and 1965 at Bowling Green, a section of the *Pan American* would split off and go to Memphis. The *Pan American* would last on the L&N until Amtrak took over the passenger business for almost all North American railroads in May 1971.

In December 1940, the L&N premiered two name streamlined, all-coach passenger trains, the Chicago-to-Miami *South Wind* and the *Dixie Flagler*. The *South Wind* ran between Louisville and Montgomery, Alabama, on the L&N, and the *Dixie Flagler* ran between Evansville and Nashville. The *Dixieland* succeeded the *Flagler* in 1954, lasting until 1957. In the fall of 1946, the L&N ordered equipment for two new name trains, including twenty coaches, four tavern-lounges, and four diners. The *Humming Bird* served between Cincinnati and New Orleans, and initially, the *Georgian* went between St. Louis and Atlanta but was later changed to Chicago to Atlanta in June 1948 with a connection to St. Louis out of Evansville. Soon, sleeping cars were added to both trains. In 1949, a new sleeping car line was added to the *Humming Bird* between New Orleans and Chicago, causing the *Humming Bird* to operate as separate trains between Chicago and Nashville and between Cincinnati and Nashville, with the trains combining south of Nashville. The only L&N passenger train to survive Amtrak Day in 1971 was the Chicago to Miami *South Wind*, which later was renamed the *Floridian*. This train struggled to maintain a schedule, eventually combining with the Louisville-Sanford, Florida Autotrain for a few years, before being discontinued in 1979. This was the last passenger service for the L&N's Louisville-Nashville main line.

No longer in the passenger business, railroads could focus completely on freight service, but competition with trucking led to many railroads' demise. The L&N was one of the major coal hauling railroads, with numerous branch lines leading to mines in eastern Kentucky, where coal was loaded, gathered, and shipped to power plants. The L&N was a progressive railroad, often staying ahead in technological advances and implementing better methods. Competition was often stifled by acquiring control of lines before rivals could do so, even if they were not needed. Expansion was always considered and the L&N acquired parts of the Tennessee Central and part of the Chicago & Eastern Illinois Railroad in 1969, providing a route into Chicago.

A larger acquisition, the Monon Railroad in 1971, provided another route into Chicago. Following this acquisition, in 1972 the L&N became controlled by Seaboard Coast Line Industries, and in 1973, along with Seaboard Coast Line, became one of a group of railroads marketed as the "Family Lines System."

In 1983, the Louisville & Nashville Railroad covered more than 7,000 miles in 13 states and was an icon of the South. The "Family Lines" railroads were all merged into Seaboard System Railroad and after serving for nearly 125 years, the L&N ceased to exist.

Seaboard gave way to CSX Transportation, which after multiple mergers and the spinning off of unwanted track creating short lines and regionals by many railroads, has become one of the dominant railroads in the United States. Even though there are some 650 railroads, just eight—CSX, Norfolk Southern (Norfolk & Western and Southern Railway merger), BNSF (Burlington Northern and Santa Fe merger), Kansas City Southern, Canadian National, Canadian Pacific, Union Pacific, and Amtrak—are classified as Class 1, signifying them as large railroads.

One

Louisville & Nashville Railroad Main Line

The main line or "main stem" of the L&N between Louisville and Amqui, Tennessee, just north of Nashville, completed in 1859, survives today as the CSX "Main Line Subdivision." It follows the same route today as it was laid during construction, south from Louisville, down through Lebanon Junction where the Lebanon Branch heads southeast, past Bardstown Junction where the Bardstown Branch runs southeast off the main line, over Muldraugh's Hill, through Elizabethtown, and farther south in the direction of Bowling Green. In this volume, the concentration will be on the line south of Bonnieville (Bacon Creek), Kentucky, through Bowling Green and Gallatin and on to the end of the main line at Amqui (Edgefield).

During the Civil War, Bacon Creek, Munfordville, and Rowlett's Station were strategic locations where battles were fought over the area bridges. The Green River Bridge was an engineering feat when constructed and is still very impressive today. To the south, the towns of Horse Cave, Cave City, and Park City occupy prominent places along the line. Farther south in Kentucky are the towns of Rocky Hill, Smith's Grove, and Oakland.

At Bowling Green, the L&N constructed large shops and facilities to support the operation of the line. Bowling Green's prominent position on the L&N made it a very heavily fortified city during the Civil War, with the defenses likely keeping it from having a major battle. As the citizens of Bowling Green attempted to charter and construct competitive railroads in the area, L&N president Milton H. Smith moved the large shops and large employee base to Paris, Tennessee. He also is said to have vowed to let the substandard depot in Bowling Green continue to fall into disrepair as long as he lived. Upon his death, Bowling Green did receive a new passenger station, and what a station it was, completed in 1925 in time to see the apex of passenger rail travel.

Just south of Bowling Green, the Memphis Branch left the main line and traveled to Guthrie, Kentucky, before continuing to Memphis. Combined Memphis Branch and main line traffic made Bowling Green a busy hub of the L&N. South of Bowling Green on the original L&N Main Line are the towns of Woodburn and Franklin in Kentucky and Mitchellville and Portland in Tennessee. South of Portland are the famous twin tunnels of South Tunnel, Tennessee, that puncture Tennessee Ridge before reaching Gallatin. Amqui (Edgefield), Tennessee, and the junction the Henderson Line is the end of the original main line, with the combined lines continuing south across the Cumberland River into Nashville. These towns were once served by L&N passenger trains such as the *Pan American*, *Humming Bird*, and *South Wind*, and a few still received service on Amtrak's *Floridian*.

Stations in these towns along the line were the center of activity, with traffic peaking during World War II. By the mid-1960s, many of the small stations had closed. The improvement of the nation's highway system and air travel contributed to a quick decline in passenger trains. Mail transport let some passenger trains hang on until the late 1960s, but by 1970, most trains had been discontinued, with the railroads claiming huge losses on nearly empty trains.

Amtrak took over passenger rail from almost all railroads in May 1971, picking a handful of routes to run the remaining passenger operations. The L&N Main Stem hosted Amtrak's *South Wind* at inception, but the name was soon changed to the *Floridian*. At one point, the Auto Train, a passenger train that would also transport people's automobiles in car carriers, began to run south out of Louisville, eventually combining with the *Floridian*.

The L&N name eventually gave way to Seaboard, as several Family Lines merged together, and, finally, the giant CSX Transportation that runs over the L&N rails today. Much has changed on the main line from the early days, and while it no longer exists, traces of the Louisville & Nashville Railroad can still be found along the line. Visits to the towns on the line show how important the L&N Railroad was to their growth or even their demise as rail travel faded.

Louisville's Union Station opened September 7, 1891. A decade earlier, the L&N had planned to replace the original station at Ninth Street and Broadway that had opened in 1858. The 11-story L&N General Office Building would be completed next door to Union Station in 1907, replacing the company's first office building at Second and Main Streets. After the last passenger services left Union Station in 1976, it became home to Louisville Transit Authority of River City. (Louisville Transit Authority of River City.)

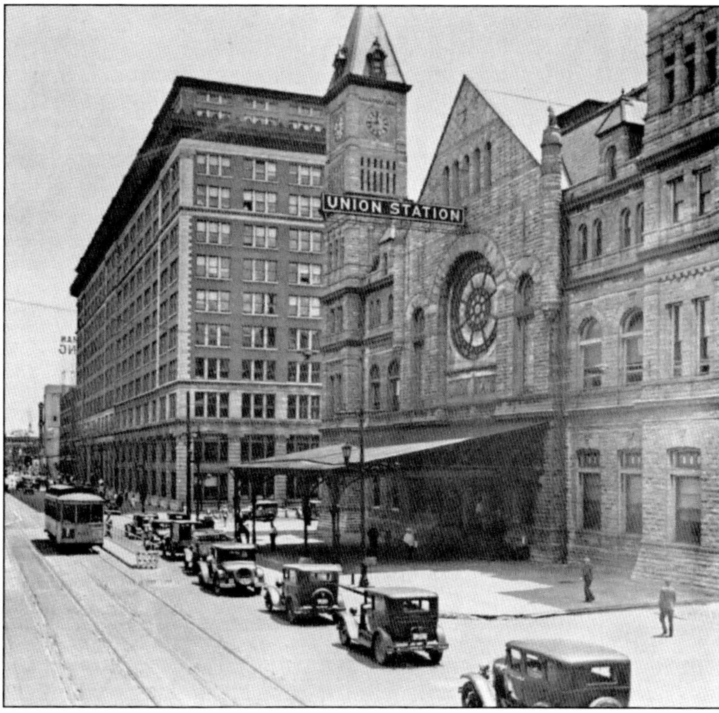

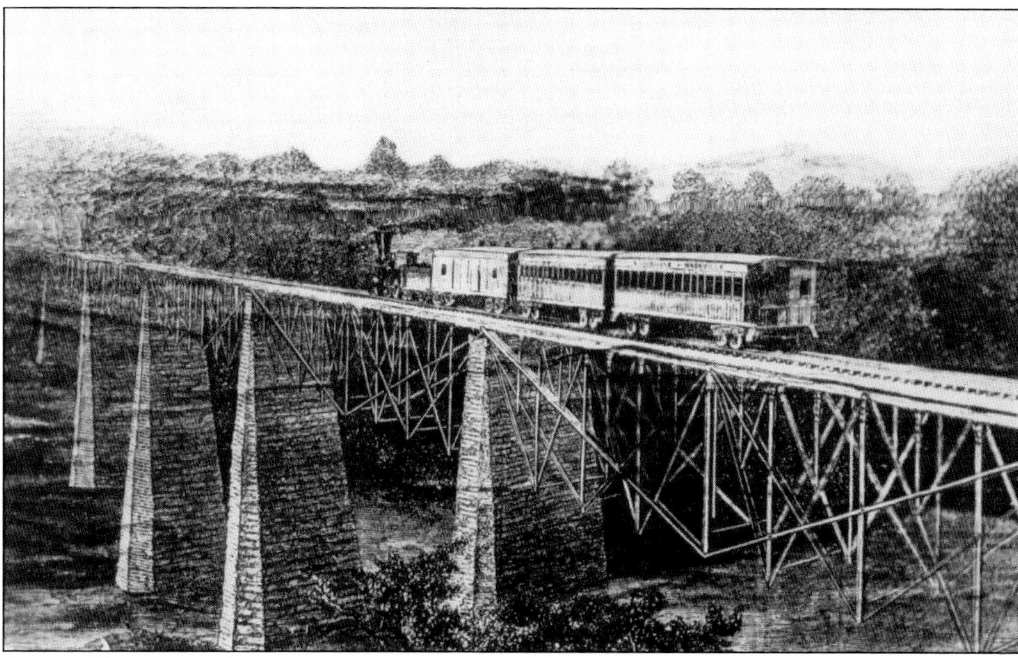

Depicted here around 1859 is a passenger train on the magnificent five-span Green River Bridge, which was 1,800 feet long and 115 feet high and designed by Albert Fink using his "Fink Truss" design. At the time of completion, this was the largest iron bridge in the United States. It was partially destroyed by Confederate general Simon Bolivar Buckner in late 1861, ironically at the hands of the Alex Key family, stonemasons who built the piers. Soon thereafter, Fink rebuilt the destroyed portion. (L&N records, University of Louisville Archives.)

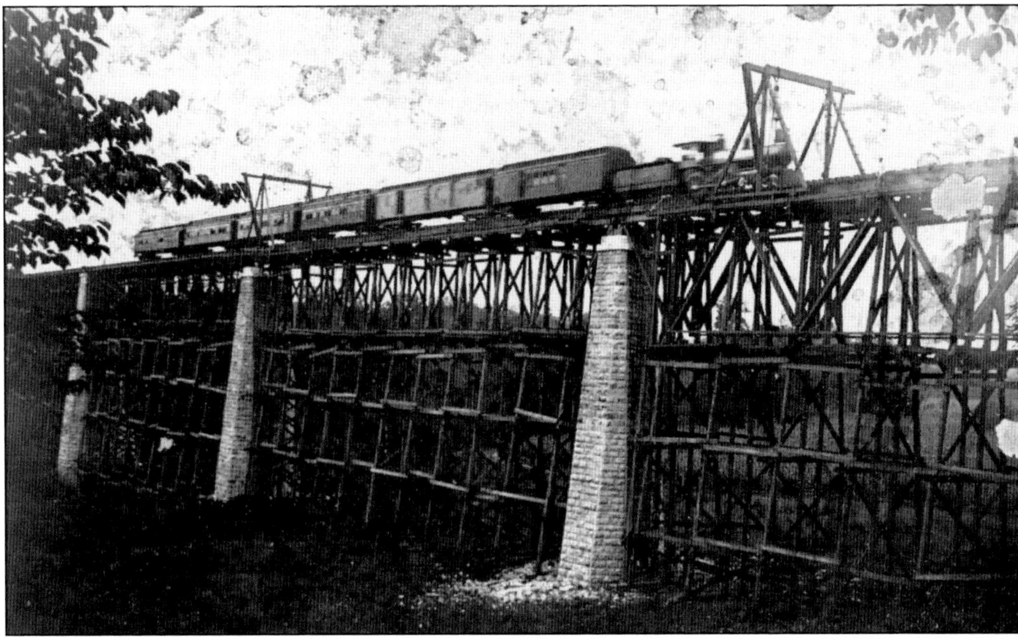

This photograph of the Green River Bridge shows the temporary trestle work during repairs. The bridge was a major objective for both sides during the Civil War, with battles fought at the site and nearby. Quick repairs were necessary to keep rail traffic moving, and troops were stationed along the line to prevent attacks. A large garrison also protected the bridge from both sides of the Green River. (L&N records, University of Louisville Archives.)

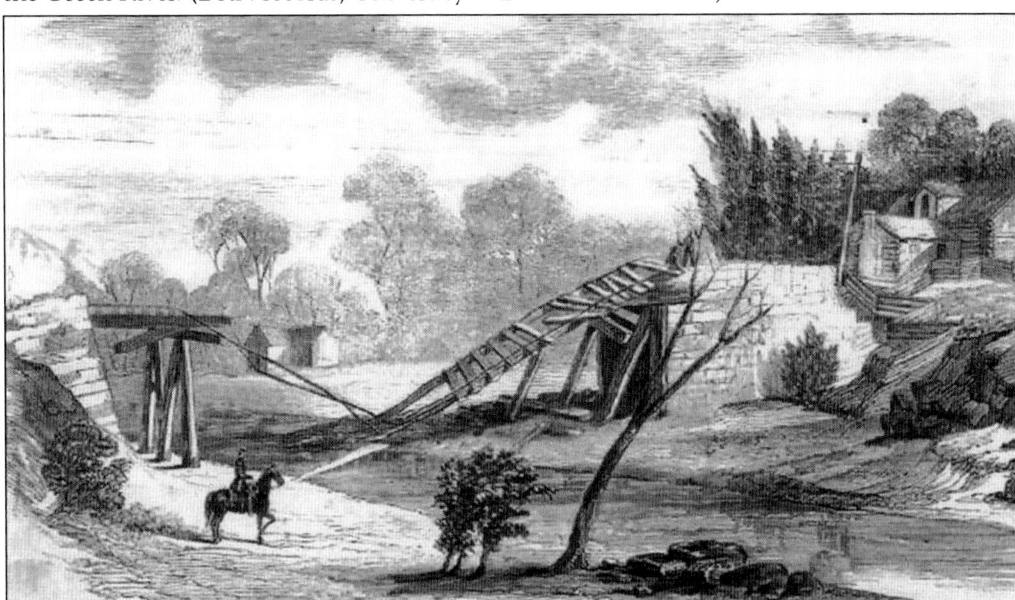

The Bacon Creek Bridge at Bacon Creek (present-day Bonnieville), Kentucky, was burned five times by the Confederates during the Civil War, twice by Gen. John Hunt Morgan. The first bloodshed of the Civil War in Kentucky reportedly happened here on October 10, 1861. This image of the aftermath of the second burning in December 1861 appeared in *Frank Leslie's Illustrated Newspaper* on January 25, 1862. (Kentucky Library and Museum-WKU.)

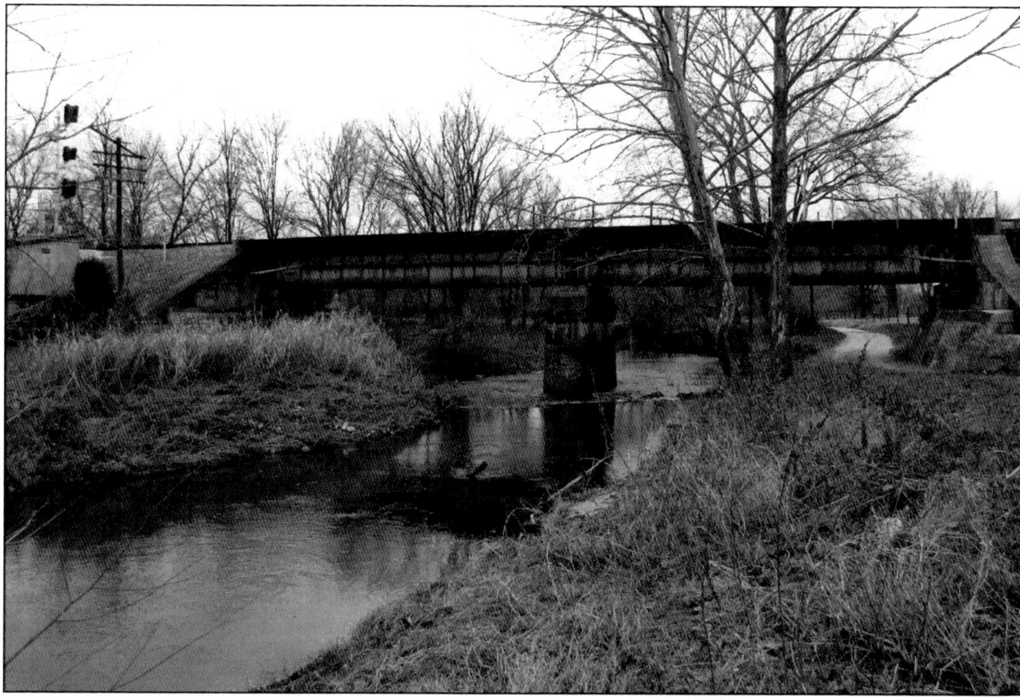

Looking at this area today, one would not suspect that the early bridges at this location were such a strategic military target. A historical marker beside US 31 West at Bonnieville, Kentucky, contains the story of the skirmishes. Today, the Bacon Creek Bridge is just north of the "Bonnieville" siding, where CSX trains meet. (Mike Dowell photograph.)

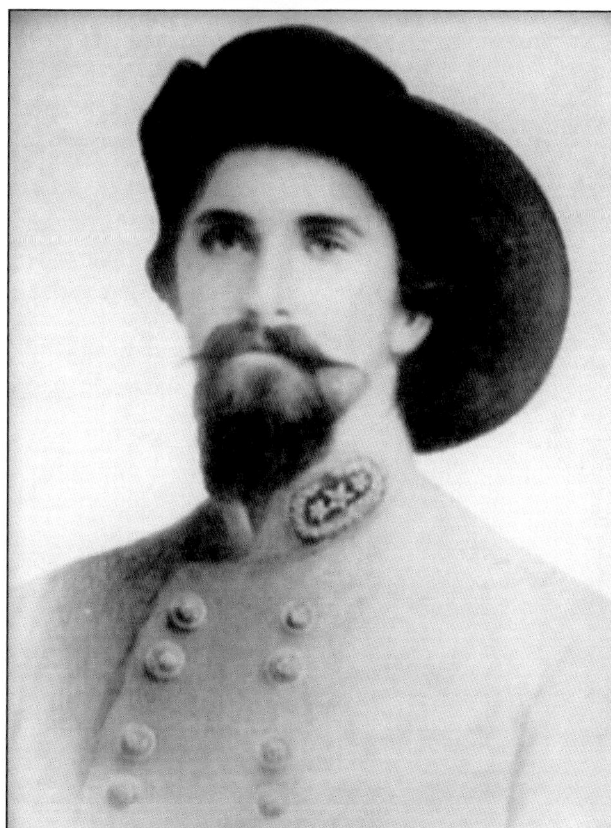

Confederate colonel John Hunt Morgan was a thorn in the side of not only the Union armies but also the Louisville & Nashville Railroad. He was responsible for many acts of destruction, including burning the Bacon Creek Bridge, a train at Cave City, trestles at Muldraugh's Hill, and collapsing one of the south tunnels, closing the line for 98 days. (Kentucky Library and Museum-WKU.)

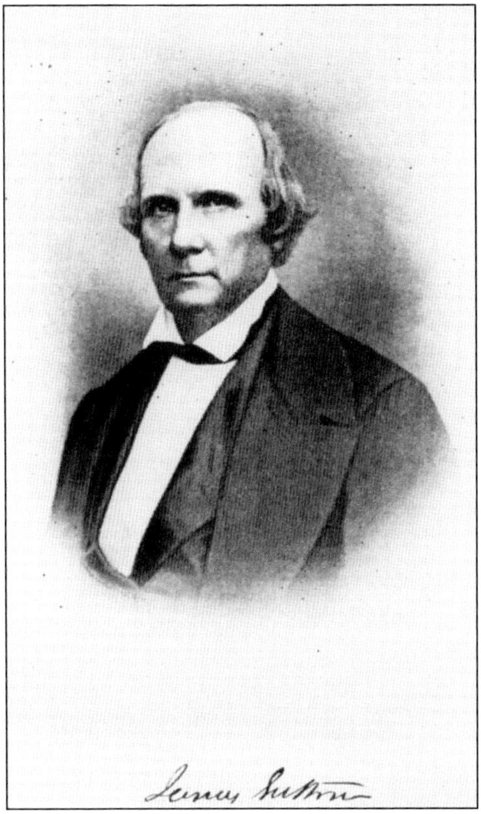

James Guthrie was president of the L&N Railroad from 1860 to 1868 and guided the company through the Civil War years. Guthrie also served in the state legislature from 1827 to 1840, was secretary of the US Treasury from 1853 to 1857, and a US senator from 1865 to 1868. The town of Guthrie, Kentucky, at the crossing of the L&N Memphis Line and L&N Evansville-to-Nashville Line is named for him. (L&N records, University of Louisville Archives.)

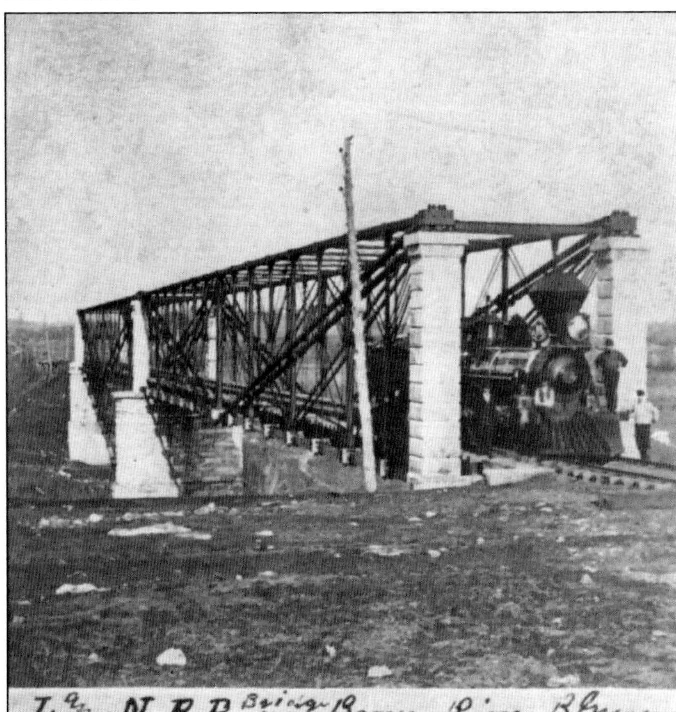

This early undated photograph of the L&N Barren River Bridge shows two truss spans. The bridge, which was destroyed by the Confederates evacuating Bowling Green on February 13, 1862, had two truss spans. During rebuilding, one was salvaged from the wreckage and used in the new temporary bridge. The bridge was completely rebuilt by 1866. (Kentucky Library and Museum-WKU.)

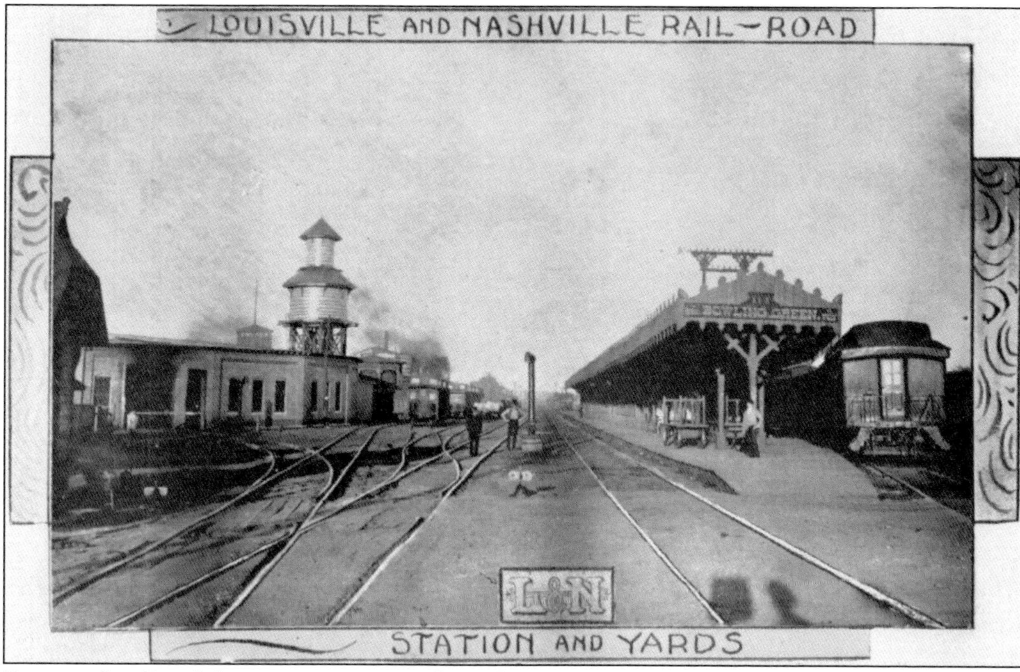

During the Confederate evacuation of Bowling Green on February 13, 1862, the railroad's roundhouse, shops, and brick depot were destroyed along with the Barren River Bridge. By 1863, the roundhouse, shops, and water station had been rebuilt, along with a new depot and express office. In 1870, the L&N constructed a new roundhouse and replaced the freight office. This view is from Main Street looking north. (Kentucky Library and Museum-WKU.)

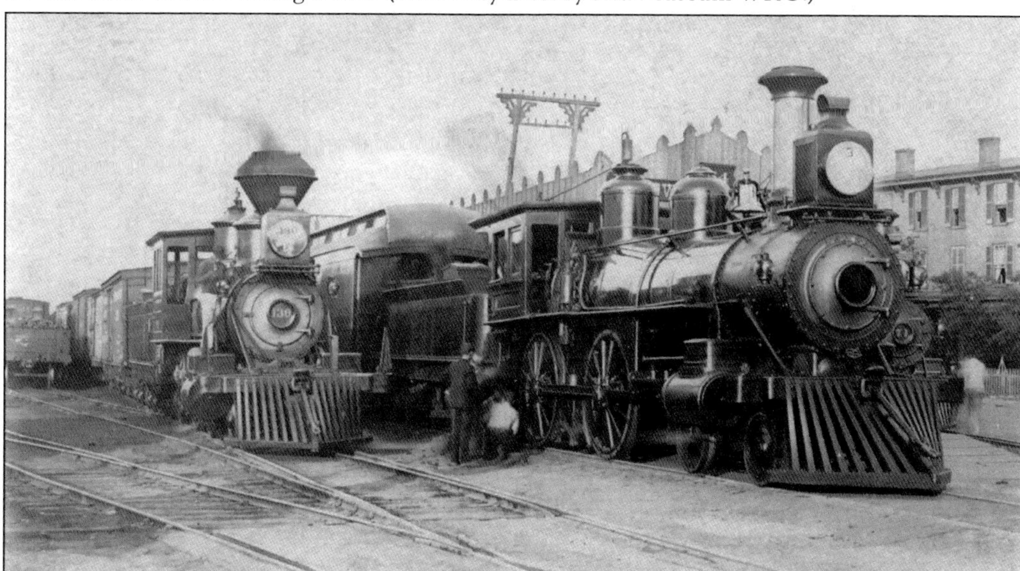

This postcard from 1887 depicts the L&N Bowling Green Station. Hand written on the back are descriptions of the following two locomotives: "L&N No. 130 (2-6-0) Rogers '81, L&N No. 3 (4-4-0) built at L&N shops in Louisville in 1886." It appears to have been a busy time at the station as a third locomotive is partially visible on the other side of the platform. (Kentucky Library and Museum-WKU.)

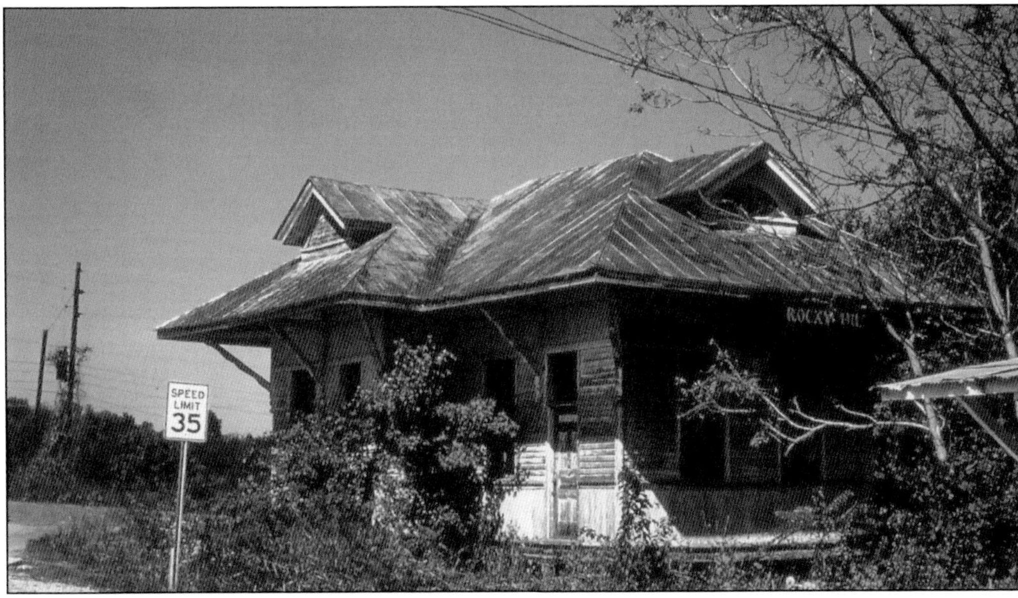

Rocky Hill in Edmonson County, Kentucky, at one time was a thriving community. A devastating fire destroyed most of the town, and it never recovered. A few homes, a post office, and volunteer fire department remain along with the relocated Louisville & Nashville Railroad Depot, pictured here in the 1970s. Rocky Hill was a shipping point for Kyrock Asphalt. The mines near Kyrock produced much of the early paving materials. They even helped cover the Indianapolis Motor Speedway track. (Rumsie Butler photograph, Rick Williams collection.)

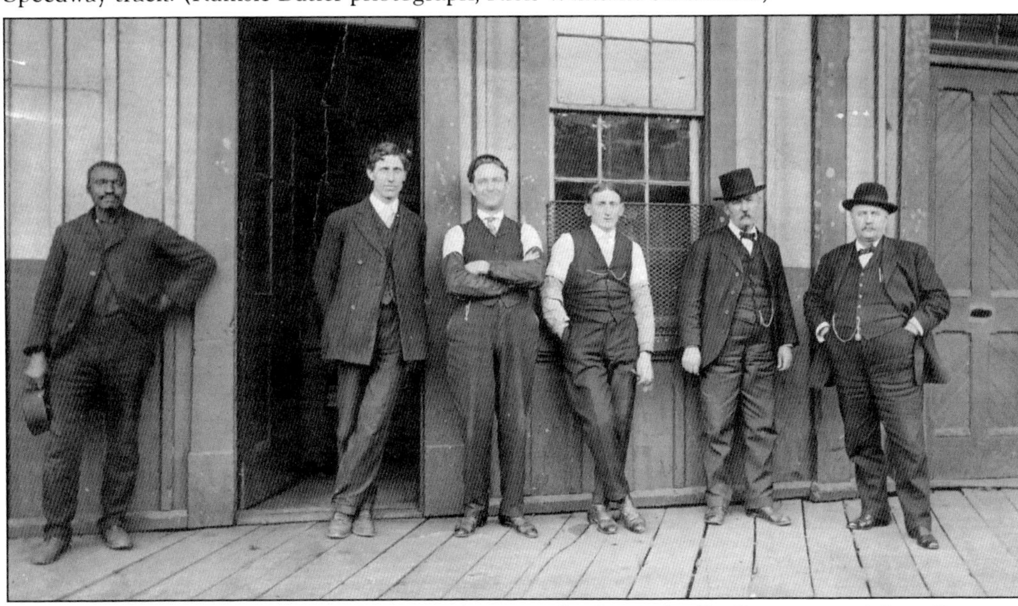

This group of men gathered at the second Louisville & Nashville Depot near Main Street in Bowling Green for a photograph. Pictured are, from left to right, Pat Clark, Andrew Ritter, J.E. Oller, Dick Bennett, J. Lewis Moore, and G.W. Thompson. Thompson was the general agent listed for Bowling Green in both 1906 and 1913. It appears that these men may have all been employees of the L&N. This depot did not stand very long after the new 1925 passenger station was completed. (Kentucky Library and Museum-WKU.)

This photograph from around 1900 shows a large force making repairs to the L&N Barren River Bridge at Bowling Green. From the looks of the repairs, it appears that a derailment may have caused damage to the bridge. (Kentucky Library and Museum-WKU.)

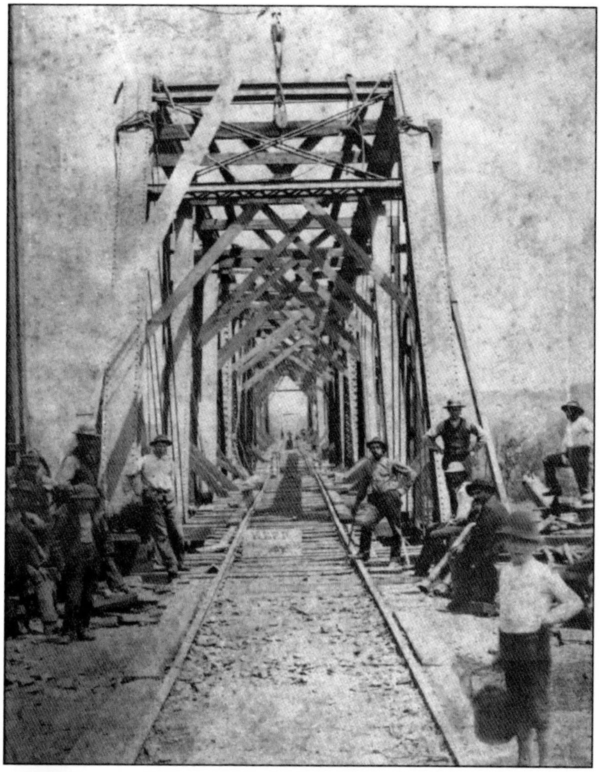

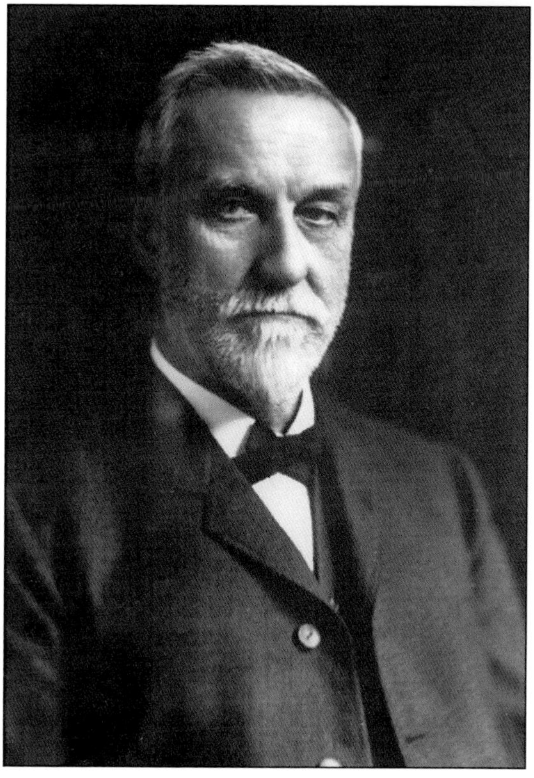

Milton Hannibal Smith began with the L&N in 1866, serving as president from 1884 until his death in 1921. Under his leadership, the railroad grew into one of the most powerful in the South. Smith fought opposition hard and battled citizens of Bowling Green about competition and facilities. Reportedly, a visit to Bowling Green left him bitter toward the town, and promptly, the shops were moved to Paris, Tennessee. Smith vowed that nothing would be built in Bowling Green as long as he was president. He died in 1921 and Bowling Green soon got its desired new passenger station. (L&N records, University of Louisville Archives.)

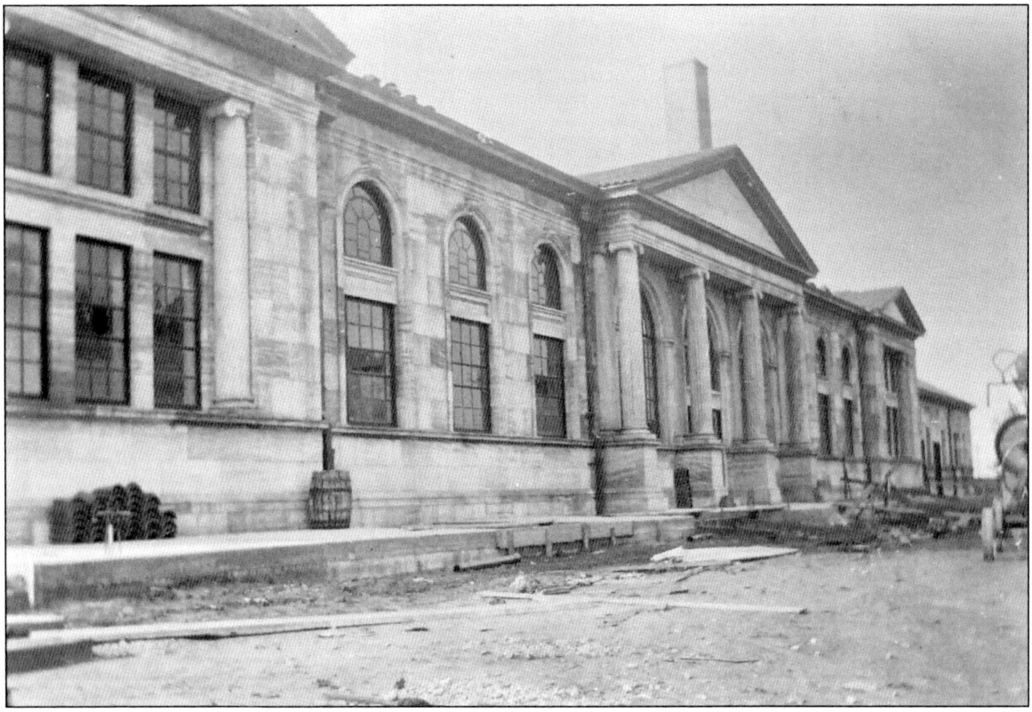

After many years of battle with the L&N Railroad to get a new station erected, the citizens of Bowling Green finally won out. The L&N purchased land in the "Shake Rag" area near Fourth and Curd Streets, just a few blocks north of the existing depot. The exterior would be faced with famous Bowling Green Limestone. (Kentucky Library and Museum-WKU.)

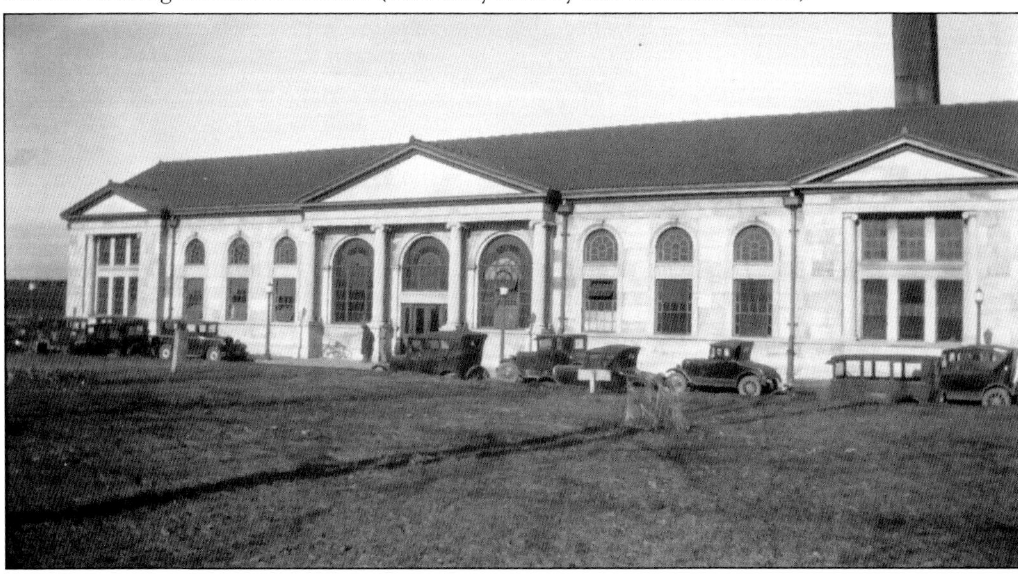

Before building the new station in Bowling Green, the L&N had been considering rerouting the line around the city, with a new station to be constructed along the new route. Eventually, this plan was forgotten, and the new L&N president, Milton Smith's son-in-law Wible L. Mapother, visited Bowling Green to resolve the conflict. His speech was well received, and the city's long battle with the L&N Railroad was left in the past. (Historic RailPark Collection.)

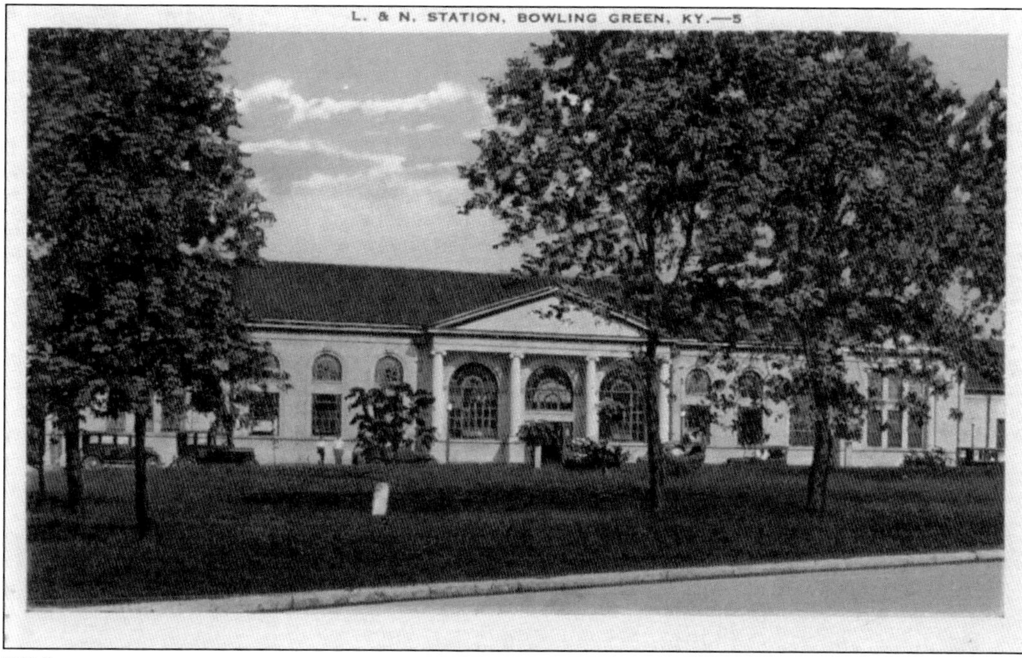

With a new spacious passenger station open in Bowling Green, there was much activity taking place there. Besides the passengers coming and going, locals conducted freight business with the L&N, and taxi companies thrived. The L&N became involved in a lawsuit for contracting with a particular taxi company to allow them a designated parking area and more access to customers than others. (Greg Hughes collection.)

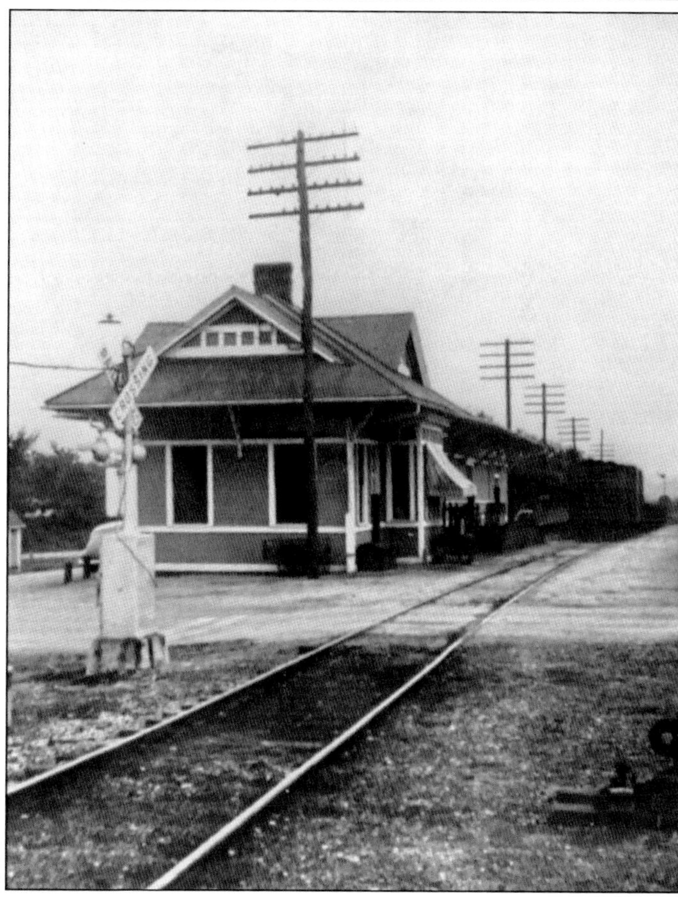

Munfordville was an important location on the L&N during the Civil War. Two battles were fought here for control of the Green River Railroad Bridge. The depot shown here no longer stands but was located on the west side of the town just north of the Green River Bridge. (Hart County Historical Society.)

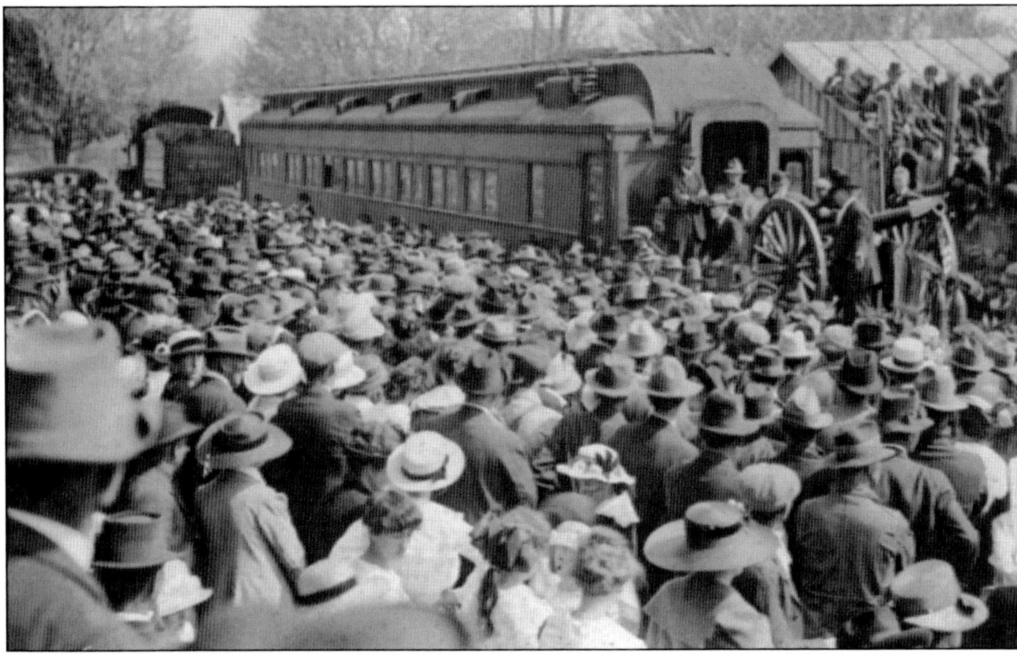

Shown at Munfordville, Kentucky, a large crowd has gathered around a Louisville & Nashville train. The occasion seems to be a Civil War veterans' gathering. Reunions such as this were held in many towns in the years following the conflict. (Hart County Historical Society.)

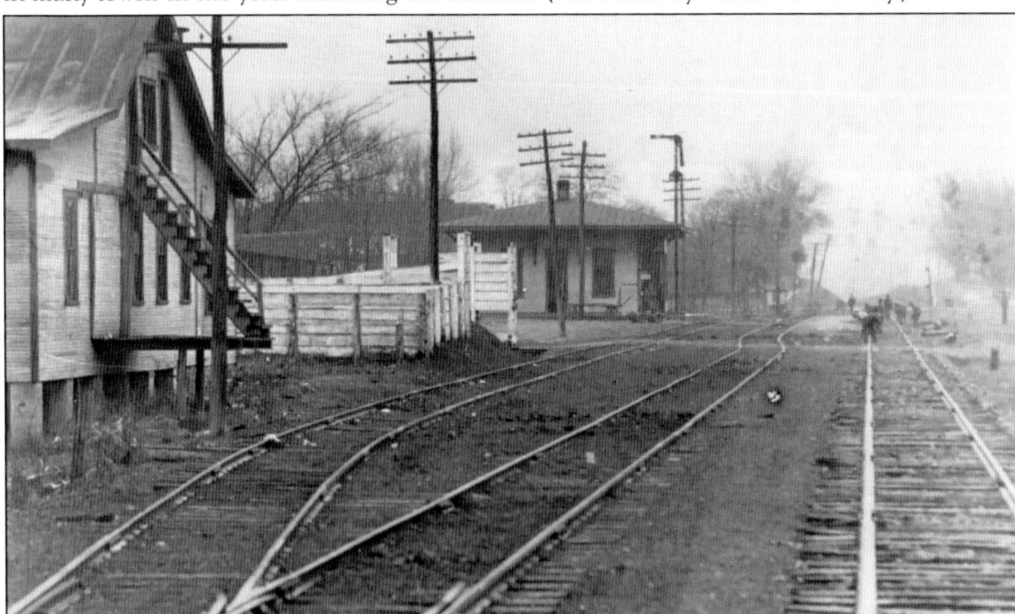

Once the L&N was completed through Cave City in 1859, notables from around the country took advantage of the easier method of reaching and exploring Mammoth Cave. On May 11, 1862, Col. John Hunt Morgan captured a train of railroad employees and sent the empty train down the tracks to explode. Another train arrived with some Union soldiers, wives, and Louisville citizens. Morgan took some soldiers prisoner, releasing the train back to Louisville with the ladies. (L&N records, University of Louisville Archives.)

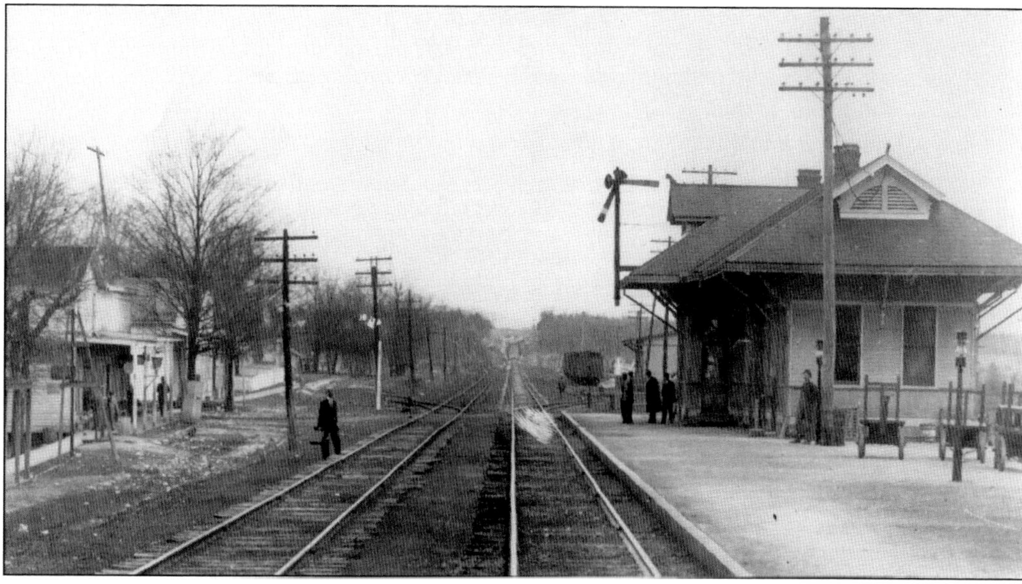

Park City, once called Bell's Tavern, Three Forks, and Glasgow Junction, once served three railroads. The Mammoth Cave Railroad ceased operation, but the CSX Main Line Subdivision passes through town, and there is a connection for the Glasgow Railway, a 10-mile line serving the Barren County seat. The depot no longer stands, but each weekday, a local CSX train out of Bowling Green serves industries at Park City and Glasgow before returning to the CSX yard. (L&N records, University of Louisville Archives.)

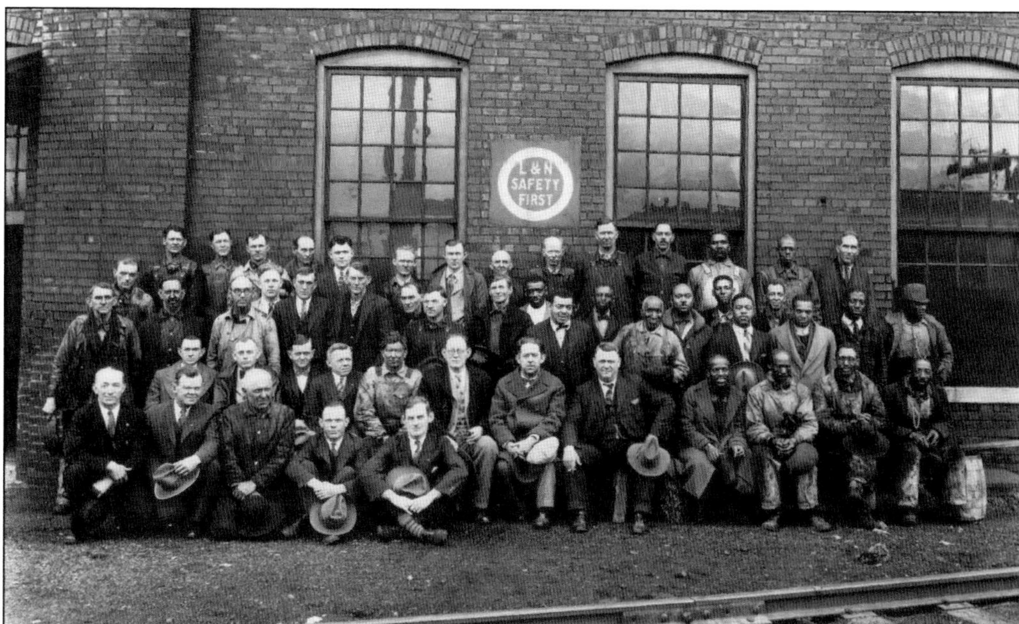

The employees of Bowling Green's Louisville & Nashville Railroad shops gathered for a photograph in front of the roundhouse in 1928. The force was recognized for being 100-percent safe for a month. The forces of Bowling Green's shops were much smaller than they had been in the past when a large workforce manned the repairs. L&N president Milton H. Smith had moved the major shops out of Bowling Green to Paris, Tennessee. (Kentucky Library and Museum-WKU.)

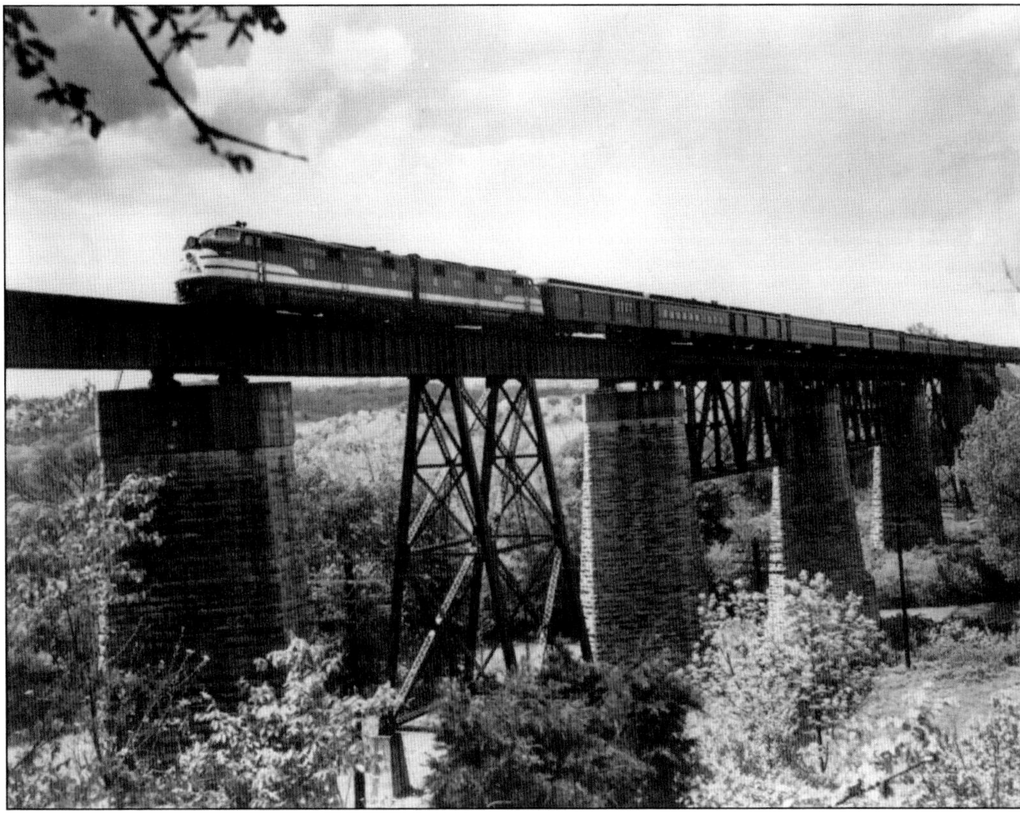

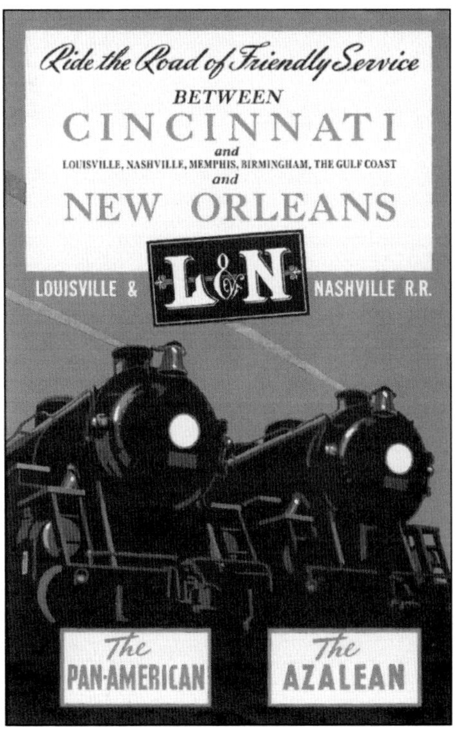

The Louisville & Nashville Railroad's *Pan American*, famous as the symbol of the L&N's passenger service, moves over the also famous Green River Bridge near Munfordville, Kentucky, around 1949. The *Pan American* and other L&N passenger trains, such as the *Humming Bird*, carried four times their normal traffic during World War II. (L&N records, University of Louisville Archives.)

This booklet promoted two of the L&N named passenger trains—The *Pan American* and the *Azalean*. The *Pan American* was the flagship train on the L&N and ran between Cincinnati and New Orleans. The *Azalean* was a New York City to New Orleans train via Louisville handled by the Pennsylvania Railroad, L&N, Southern Railway, and West Point Route. (Historic RailPark collection.)

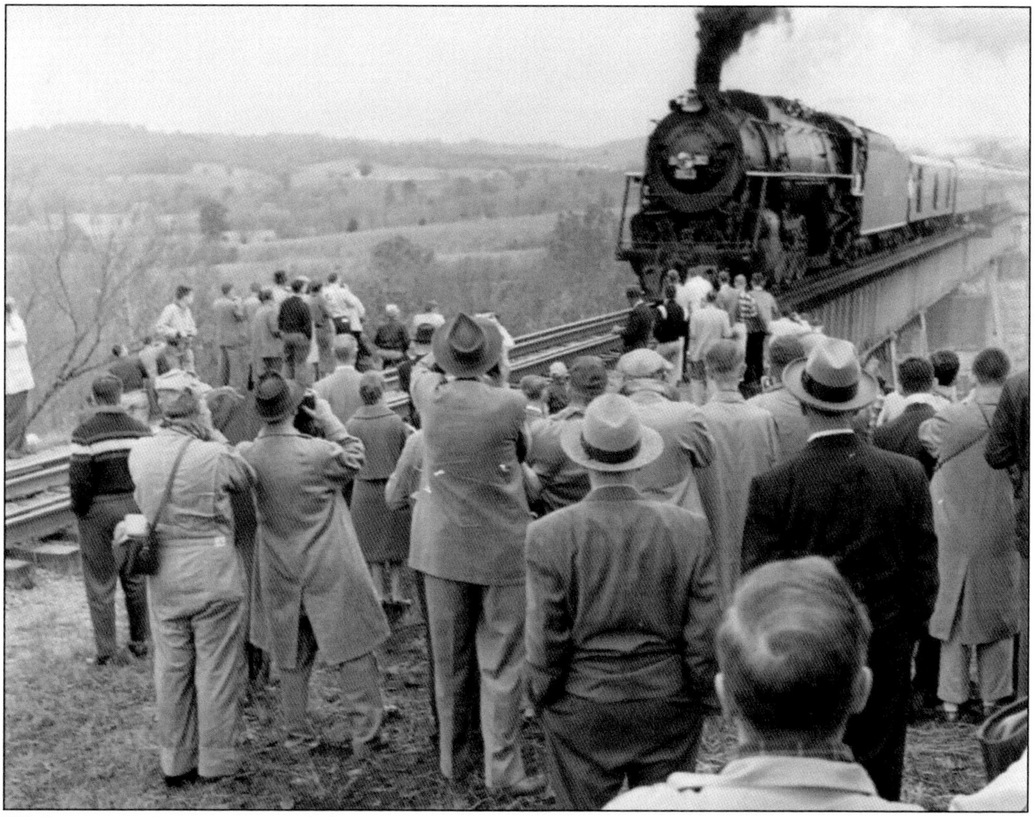

With no L&N steam power left to run, Illinois Central 4-8-2 2613 led the Louisville & Nashville's centennial anniversary train south from Louisville to Nashville on October 24, 1959. The 15-car train with more than 850 riders posed here for photographs at the Green River Bridge. After two hours for lunch at Bowling Green, the trip continued briefly until the tender ran out of coal near Gallatin, Tennessee. Diesels assisted in completing the run to Nashville. (L&N records, University of Louisville Archives.)

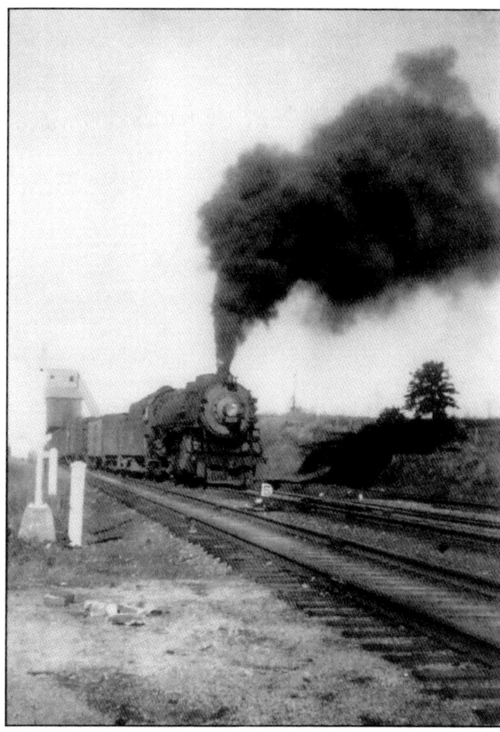

The massive double-track coaling tower seen in the distance was built in 1926 and held 500 tons of coal with a conveyor attached for reloading. Here, the steam engines on the main line or Memphis Line received coal. On December 5, 1956, the abandoned tower was dynamited to fall into a hole dug for that purpose. This 1942 photograph was taken from the yard of L&N employee David Craft. At the time of the photograph, Elijah C. Lee was 12 years old and visiting with his foster brother James W. Craft. (Elijah C. Lee.)

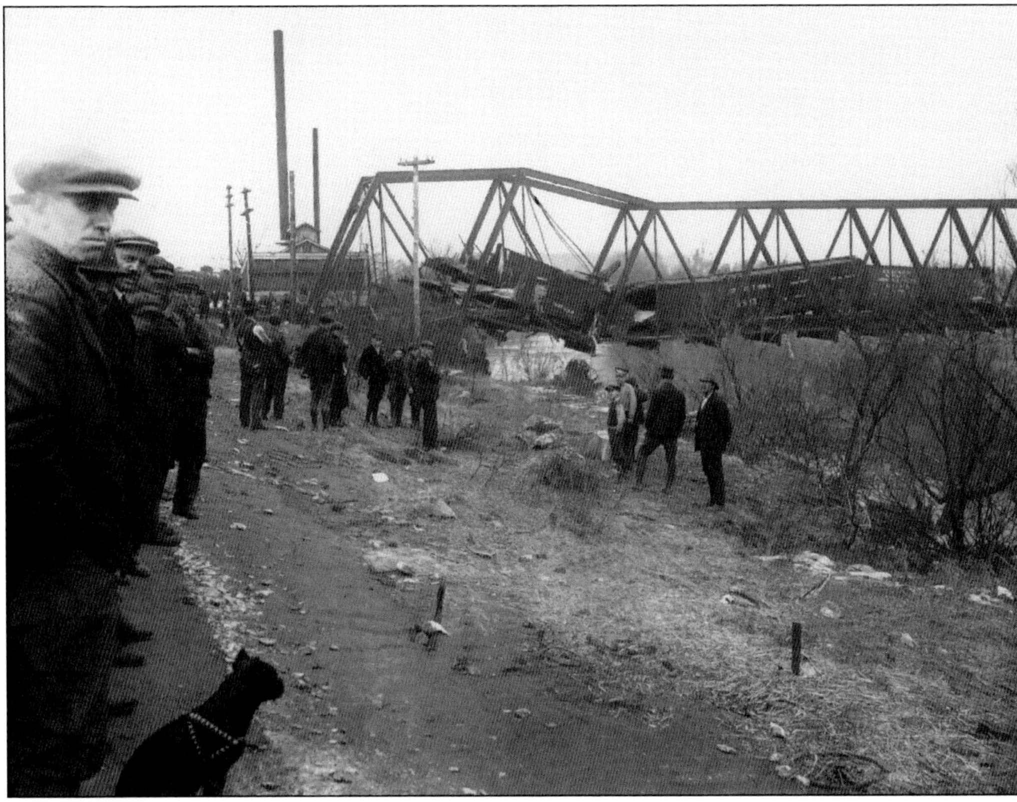

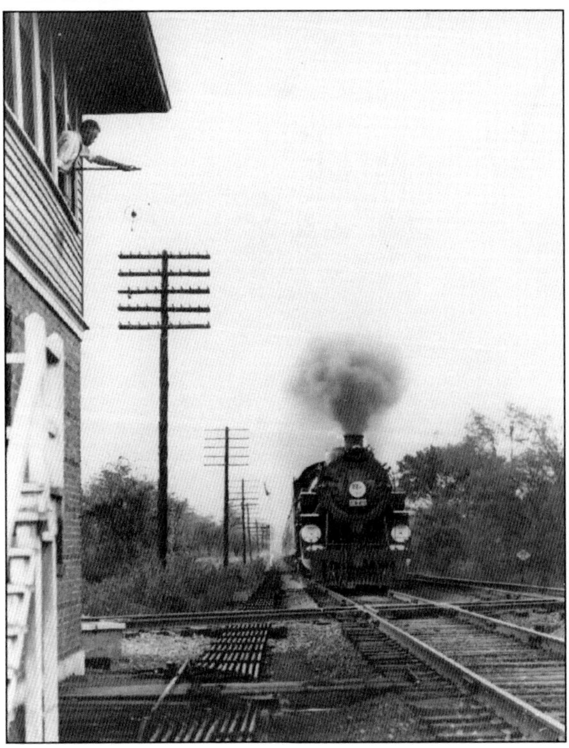

On February 15, 1921, L&N freight No. 74 derailed eight cars on the Barren River Bridge. Overnight, crews worked to salvage materials from the cars, with pieces of wrecked cars and contents dumped in the river. On February 16, as spectators gathered, some bridge girders were dynamited. During the explosion, Dan Cornwell, a carpenter, was struck in the head and killed by a flying piece of steel. (G. Marshall Love collection.)

In 1933, WSM Radio in Nashville began broadcasting live on the radio the sound of Louisville & Nashville's *Pan American* passing the station's 878-foot tower, located 12 miles south of the city. Later, the microphone was moved to Vine Hill tower, just to the north. Furthermore, with the *Pan American* offering radio and headphones on board, patrons could hear their own train passing via radio broadcast. (L&N records, University of Louisville Archives.)

Salmons, just north of Franklin, Kentucky, is where the southbound and northbound *Pan American* passenger trains met for many years. Today, the siding is still used for meets, and there is an industrial park off the main line that is worked often by the southbound local out of Bowling Green. Customers at Salmons include Key Oil Company and Dana Films. (L&N records, University of Louisville Archives.)

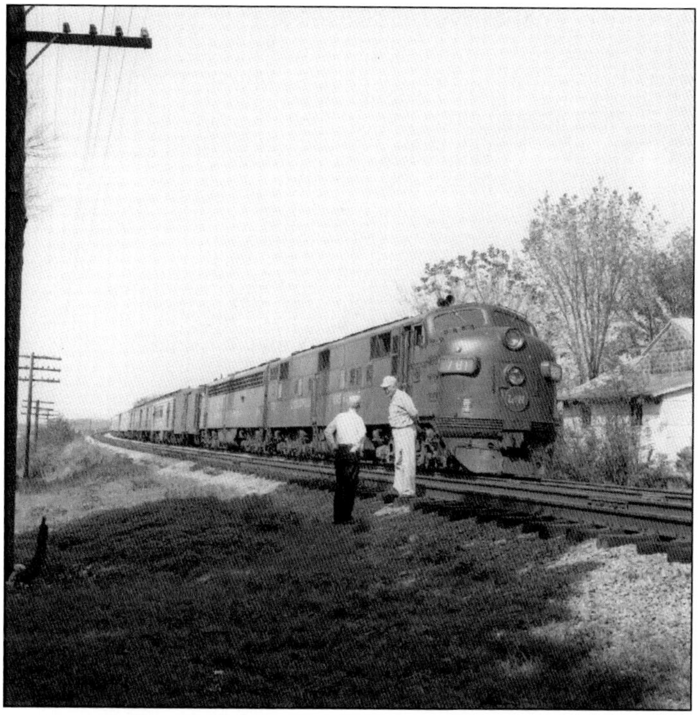

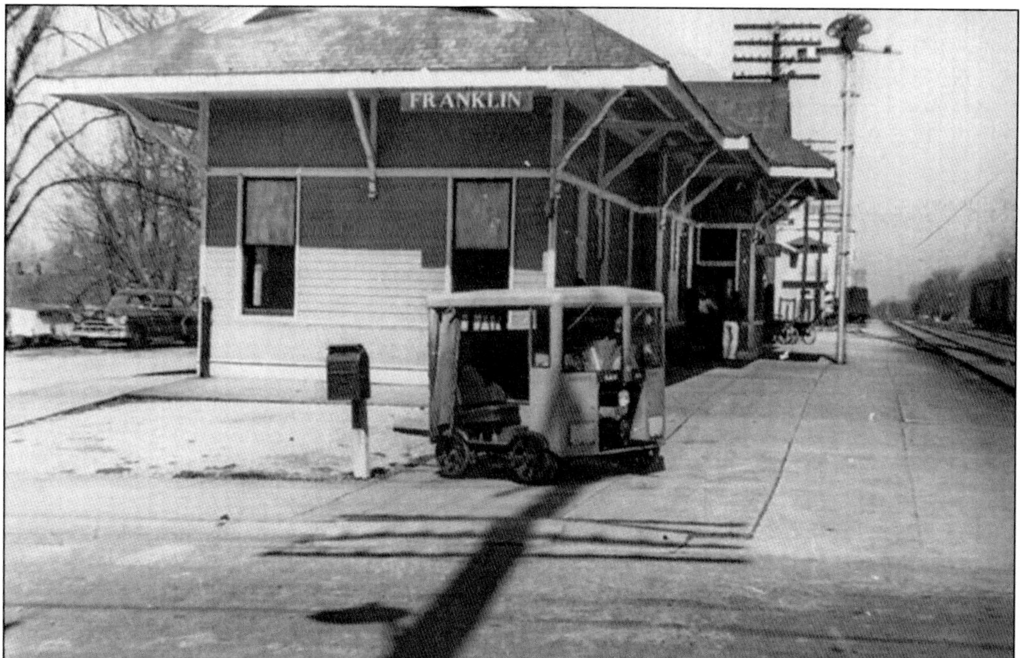

This image of Franklin, Kentucky, shows the depot at Railroad and Cedar Streets. An early robbery of an L&N train took place at Franklin. The robbers were caught and some were hanged. The freight house and depot were both razed long ago, but the concrete platform is still visible in 2011. Franklin has various industries still served by L&N successor CSX every weekday by a local train out of Bowling Green. (L&N records, University of Louisville Archives.)

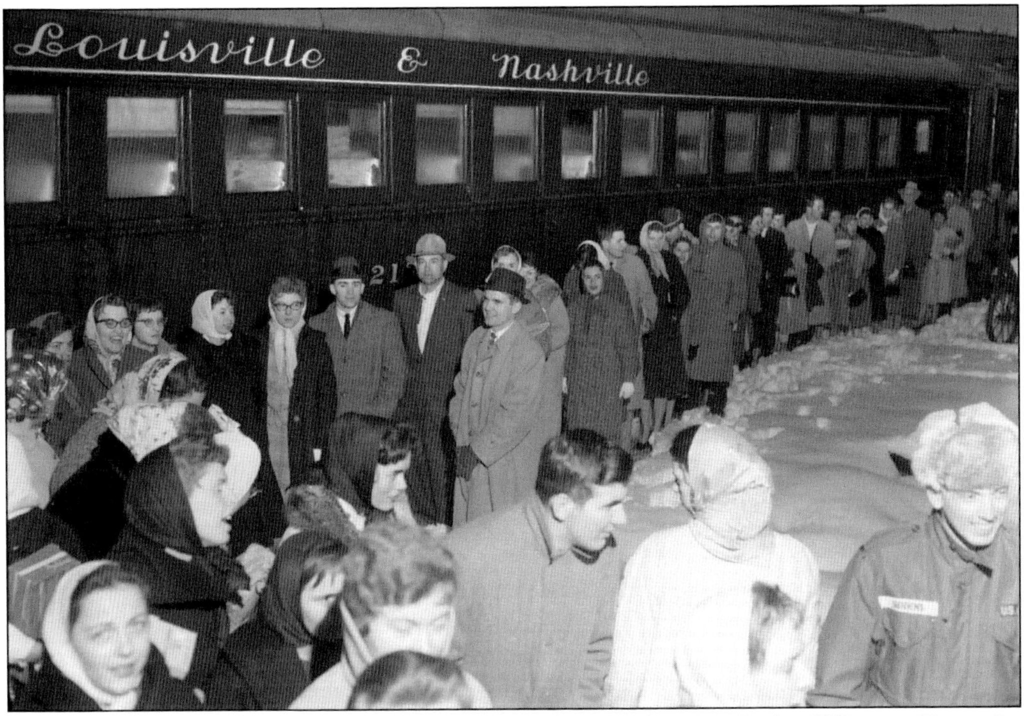

On March 8, 1960, a large snowfall crippled central Kentucky. Hundreds of Western Kentucky State College Hilltopper fans had traveled to Lexington for an NCAA basketball game versus Miami. Many small groups and 13 chartered buses became stranded overnight as they tried to return to Bowling Green. On the morning of March 9, the L&N added four cars to the southbound *Pan American* to pick up travelers and then ran a 10-car train, the "Snowball Special," from Louisville to gather the rest of the groups, shown here at Bowling Green. (L&N records, University of Louisville Archives.)

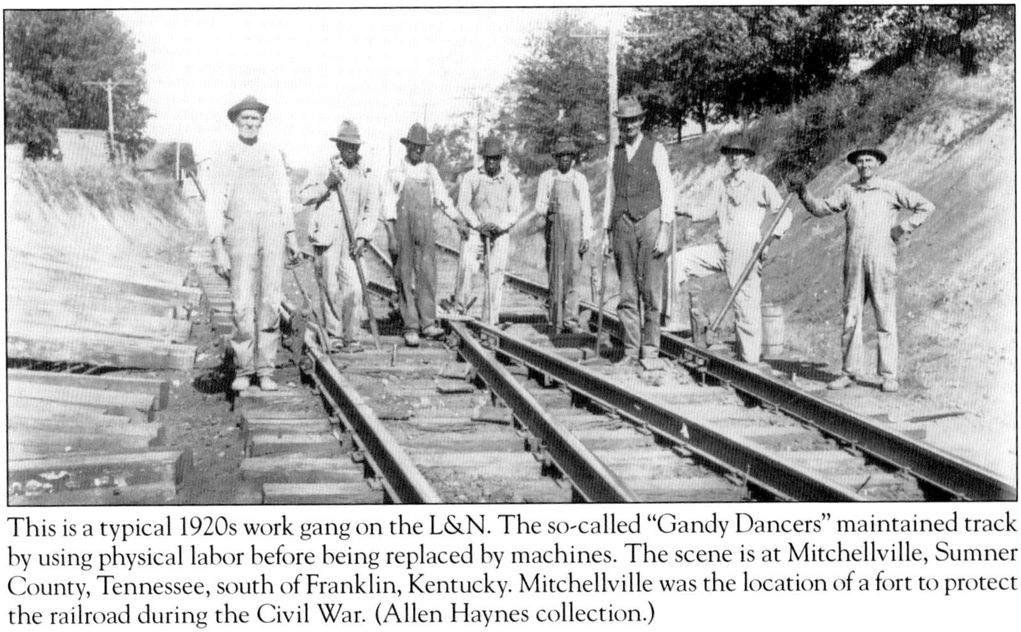

This is a typical 1920s work gang on the L&N. The so-called "Gandy Dancers" maintained track by using physical labor before being replaced by machines. The scene is at Mitchellville, Sumner County, Tennessee, south of Franklin, Kentucky. Mitchellville was the location of a fort to protect the railroad during the Civil War. (Allen Haynes collection.)

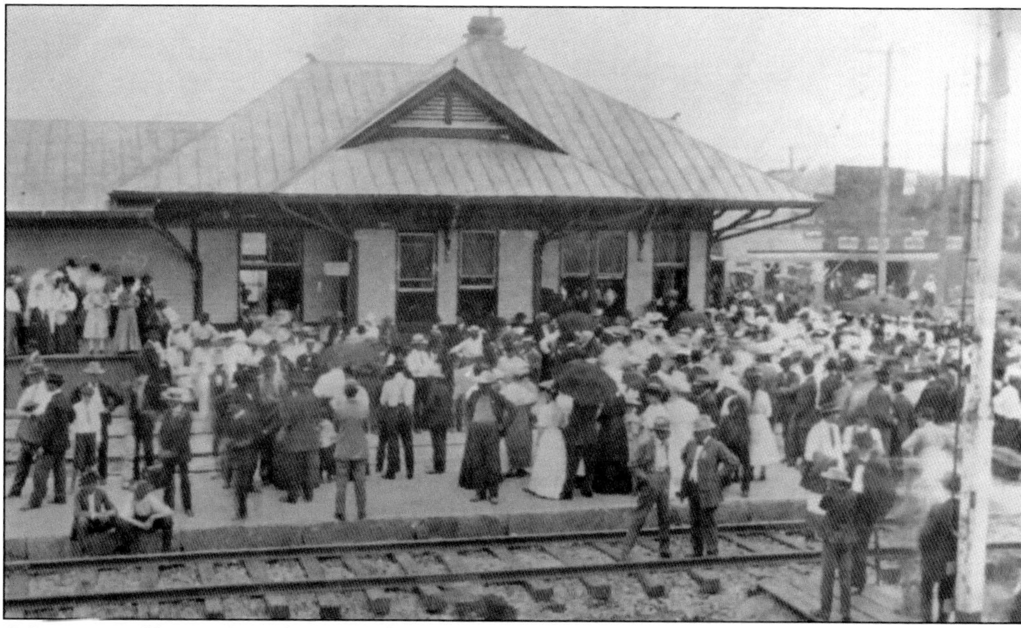

A large crowd has gathered around the L&N Depot at Portland, Tennessee. In many small towns, the local railroad station was the gathering place for speeches and events. Newspapers, people, and goods arrived by train, so the depot could have been the center of activity on any given day. Businesses without rail service might have had a car dropped at the station for unloading. (Allen Haynes collection.)

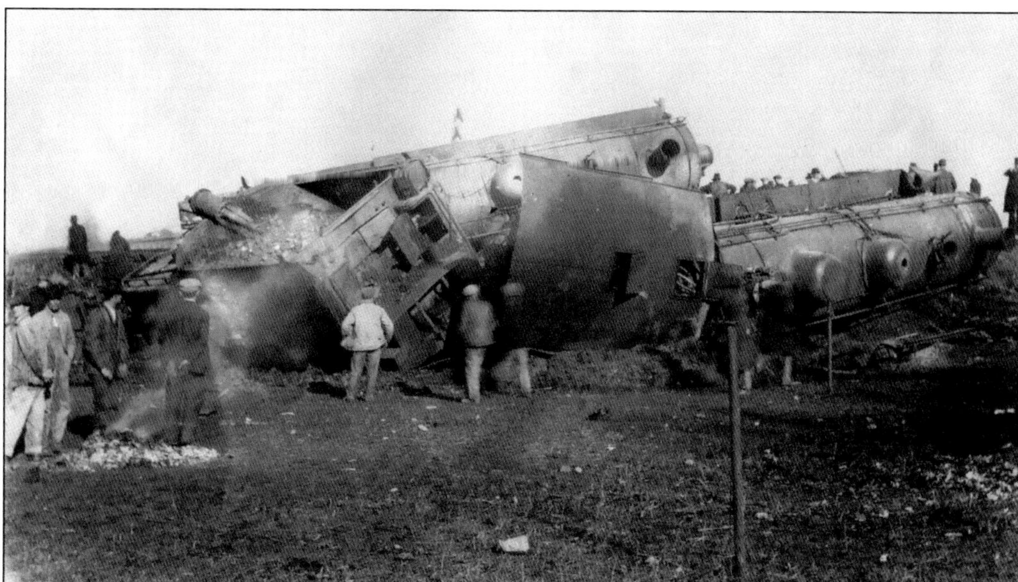

On November 24, 1924, at 7:42 p.m., Louisville & Nashville southbound passenger train No. 7, a Cincinnati-to-Birmingham express, derailed 200 yards north of the Portland, Tennessee station. The diner and passenger cars, including the private car of L&N president Wible L. Mapother, remained on the track, and no passengers were seriously injured. The engine crews received injuries and burns as the locomotives plunged down a 20-foot embankment. (J.E. Flanagan photograph, Allen Haynes collection.)

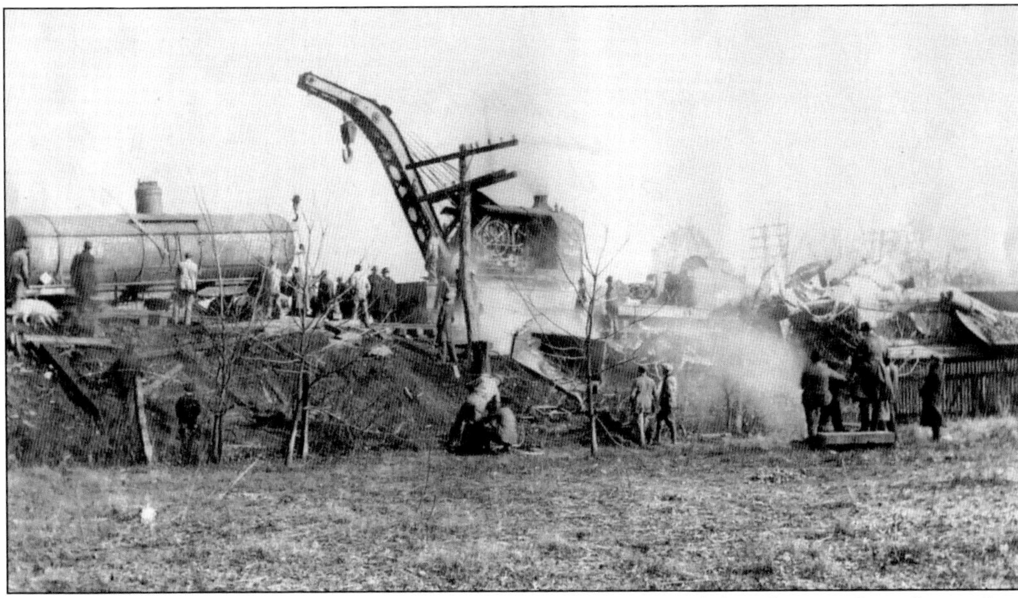

The November 24, 1924, accident was caused by the collapse and derailment of a pulpwood car on passing fast freight No. 78. Five freight cars were smashed to kindling. Engineers Burks and Trout as well as firemen Helwige and I.E. Brown were scalded and bruised when they were thrown against the hot fireboxes. The photograph shows L&N steam wrecker working to clear the debris. A Pizza Hut stands near this site today. (J.E. Flanagan photograph, Allen Haynes collection.)

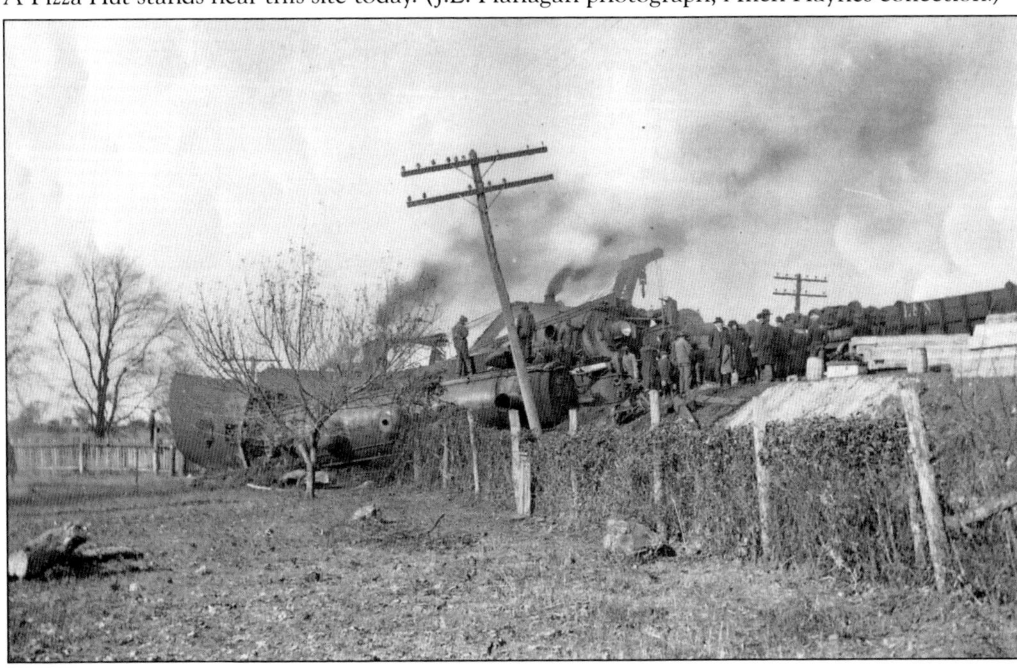

Another view of the November 24, 1924, accident at Portland, Tennessee, shows the wreck scene. The double-headed steam engines were traveling 45 miles per hour when the impact occurred, derailing two heavy locomotives, two express cars, and a baggage car, and destroying five freight cars on the passing train. Amazingly, nobody was killed. Most of the injuries were to members of a traveling football team. (J.E. Flanagan photograph, Allen Haynes collection.)

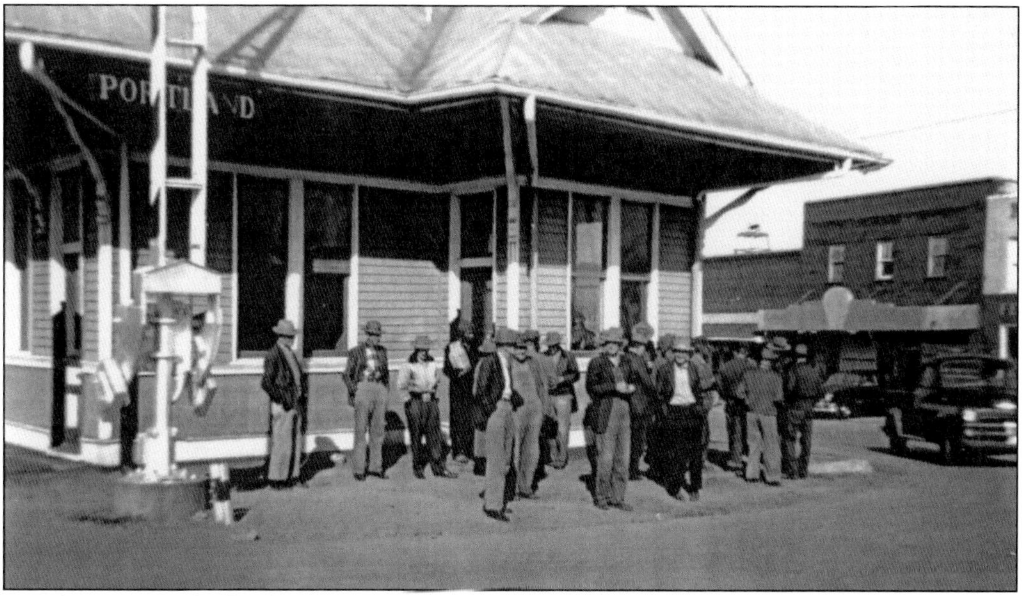

Another scene at the Portland, Tennessee, L&N Depot shows a group of knife traders and whittlers passing the time. For many years, in most towns, the wise older men of a community would gather at a train station or courthouse lawn and impart their wisdom and knowledge on one another or just find out the latest news. (J.E. Flanigan photograph, Allen Haynes collection.)

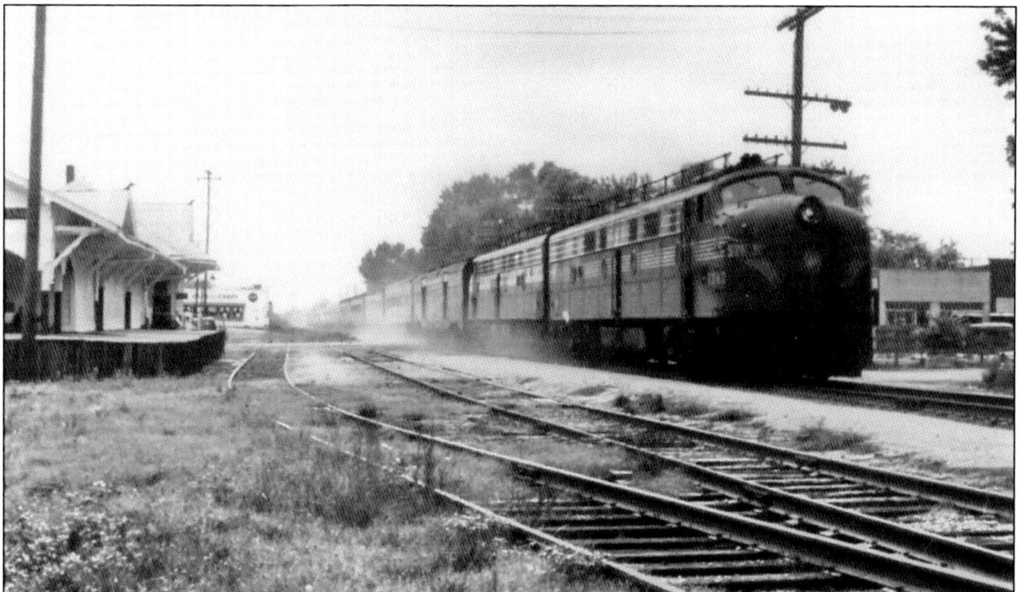

In late 1962, at Portland, Tennessee, northbound train No. 16, the *South Wind*, is making track speed by the depot. The *South Wind* served between Chicago and Florida in 1962 as an every-other-day train alternating with the Illinois Central's *City of Miami*. The *South Wind* traveled 313 miles on the Pennsylvania Railroad (PRR) to Louisville, 490 miles on L&N track from Louisville to Montgomery by way of Nashville and Birmingham, on to Jacksonville on the Atlantic Coast Line for 389 miles, and then 366 miles to Miami for the final leg. (David Englert photograph, Charles Castner collection.)

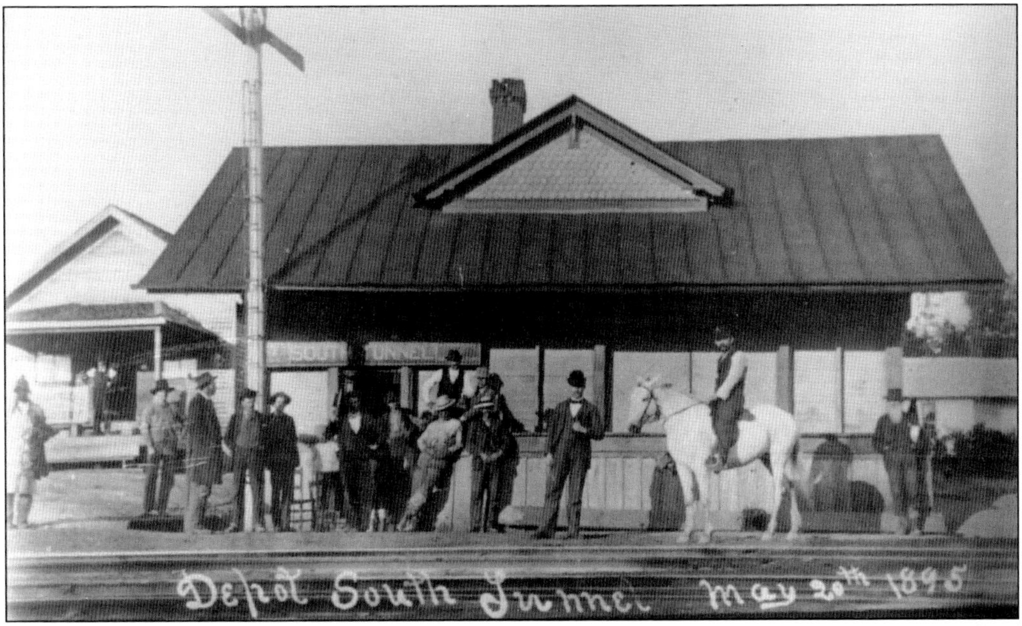

This rare photograph shows the L&N Depot at South Tunnel, Tennessee, in 1895. Just south of the station were the two tunnels through Tennessee Ridge. This area was very busy during the Civil War, with soldiers from both sides battling for control of the railroad and tunnels. A few homes dot the landscape in the area today, but the depot has been gone for a long time. (J.E. Flanigan photograph, Allen Haynes collection.)

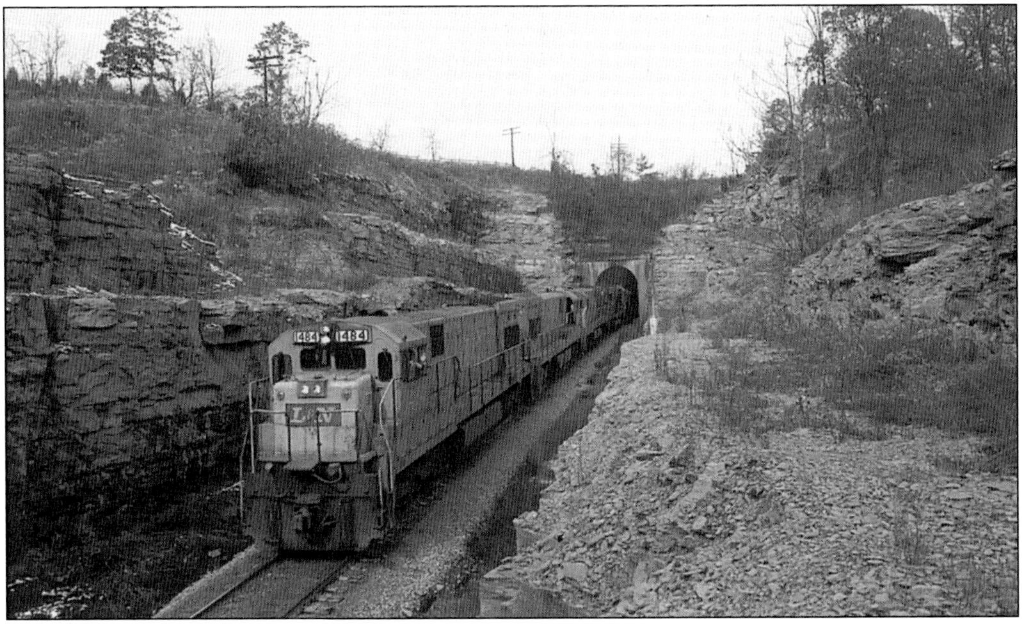

L&N U30C 1484 is seen emerging from "Little South" Tunnel, the northernmost of the twin tunnels of South Tunnel, Tennessee, in the early 1970s. This tunnel is about 600 feet long, and the community of South Tunnel is just north of the northern portal. The train is traveling through the short, deep open space between the tunnels before plunging into the darkness of the southernmost tunnel, or "Big South." (David P. Oroszi photograph.)

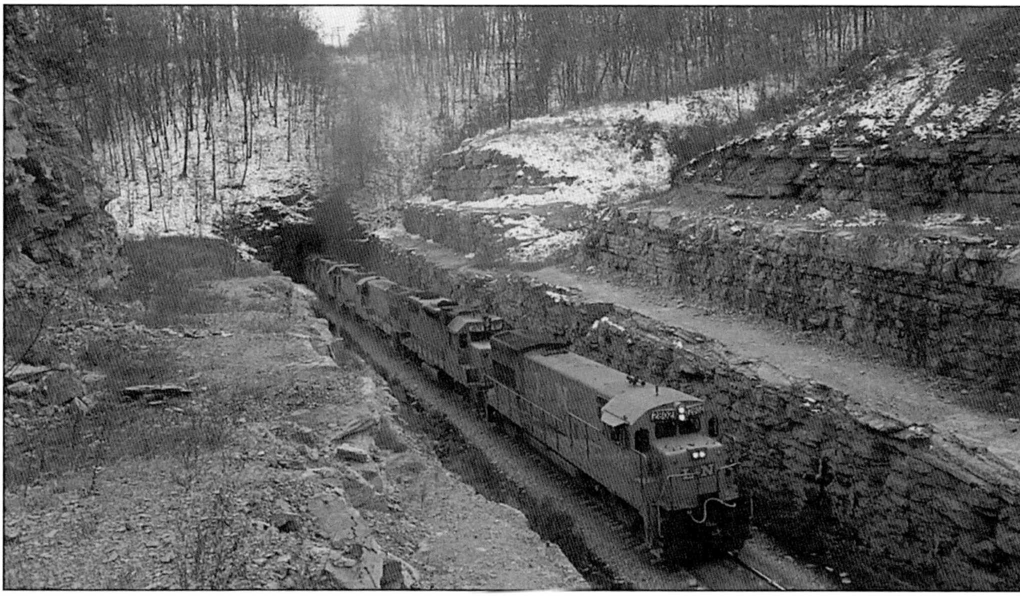

L&N U23B 2802 leads a power-laden consist north out of the southernmost tunnel of the twin tunnels at South Tunnel, Tennessee. The train is climbing Tennessee Ridge out of the Big South Tunnel, nearly 1,000 feet in length. On August 12, 1862, Confederate raiders under Col. John Hunt Morgan plunged a burning locomotive and cars into debris piled inside, causing a fiery crash and 800 feet of collapsed superheated rock. It took 98 days for the L&N to reopen the tunnel, the biggest accomplishment of Morgan's many raids. (David P. Oroszi photograph.)

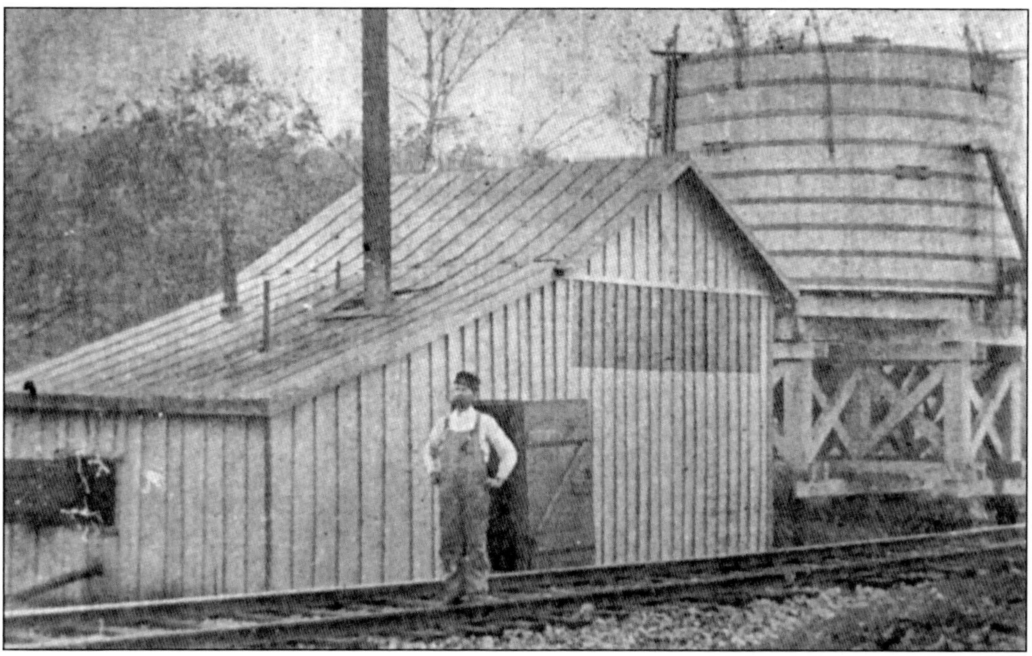

Buck Lodge lies between Portland and South Tunnel, both in Tennessee. The image shows the depot and water tank that occupied the area long ago. A passing siding is in use here today by CSX. The southbound local from Bowling Green will run around their train at Buck Lodge before returning north on the evenings that they work at Portland. (Allen Haynes collection.)

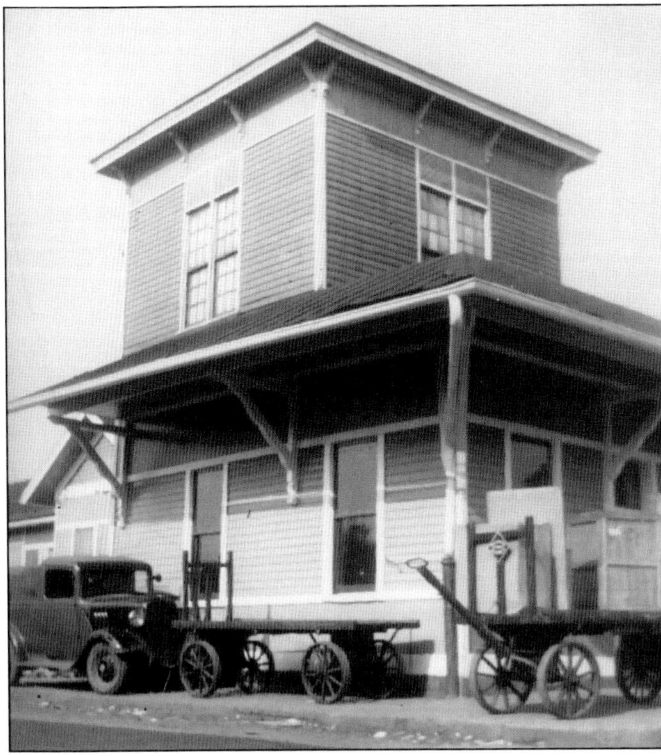

This Gallatin L&N Depot tower, built in 1861, is where John Hunt Morgan and telegrapher Elsworth posed as Union soldiers for several hours in early 1862 tapping into Union communications. In August of the same year, they pulled the then-routine ruse again at Gallatin with the Union troops unaware of their presence. The famous tower was razed during a remodel in August 1942. (Walter Durham photograph, Allen Haynes collection.)

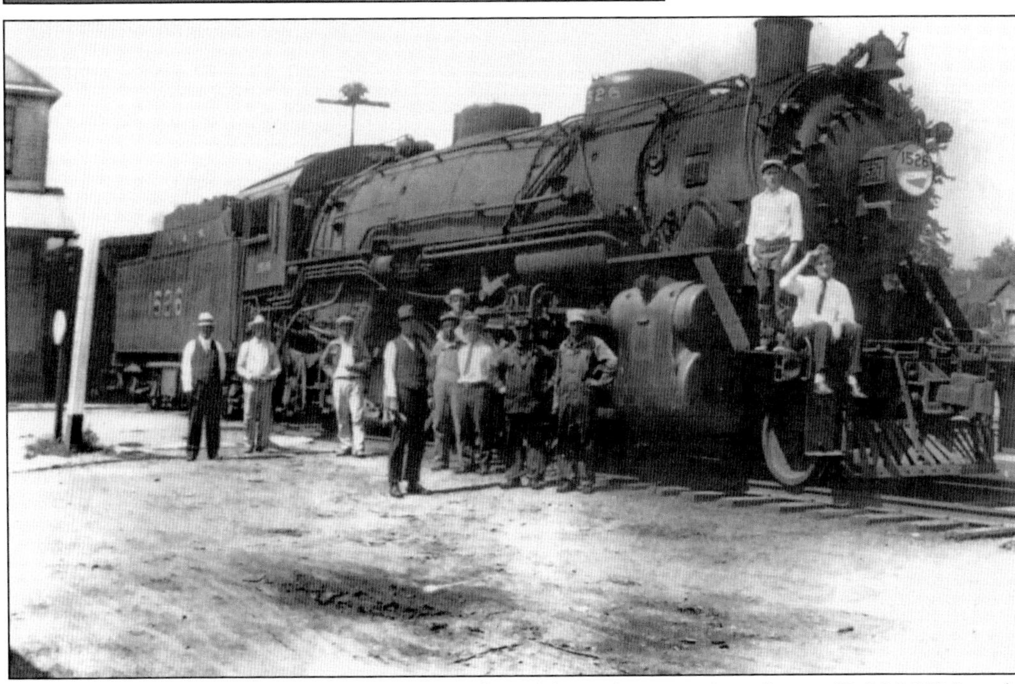

At Gallatin, Tennessee, a large group has gathered for a photograph in front of L&N 1526 in the late 1920s or early 1930s. The engineer and fireman have included themselves in the photograph. The large steam-powered giants captured onlookers' attention, a fascination that continues today when preserved steam runs in the 21st century. (Allen Haynes collection.)

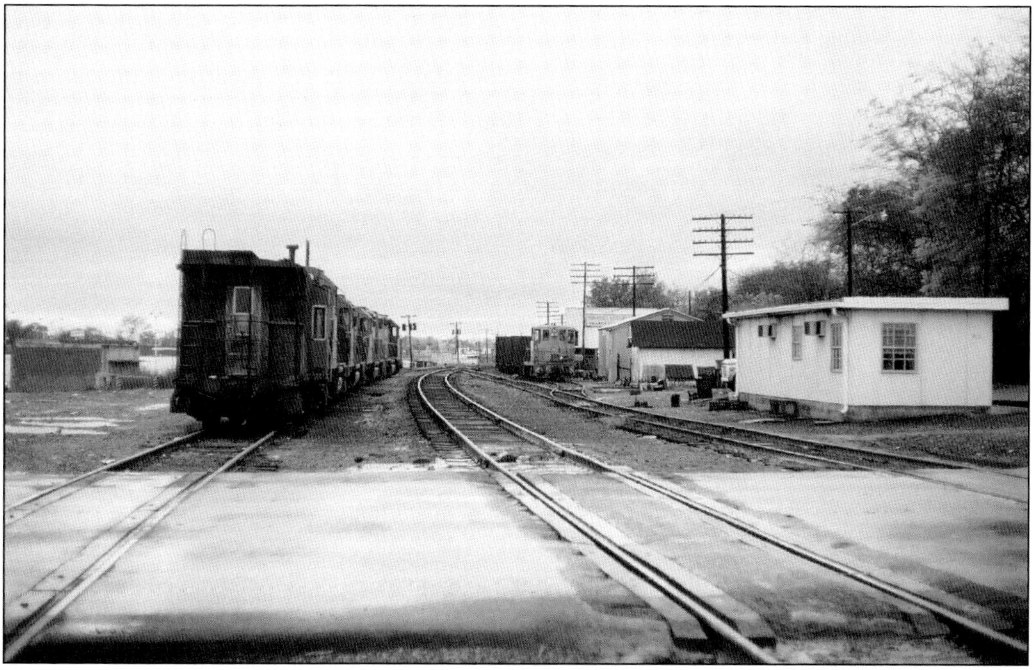

On October 27, 1972, L&N GP 38ACs 4027, 4026, and 4045, along with GP 38 4010 and red caboose 1278 await their next run on a Tennessee Valley Authority (TVA) coal train between Paradise, Kentucky and Gallatin, Tennessee. L&N purchased 50 four-axle, 2,000-horsepower GP (General Purpose) 38s in 1970 and 1971. (Dennis Mize photograph.)

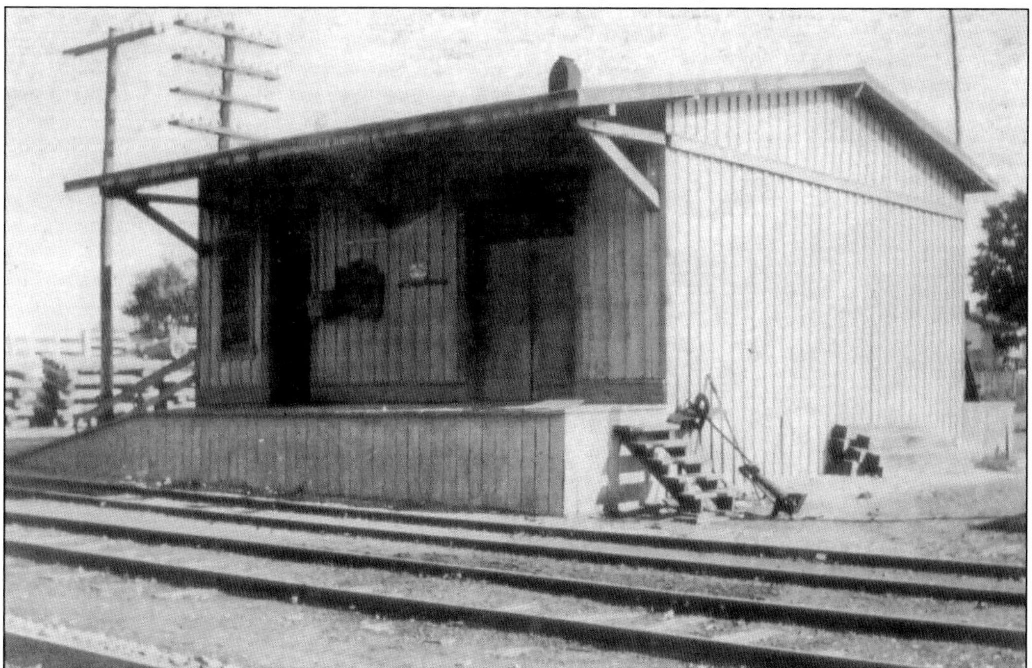

This rare photograph shows the Louisville & Nashville depot at Fountain Head, Tennessee around 1878. This is one of the many long-ago stations that no longer exist. (Allen Haynes collection.)

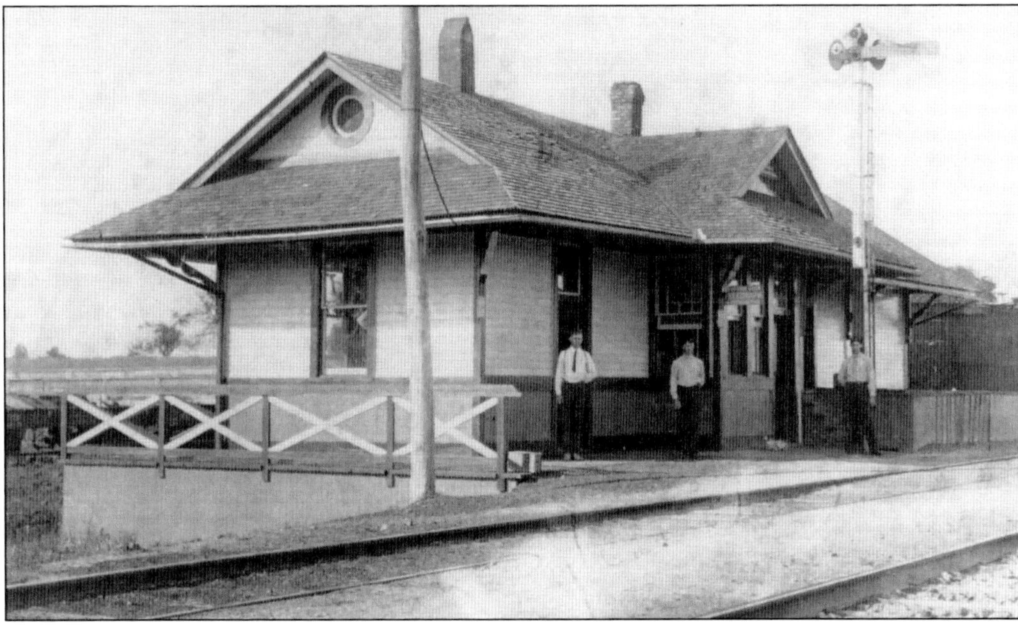

Between Gallatin and Hendersonville, Tennessee, was the St. Blaise-Peytona Station on the L&N Main Line. Note the Western Union telegraph sign, the cars on the tracks behind the station, and the semaphore signals. (Allen Haynes collection.)

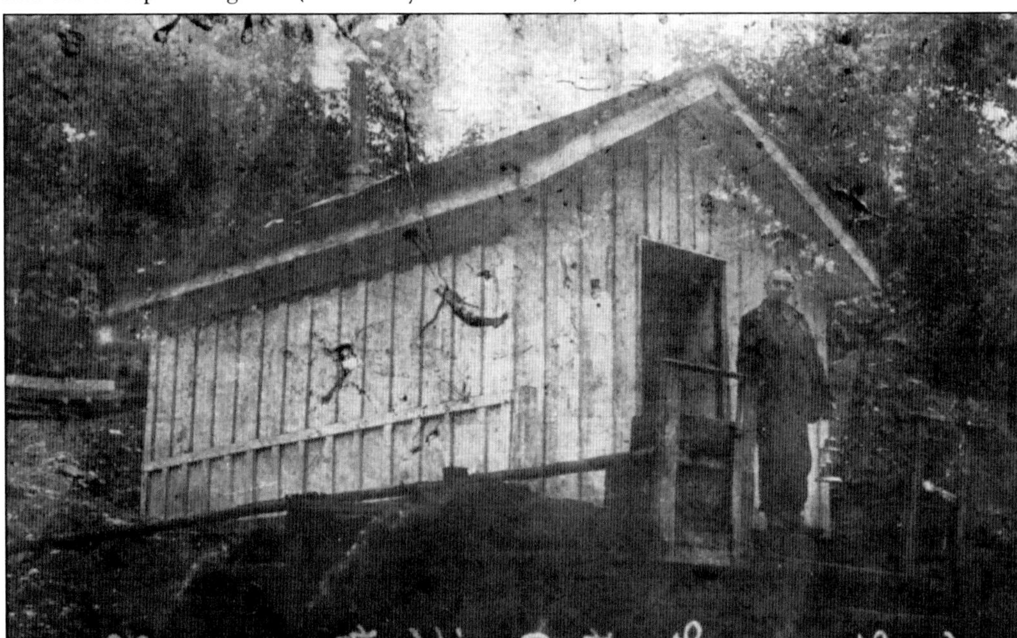

Railroads employed "walkers" to check tracks for debris, especially in areas with tunnels and rock cuts. George Taylor was a watchman on the Louisville & Nashville Railroad for 33 years, walking the tracks near South Tunnel, Tennessee. He was killed in the 1890s when a calf fell from the edge of the rock cut at the tunnels and landed upon him, breaking his neck. (Alan Haynes collection.)

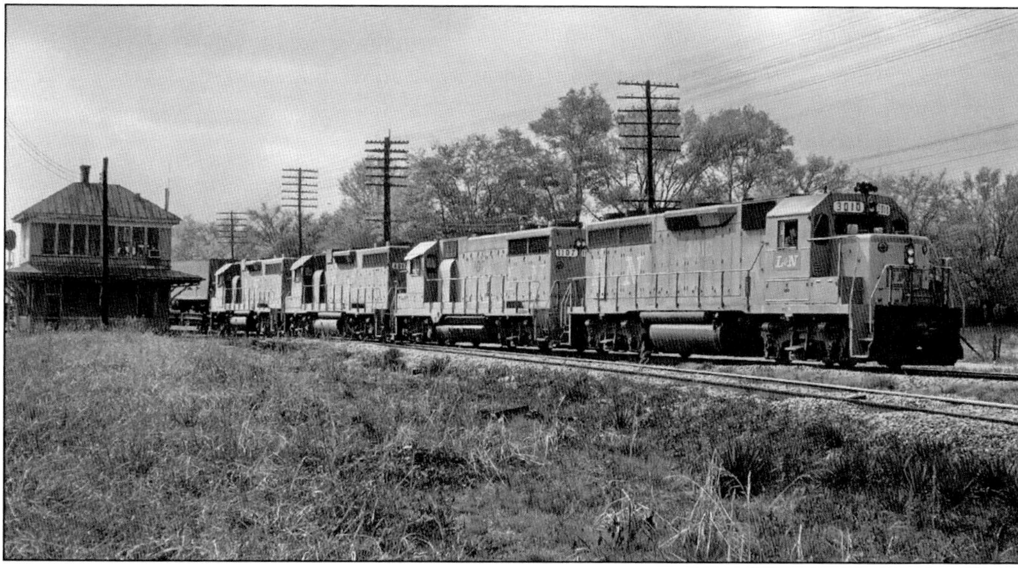

At the junction of the Louisville to Nashville main line and the Evansville to Nashville line in Amqui, Tennessee, a northbound train passes the tower at 12:20 p.m. on October 29, 1972. The Evansville-bound 42-car piggyback train is led by L&N GP 40 3010, GP35 1107, and GP38s 4017 and 4069 and trailed by red caboose 1212. As many as 35 to 40 trains pass this junction daily. (Dennis Mize photograph.)

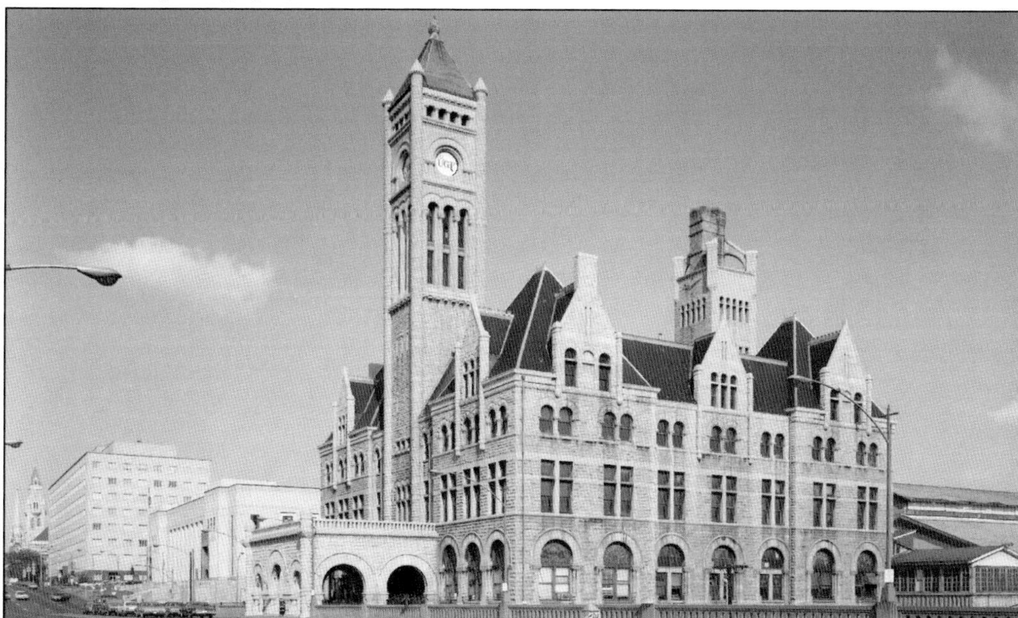

The L&N had operated out of a cramped station in Nashville built in the 1850s, until it burned in 1886. This led to the railroad moving passenger operations into the subsidiary Nashville, Chattanooga & St. Louis Railroad Depot, which was also undersized. This new Romanesque-style Union Station, constructed of Tennessee marble and Bowling Green Limestone, opened September 3, 1900. After the end of passenger service, the station became an upscale hotel, which it remains today. The train shed burned in 1996 and was demolished in 2001. (Historic RailPark Collection.)

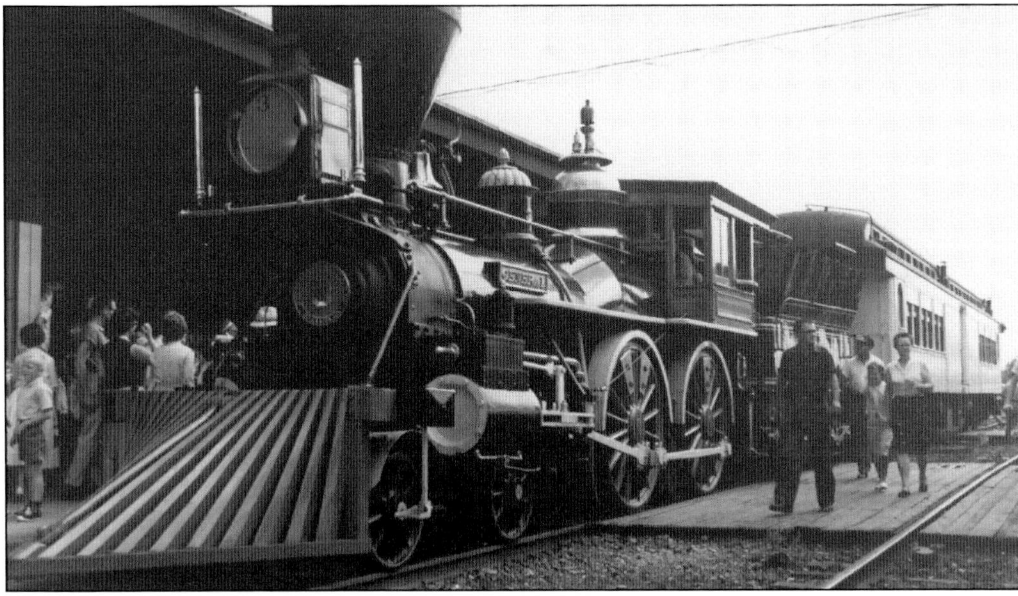

The Western and Atlantic Civil War steam locomotive, the *General*, was stolen by James J. Andrews's Union raiders at Big Shanty (Kennesaw), Georgia, on April 12, 1862. Pursued by Confederates and conductor William Fuller, the Great Locomotive Chase ended with the capture short of Chattanooga. Later rebuilt, the *General* was exhibited at special events and displayed at Chattanooga. The L&N acquired the *General* with the Nashville, Chattanooga & St. Louis in 1957 and, in 1961, began to restore the now famous 4-4-0 for the 100th anniversary of the chase. Afterward, the *General* stopped at Bowling Green during a 12-state, 120-city tour in 1962. (G. Marshall Love collection.)

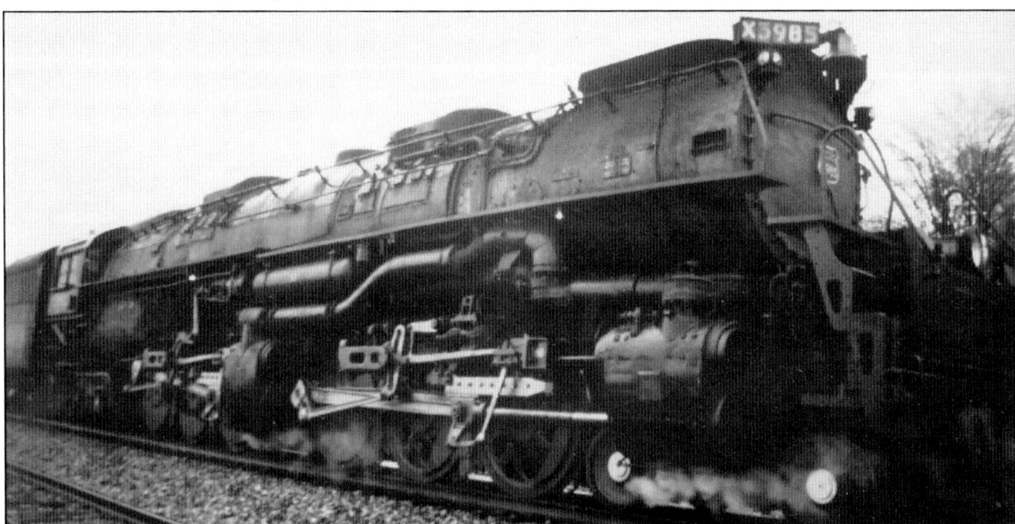

In November 1992, Union Pacific Challenger steam locomotive 3985 traveled north on the former L&N Main Line. Running late, the world's largest operating steam locomotive, built in 1943, is shown at Gallatin, Tennessee. Hundreds gathered along the line to see the million-pound, 122-foot-long, hinged 4-6-6-4. The 3985 was making an 11-state, 4,307-mile tour. It also pulled the annual Santa Special between Shelby, Kentucky and Kingsport, Tennessee on November 21. (James Lee photograph.)

Two

Bowling Green

Bowling Green's railroad history began with the Portage Railway. With a growing river trade bringing packets and steam boats into the city's boat landing daily, a way to move passengers and goods between the commercial district and the river became necessary. In February 1836, James Rumsey Skiles, James G. Pitts, and Jacob Van Meter received a charter "to construct one or more tracks together with wharves or landings, depots and warehouses as deemed necessary" to connect the boat landing with Bowling Green's city center, 1.5 miles away. Using slave labor, the line was completed in 1837 as the second railway built in Kentucky. Vertical cedar rails with steel straps attached carried "platforms" on wheels, pulled by horses. The line ran from a point on the Barren River adjacent to Skiles steam mill, along Church Street to a point at Main and Adams Streets, between Adams and Kentucky Streets to 10th Street, finally turning east along 10th Street to a small depot area now occupied by the old Warren County Courthouse. Later, iron cars would be purchased, and the line strengthened, but eventually it fell into a state of disrepair. The line was sold to the Louisville & Nashville Railroad in 1853, and would be used as an industrial spur line for more than 130 years.

During the late 1840s, towns in Kentucky wanted railroads. Meetings were held in Glasgow and Bowling Green to push for connections to existing lines or new railroads. With a Louisville to Nashville line in the planning stages, Bowling Green citizens badly wanted the railroad to pass through their town. Glasgow residents also wanted the line. The Louisville & Nashville Railroad was chartered on March 5, 1850, to construct a line south from Louisville to Tennessee with the company determining the route based on financial commitments from counties toward construction. On the same day, the Bowling Green & Tennessee Railroad also received a charter to construct a line from Bowling Green to Tennessee in the direction of Nashville. By early 1852, the L&N had not decided upon a route. The BG&T amended its charter in hopes of also connecting to a line to Memphis. Being unable to ignore the possibility of the Bowling Green & Tennessee Railroad starting construction, the L&N chose the route through Elizabethtown and Bowling Green over the route via Bardstown and Glasgow. The L&N board of directors negotiated the consolidation of the two railroads. Work began on the L&N in 1853, continuing throughout the decade to the laying of the final rail at Bells Station, now Park City, Kentucky on October 8, 1859.

Bowling Green's Barren River Bridge was completed in August 1859, and a two-story brick passenger station was constructed at Main and Adams Streets. Over the years, Bowling Green was an important junction for the L&N, with shops and passenger and freight operations for both the main line and Memphis line, along with the Portage spur. The rail operations helped Bowling Green grow into an industrial and educational center for southern Kentucky.

During the Civil War, forts were constructed around the city to protect the Confederate position and the railroad. Bowling Green was an important point for moving men and supplies. As Fort Henry to the south fell into Union hands, Gen. Albert Sidney Johnston, commander of the Confederate army in Bowling Green, feared being cut off and began evacuating on February 11, 1862. On February 13, Johnston destroyed the L&N iron bridge across Barren River. On February 14, Union troops began lobbing shells into town from across the river in hopes of speeding the Confederate retreat before they could destroy supplies and infrastructure. The brick depot, roundhouse, shops, warehouses, and many businesses were burned. The Union occupied Bowling Green for the remainder of the war, and the railroad facilities were all rebuilt.

This second Bowling Green station at Main and Adams Streets would serve from 1862 until the citizens of Bowling Green finally received the magnificent station completed in 1925 that still stands today. The town had battled with the L&N for years to get a replacement for the outdated, shabby, decrepit station from the Civil War era, and when it happened, the new structure became a source of great pride for the community. Many passenger trains stopped at Bowling Green daily during the pinnacle of rail travel and the station was a busy hub of activity. Trains from the main line and Memphis line interchanged cars and passengers, and much freight was handled. During World War II, the number of soldiers departing and arriving or just passing through on troop trains was tremendous. Main line trains such as the *Azalean*, *Pan American*, *Humming Bird*, and *South Wind* were well patronized. Memphis line connecting trains 101 and 104, the "Fast Mail," connected with the *Azalean*, and 102 and 103, the "Fast Line," also connected Bowling Green with most Memphis line towns. Trains 198 and 199, the "Up Pan" and "Down Pan," had to operate on time to keep up the connection with the main line *Pan American* at Bowling Green, where cars were switched between the two trains. From Bowling Green, a person could depart for most any destination by train.

As highways improved, and more people started driving and flying, rail travel declined. Trains began to be discontinued, and eventually the railroads wanted out of the passenger business by the mid-1960s. Amtrak was formed in 1971 and took over the nation's now limited rail service. Bowling Green had only two scheduled trains make stops, the northbound and southbound trains 52 and 53, the *South Wind*, later renamed *Floridian*, which lasted until 1979. After 1979, all rail operations in Bowling Green moved a few miles south to Memphis Junction, vacating the downtown yard and station.

Eventually the L&N became Seaboard System, and now CSX Transportation, and more than a dozen freight trains roll through the city daily between Louisville and Nashville. CSX also maintains a yard and originates several local trains to serve various industries in the area. Even though the Louisville & Nashville Railroad is no more, Bowling Green still plays a role in area railroad operations, and with the passenger station restored and functional as the Historic RailPark and Train Museum, one can revisit the glory days of the L&N.

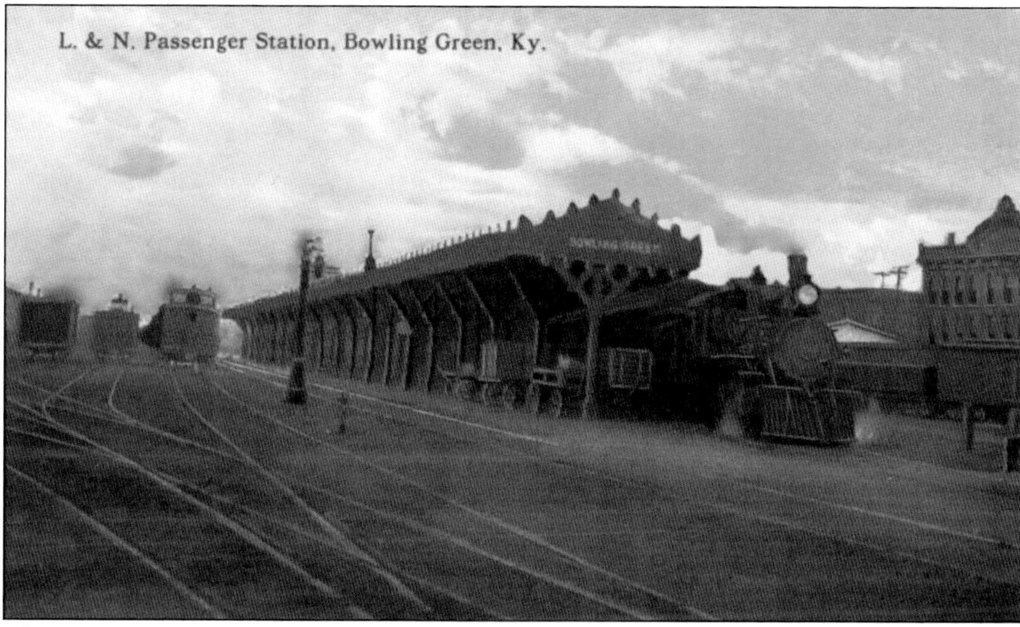

This station replaced Bowling Green's first L&N station, which was burned during the Civil War. A series of expansions left two structures separated by a 14-foot breezeway on a cigar-shaped 410-foot-long platform with tracks surrounding. Years of neglect left the town's citizens clamoring for a new station for 24 years. (Greg Hughes collection.)

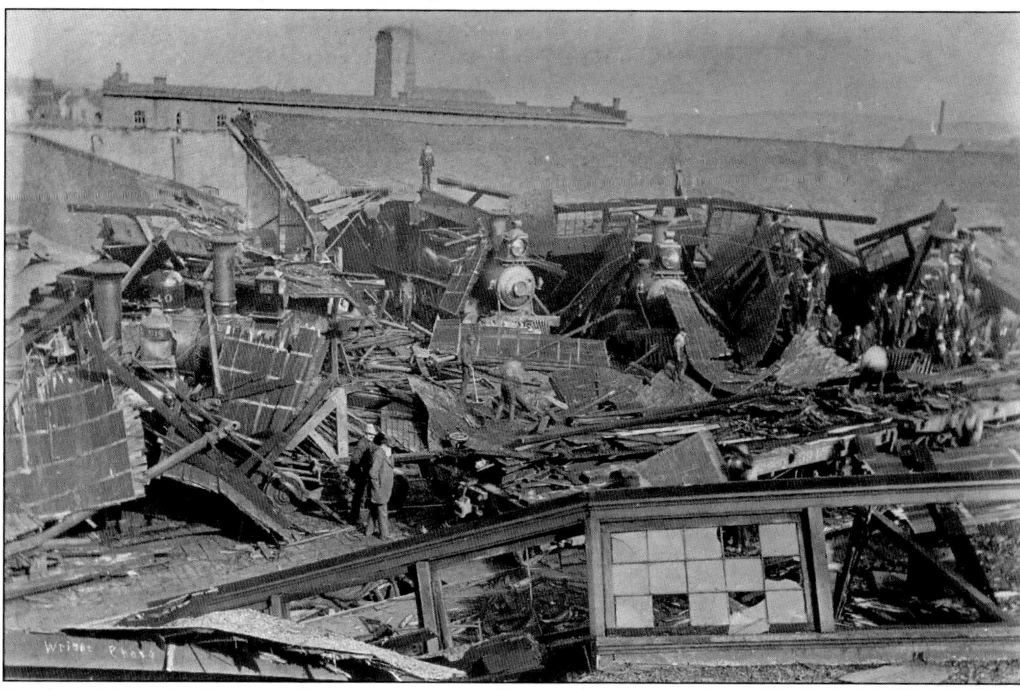

Bowling Green had received a new large roundhouse for engine servicing in 1870. The structure was destroyed on March 24, 1893, when a "death wind" cut through the southern United States. Much damage was also done to other Bowling Green structures. There were no injuries, and little damage was done to the locomotives that were inside. (Kentucky Library and Museum-WKU.)

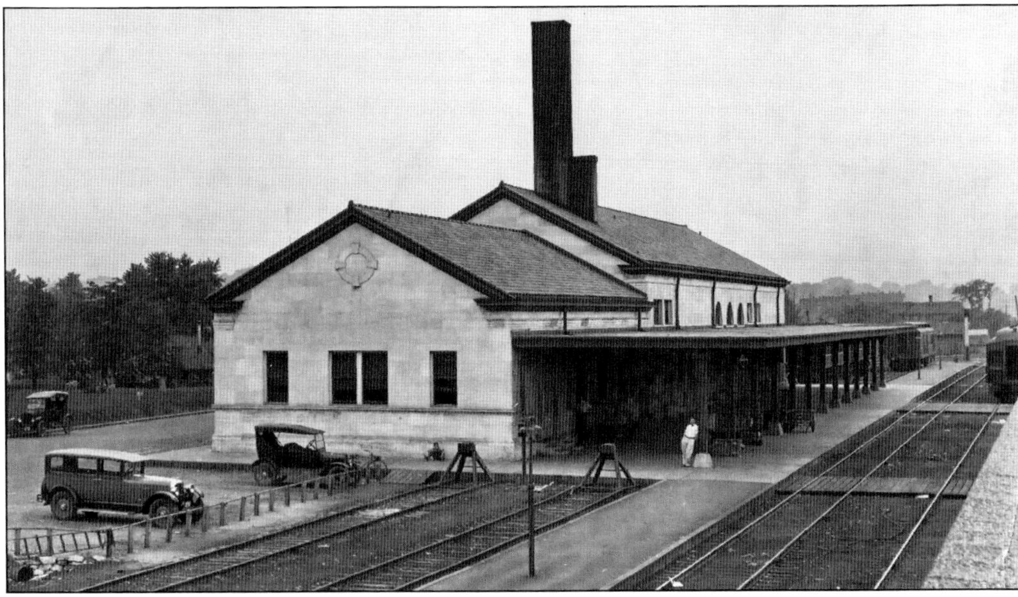

This view from the top of the roof of the butterfly shed shows Bowling Green's new passenger station soon after opening. Notice the passenger cars to be added to outbound trains on the station track. The freight operations were handled in the near end. Today, the entire station platform is enclosed, housing offices and museum space. (L&N records, University of Louisville Archives.)

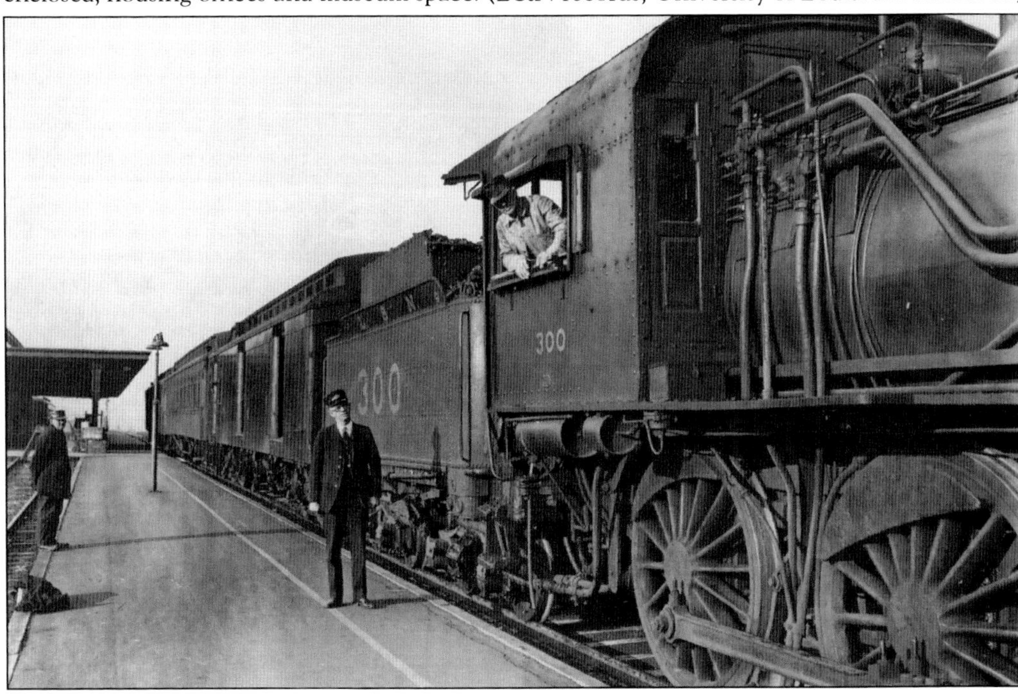

L&N 300 waits at Bowling Green's new passenger station in 1935. A baggage car and coaches stretch along the east platform and station canopy. While some of this near the platform has been removed for green space and parking, much of it exists intact in an overgrown area just north of the building. Some of this area is being reclaimed for restored railcars, exposing the lost platform. (L&N records, University of Louisville Archives.)

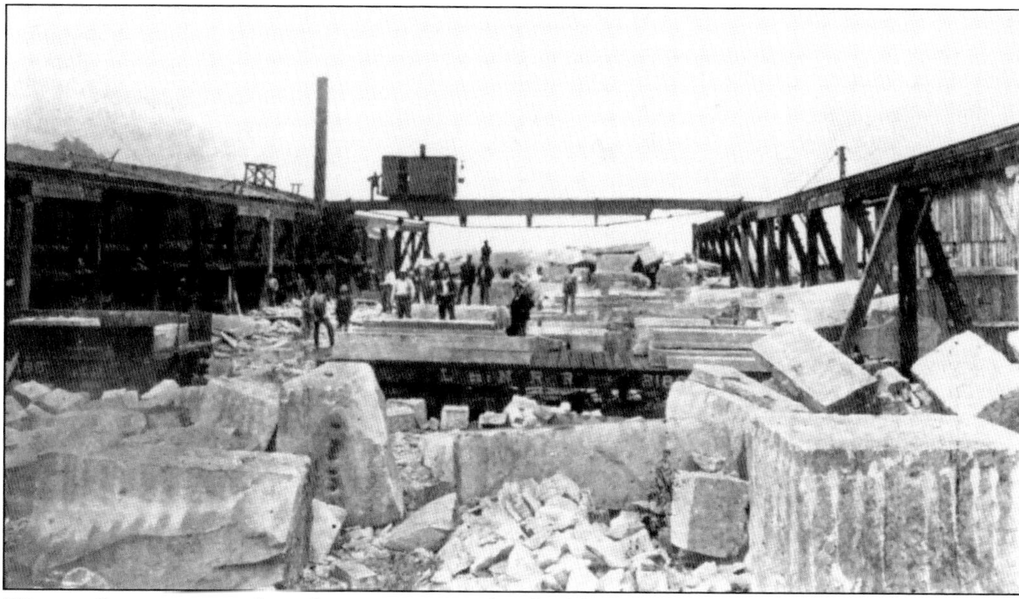

Warren County was rich with a superior quality building stone, and there were many quarries. The largest, White Stone Quarry, had a spur line constructed in 1872 to connect the quarry with the L&N. Stone blocks were transported to Southern Cut Stone Company on the Portage Railroad in Bowling Green and finished into assorted stone building products. The stone bleaches white in the sun and was used on the exterior of the Bowling Green Station. (Kentucky Library and Museum-WKU.)

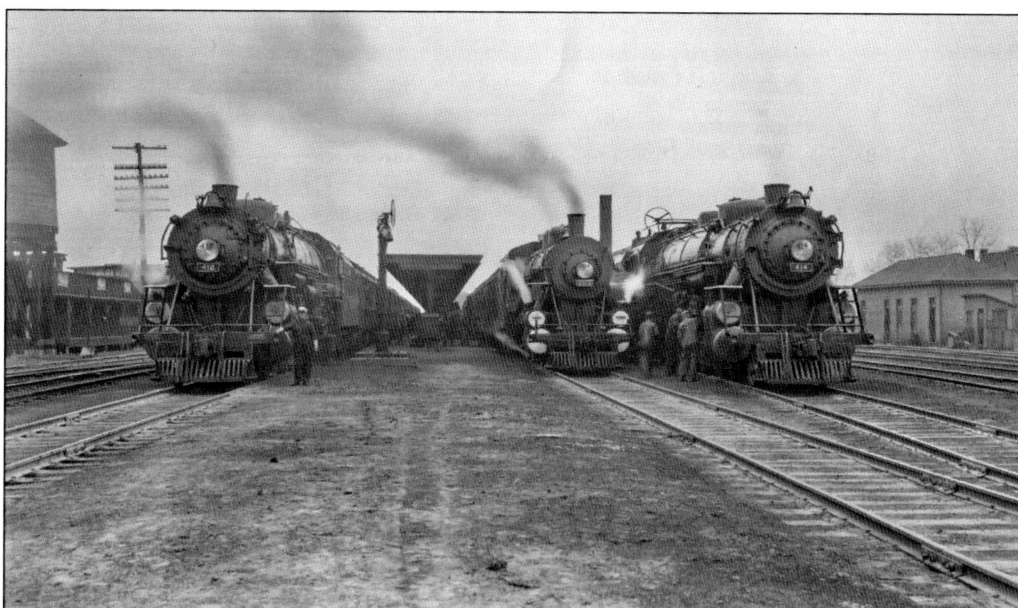

In this 1930s photograph, the trains pictured are speculated to be (from left to right) southbound train No. 7, the *Atlantic Flyer*; southbound train No. 99, the *Pan American*; and southbound train No. 199, the Memphis Line section of the *Pan American* or "Memphis Pan." L&N 412 and 414 were L1 Mountain-type locomotives, while L&N 204 is a K3 Pacific type. (Kentucky Library and Museum-WKU.)

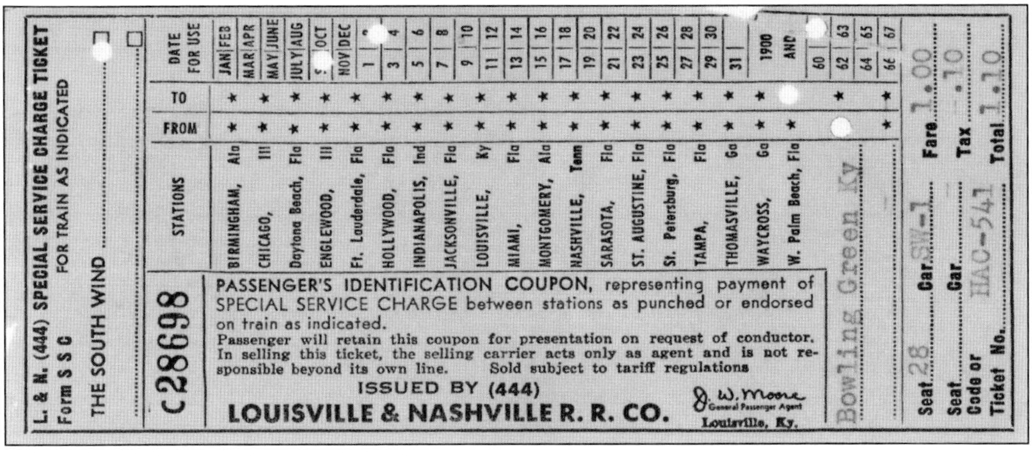

This L&N ticket shows that the customer paid $1.10 for a "Special Service Charge" from Bowling Green, Kentucky, to West Palm Beach, Florida, on the *South Wind* on September 2, 1962. (Historic RailPark Collection.)

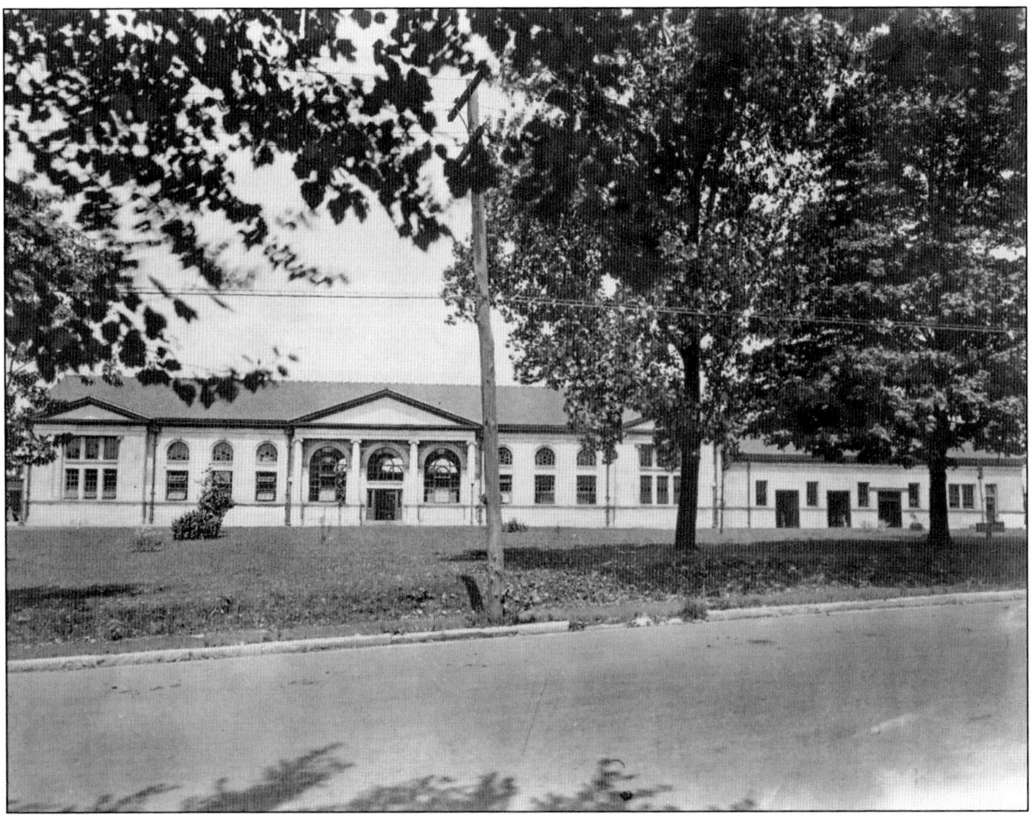

This front view of the Bowling Green L&N Station shows the passenger services on the left and the freight operations on the right. When constructed, a park was to be a focal point in front of the depot. Small trees are visible so it seems that purpose was beginning to be fulfilled at the time of the photograph. (Kentucky Library and Museum-WKU.)

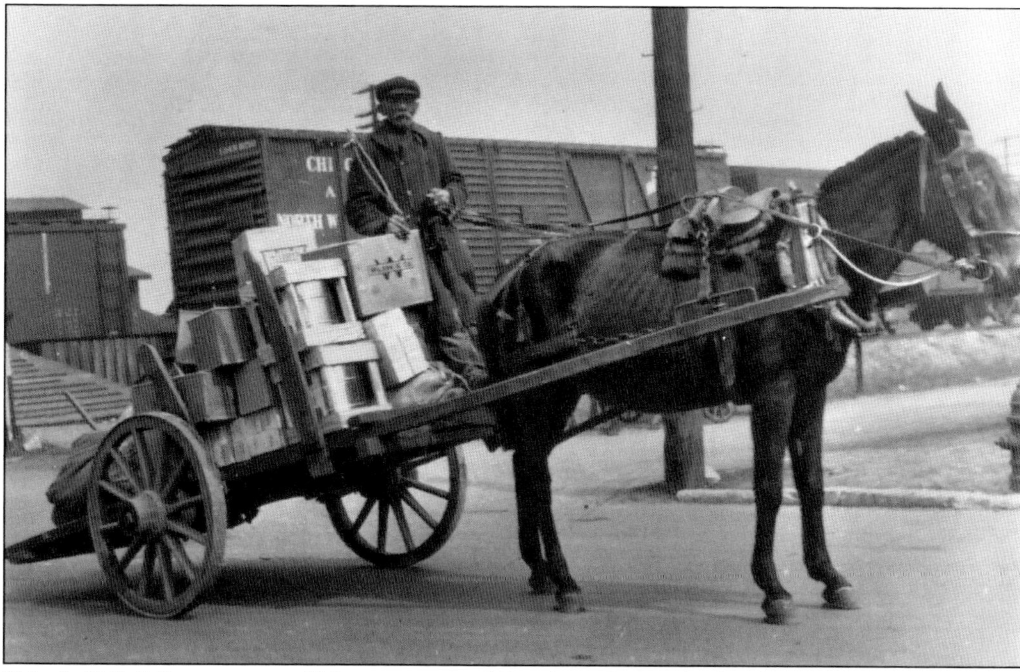

"Uncle Billy" Porter was well known around Bowling Green for hauling freight around town with his mule-drawn dray. This photograph appears to have been taken across from the L&N freight house along Adams Street at Eighth Street. Porter has quite a load going out for delivery. (Kentucky Library and Museum-WKU.)

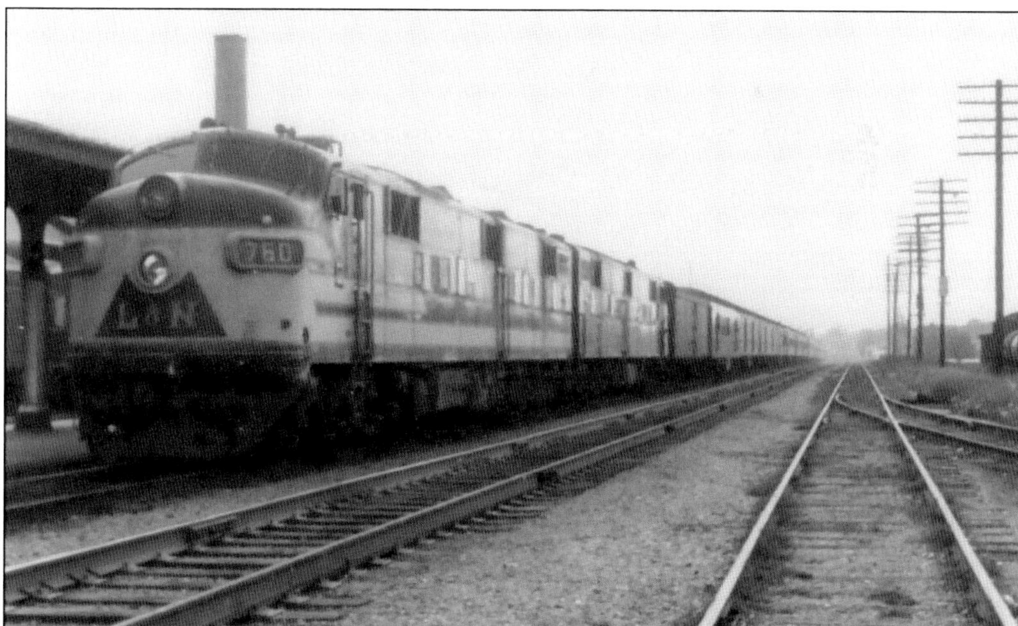

Northbound train No. 98, the L&N *Pan American*, makes the stop at Bowling Green in November 1962. The classic E7 passenger unit is in the original color scheme as delivered in 1945. The original number was L&N 460A. None of the L&N's E7 locomotives survive today. (David Englert photograph, Charles Castner collection.)

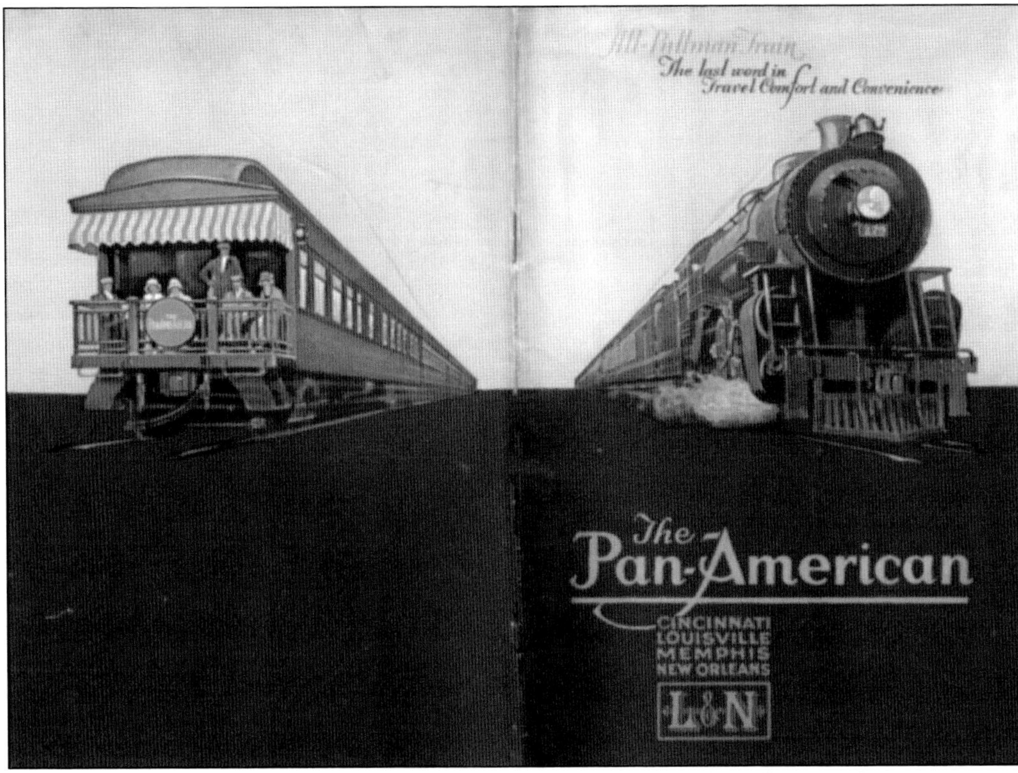

This L&N booklet features the company's flagship passenger train, the *Pan American*. From the inaugural run on December 5, 1921, until May 1971, when Amtrak took over the nation's passenger service, the *Pan American* offered first class dining, comfort, and service. In 1928, the overnight run between Cincinnati, Louisville, Nashville, and New Orleans offered valet and maid service, showers, lounges, and radio on board. The train was advertised as "All-Pullman," meaning sleeping cars instead of day coaches. (Historic RailPark Collection.)

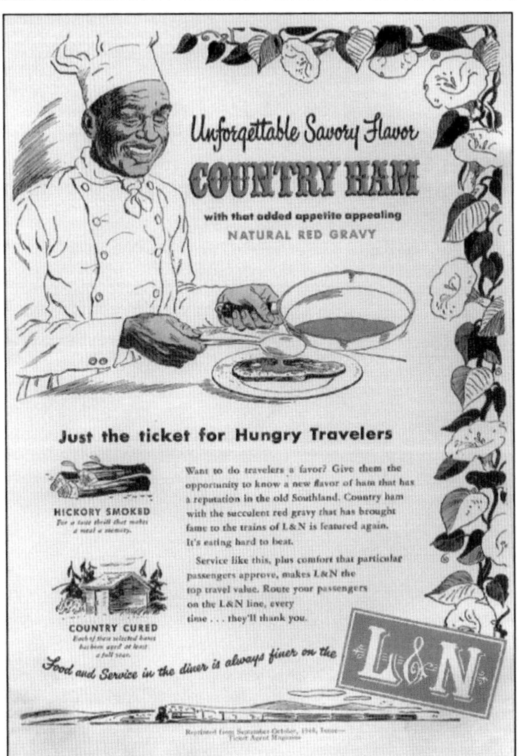

The food served on L&N's dining cars was first class. The "Kentucky Country Ham" breakfast was one of the most popular items on the menu. The hams were sugar cured and hickory smoked and provided by the Old Hickory Farm, located near Pee Wee Valley, Kentucky. Fresh seafood was another popular item for patrons. (L&N records, University of Louisville Archives.)

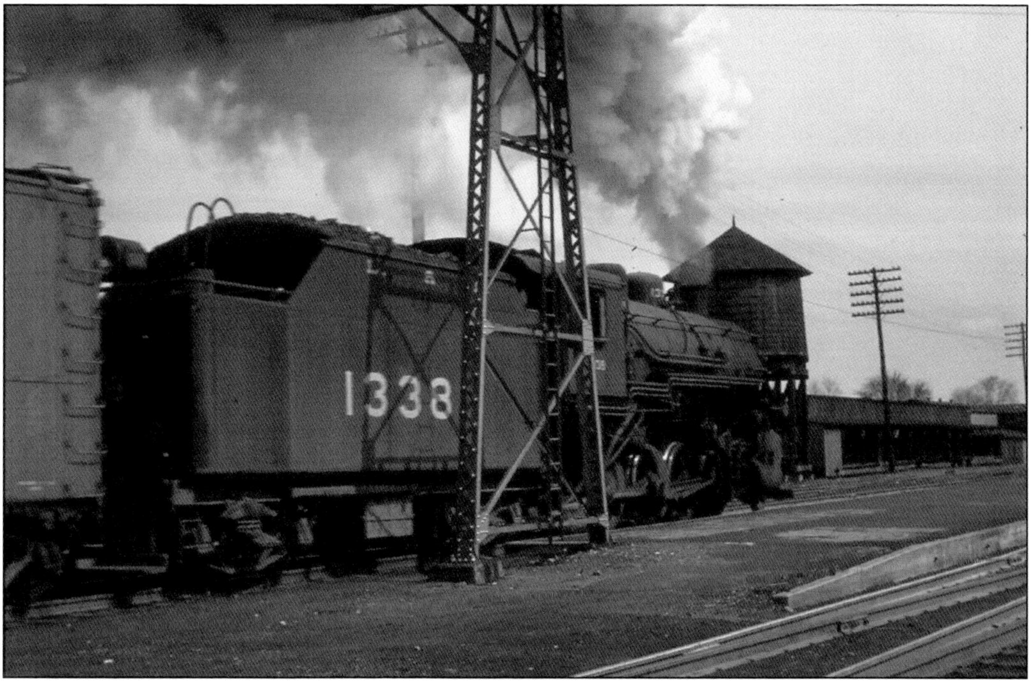

L&N No. 1338 passes under a signal bridge approaching the passenger station and platform areas at Bowling Green. The supports for the visible water tank can still be found along the track. The train is sorting cars on the storage tracks between the Portage wye and Sixth Street. (Leon Garrett photograph.)

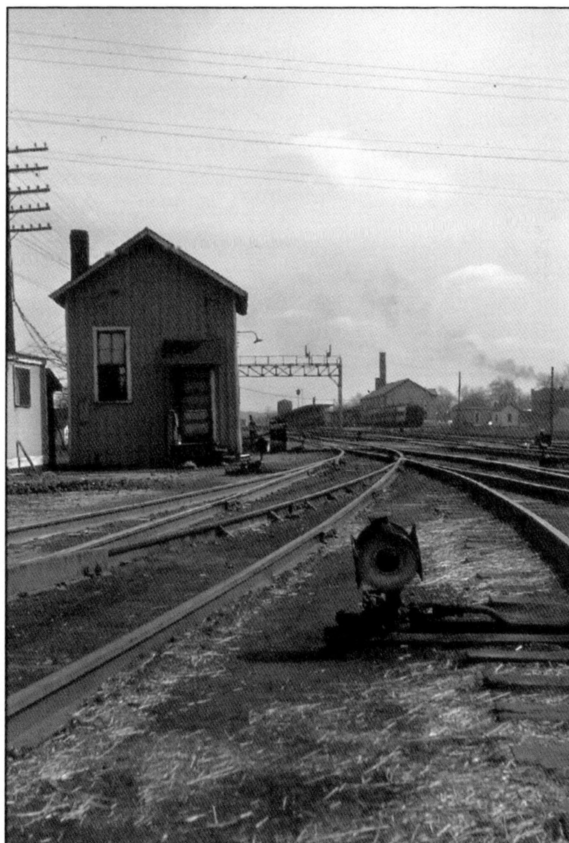

This view shows the north end of the busy Bowling Green yards in 1949. In the distance is the Bowling Green Limestone–clad passenger station and sheds. Farther north, a water tank stood on the east side. The tracks at left lead to the shops and the Portage Railroad Line across Clay Street. Passenger cars wait on the station tracks for movement to arriving trains. (Leon Garrett photograph.)

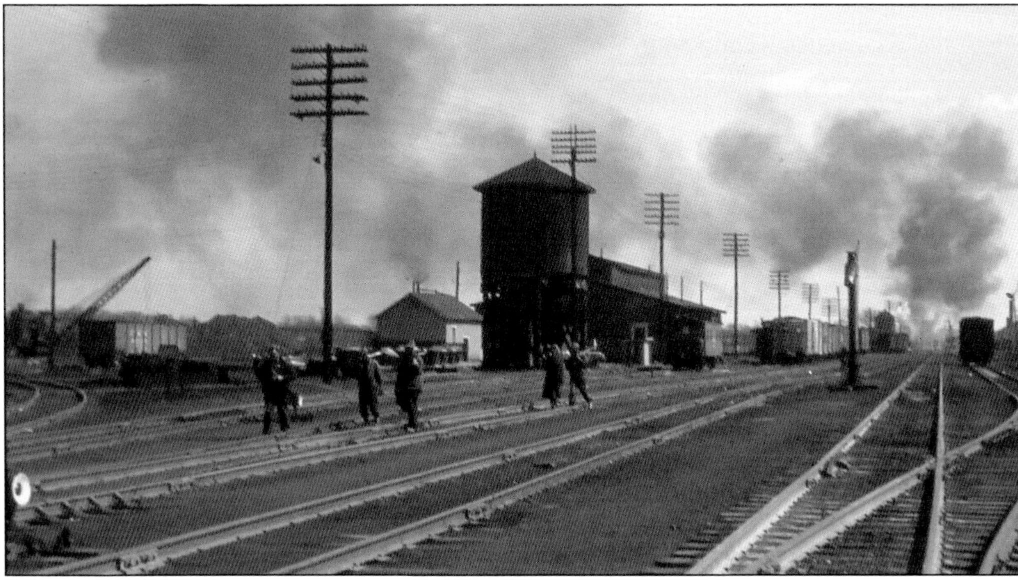

This late-1940s view shows L&N workers with shovels walking toward the south end of the yards. The center of the Portage wye is visible. The roundhouses are gone, but the old shop building remains. A clamshell scoop is available to load coal to locomotives from the coal pile. The north and south legs of the wye merged at Clay Street into the "River Track" or Portage Railroad, directly to Barren River. A branch off of that line ran north to the local power plant. (Leon Garrett photograph.)

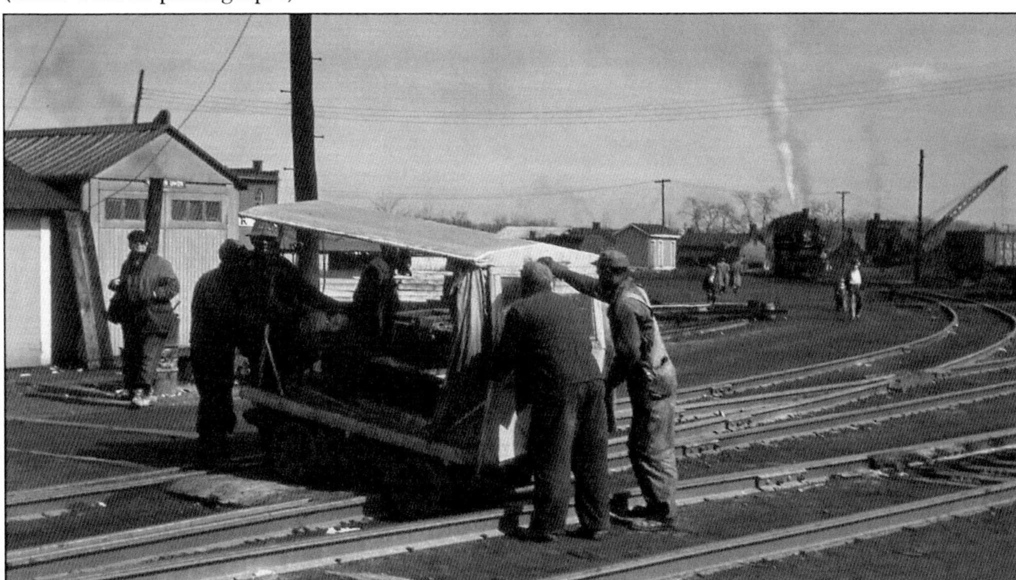

On a cool day in 1949, workers manhandle a motorcar or "track speeder" in Bowling Green. The shed at left is the storage place for the track gang's equipment. Note the rails leading to the storage building. In the distance, the Clay Street crossing can be seen, and the track is the Portage Railroad, which crosses Clay Street and runs to industries along Church Street and the Barren River. The corner of the Roemer Brothers Lumber Co. can be seen next to the pole. That building still stands on Clay Street. (Leon Garrett photograph.)

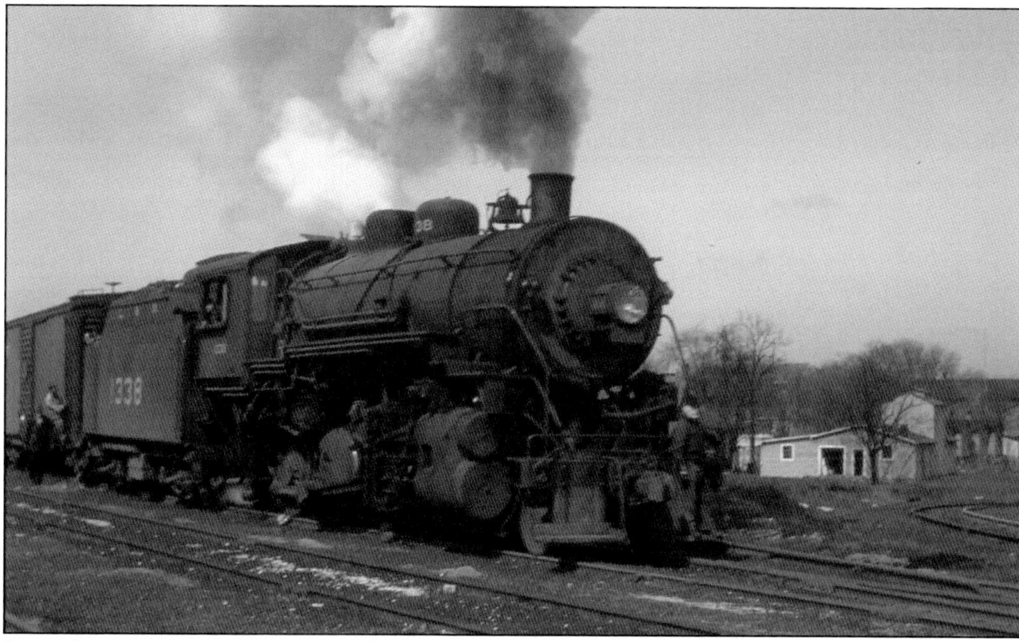

Leon Garrett spent some time at the downtown Bowling Green Louisville & Nashville yards in 1949. This group of images captures various scenes that one will never find again. L&N 1338 is switching cars in the yard. Note the switchman riding on the step at the front of the locomotive. (Leon Garrett photograph.)

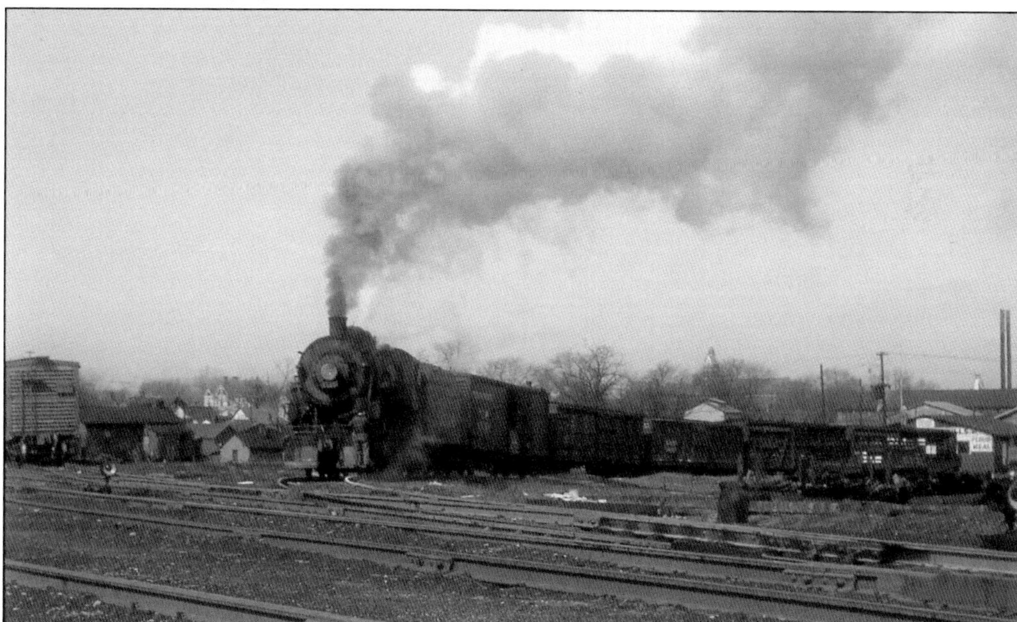

L&N 2-8-0 Consolidation locomotive leads a string of cars out of Bowling Green's stockyards just across Clay Street. In 2011, a portion of the track can still be seen exiting the Southern Recycling complex and crossing Clay Street to the remains of the old Bowling Green Stockyard. Note the men riding on the footboards at the front of the locomotive and on top of the last car. (Leon Garrett photograph.)

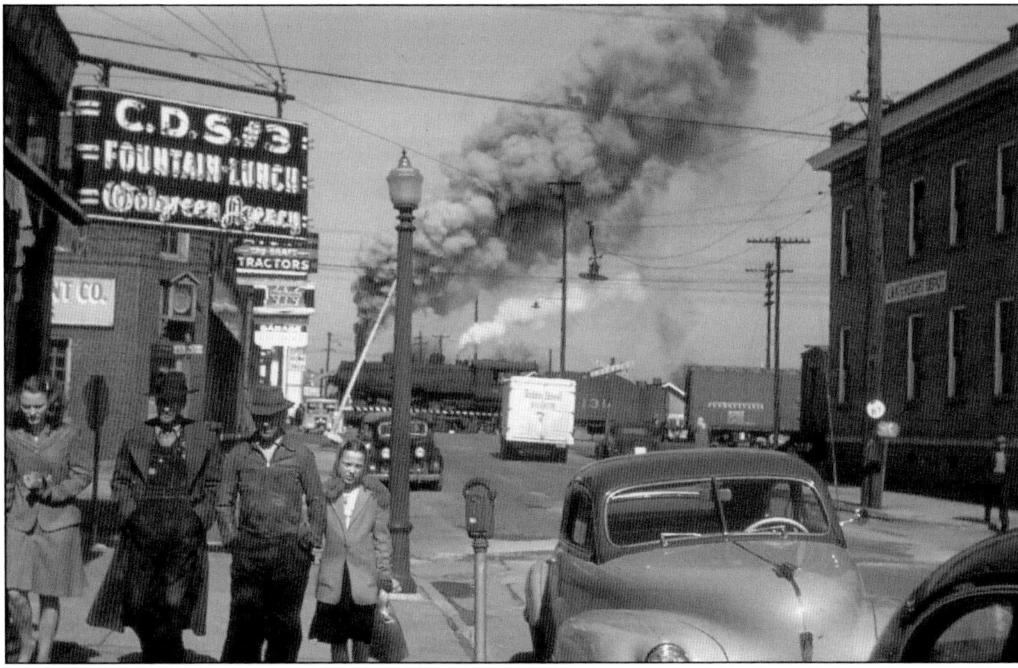

The L&N yards at Bowling Green stretched from the passenger station at Fourth Street to near Tenth Street. Shown here is the Main Street crossing of several tracks. A crossing watchman's tower is out of view to the left. The L&N Freight House is at right. None of the pictured buildings remain, just a single track, the CSX Main Line, crosses Main Street today, and the CSX Bowling Green yard is nearly five miles to the south at Memphis Junction. (Leon Garrett photograph.)

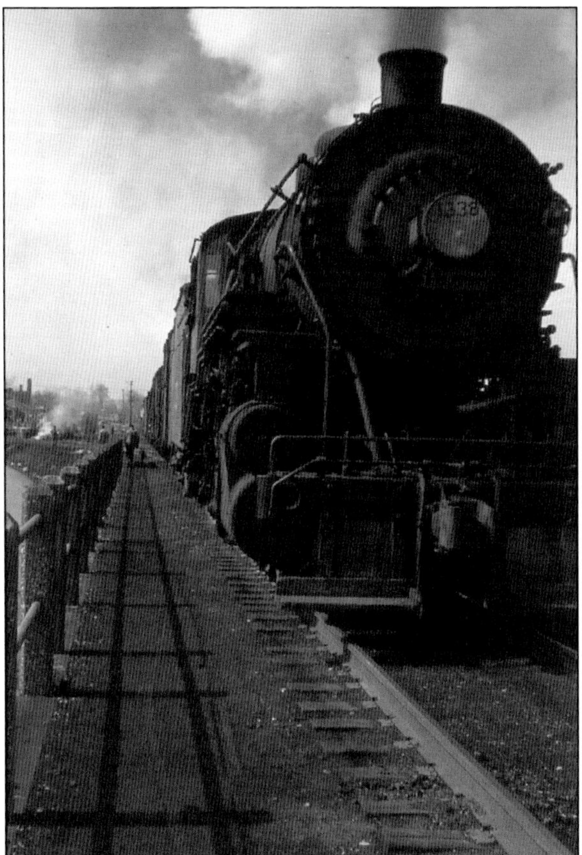

Here, L&N 2-8-0 Consolidation works near the end of Adams Street close to the Sixth Street viaduct in 1949. In the distance at left, one can see construction near the L&N freight house. Switchmen mill about the yard handling switches for the moves of the locomotive. After the L&N yard moved five miles south to Memphis Junction, this area became home to a brick yard, and most of the old yard site west of the main line has been consumed by Southern Recycling, which ships loads of scrap by rail on CSX. (Leon Garrett photograph.)

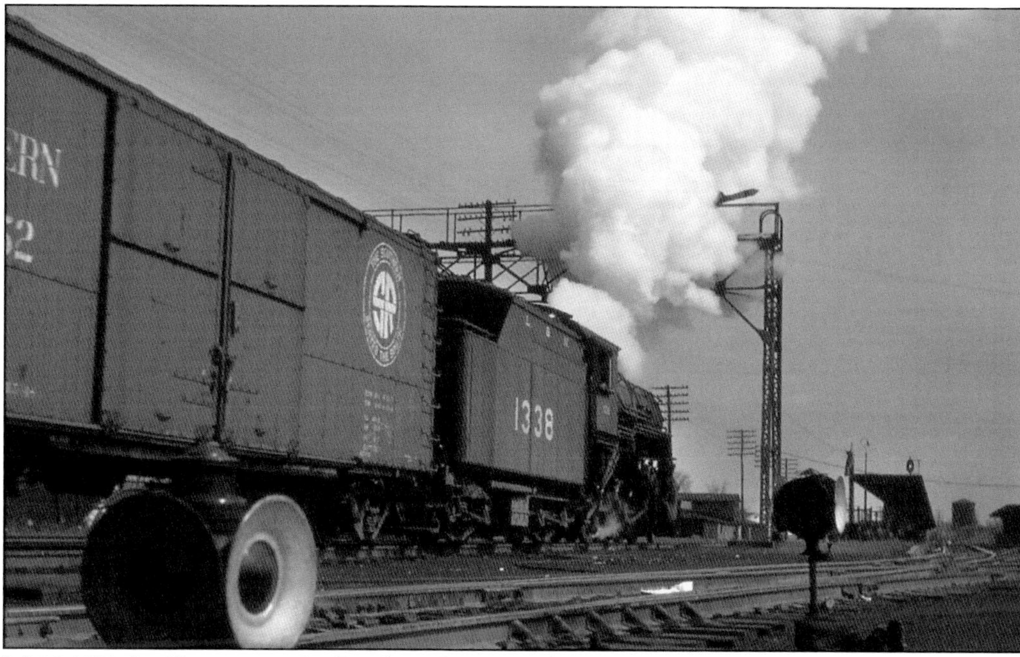

L&N 1338 shuffles cars in the Bowling Green yards as it passes under a signal bridge just south of L&N's passenger station. The station platforms are visible with baggage carts lined up. The signal on top of the platform directs crews whether they need to stop at the station for train orders. (Leon Garrett photograph.)

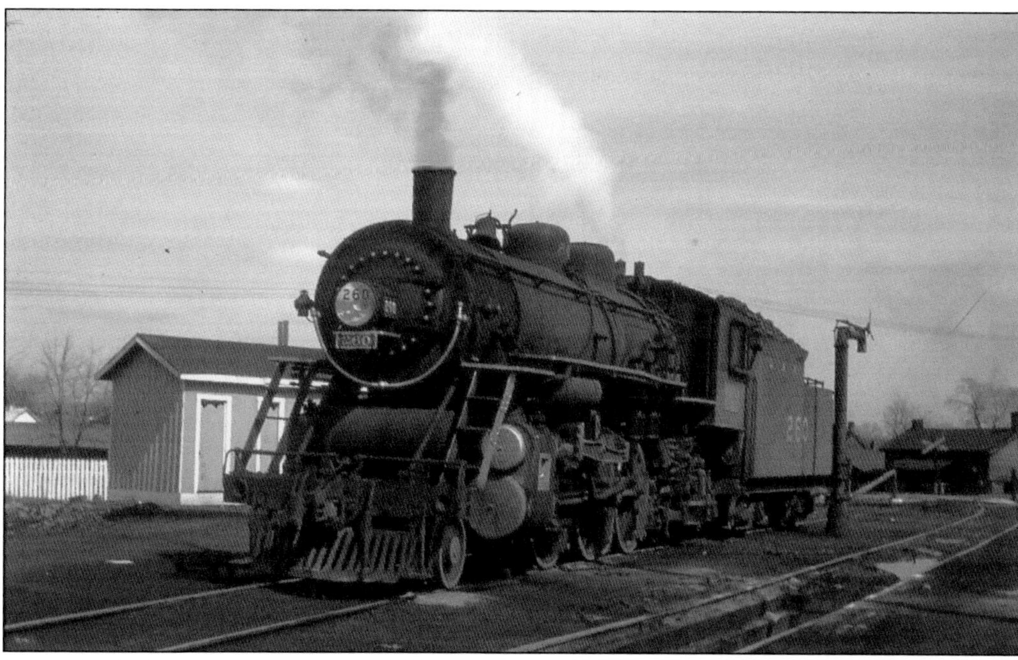

In this 1949 photograph, Louisville & Nashville K4B class Pacific-type 260 rests on the wye in the Bowling Green yard. The engine likely is between runs on the *Pan American*. Note that the trimmings on the engine have been enhanced with silvered running boards, driver tires, and smokebox door nuts. The Clay Street crossing is in the background. (Leon Garrett photograph.)

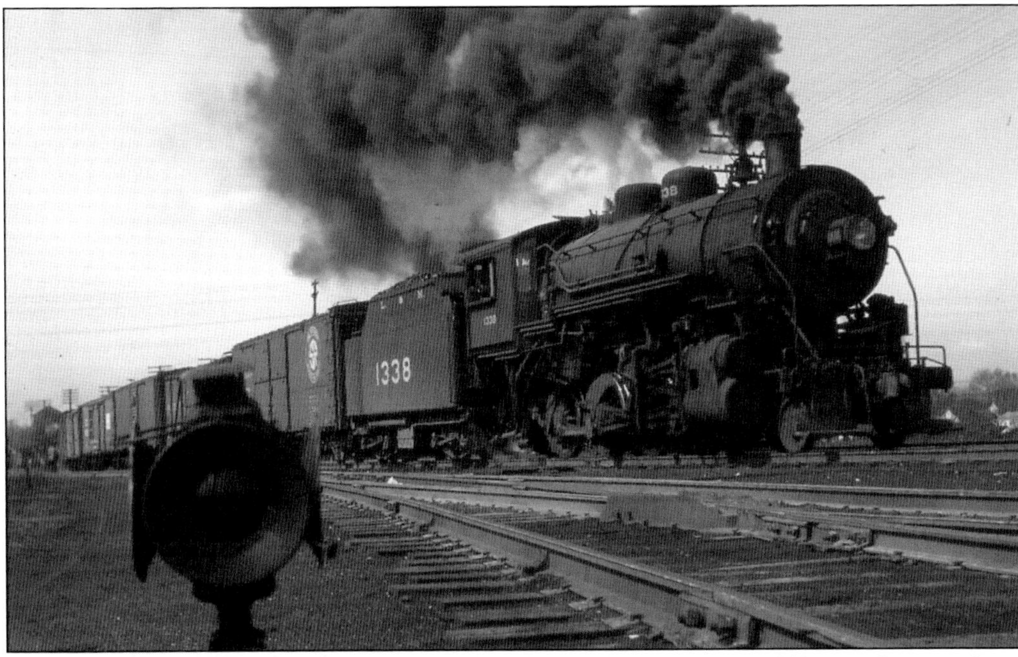

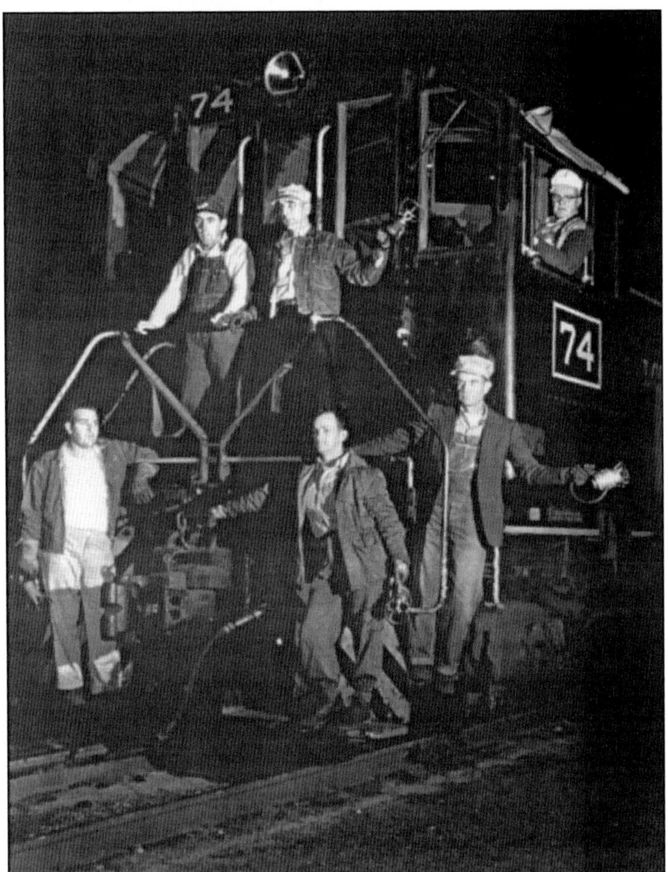

L&N 1338 is working in the yard near the station tracks just south of the Bowling Green passenger station in 1949. The 2-8-0 H29 Consolidation locomotive would be retired just two years later. One of three large water tanks is visible near the shop buildings inside the Portage wye. (Leon Garrett photograph.)

These Bowling Green L&N employees were featured in an L&N employee magazine story about the average Louisville & Nashville Railroad employee. Pictured in the photograph on switcher No. 74 are, from left to right, (first row) J.F. Buttrum and H.E. Taylor, switchmen; and Willis Taylor, switch foreman; (second row) N.D. Cole, fireman; H.C. Roe, switchman; and B.H. Williams, engineer. (L&N records, University of Louisville Archives.)

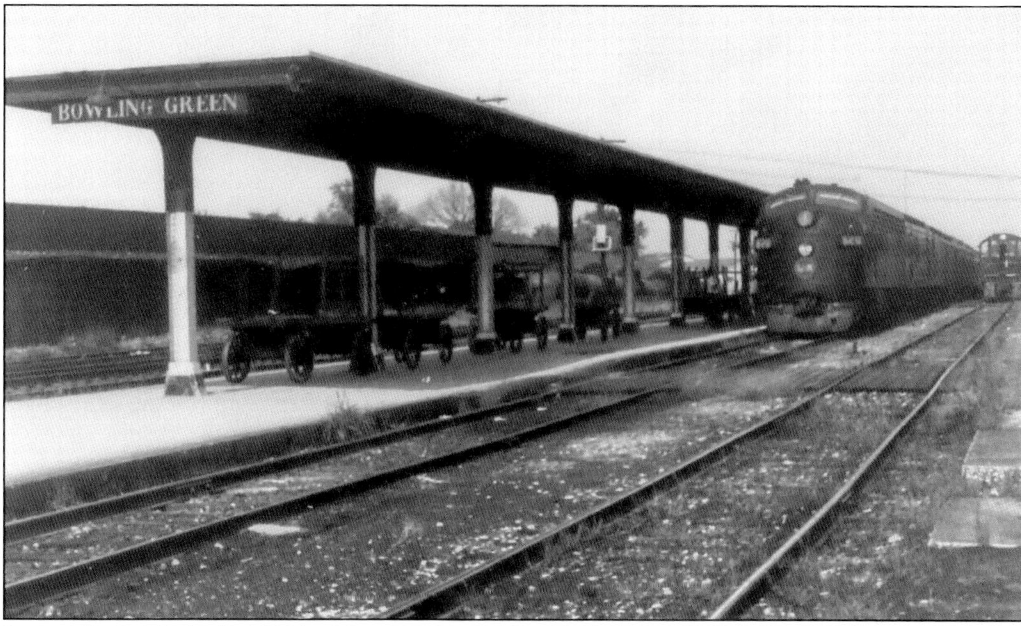

Louisville & Nashville FP7A 620 is southbound with the Memphis section of the *Pan American* in late 1962 at the Bowling Green Station. The "Down" *Pan*, train No. 199, will leave shortly after the No. 99 *Pan American* and veer off the main line onto L&N Memphis Line at milepost 118 about five miles south, continuing on to Memphis, Tennessee. (David Englert photograph, Charles Castner collection.)

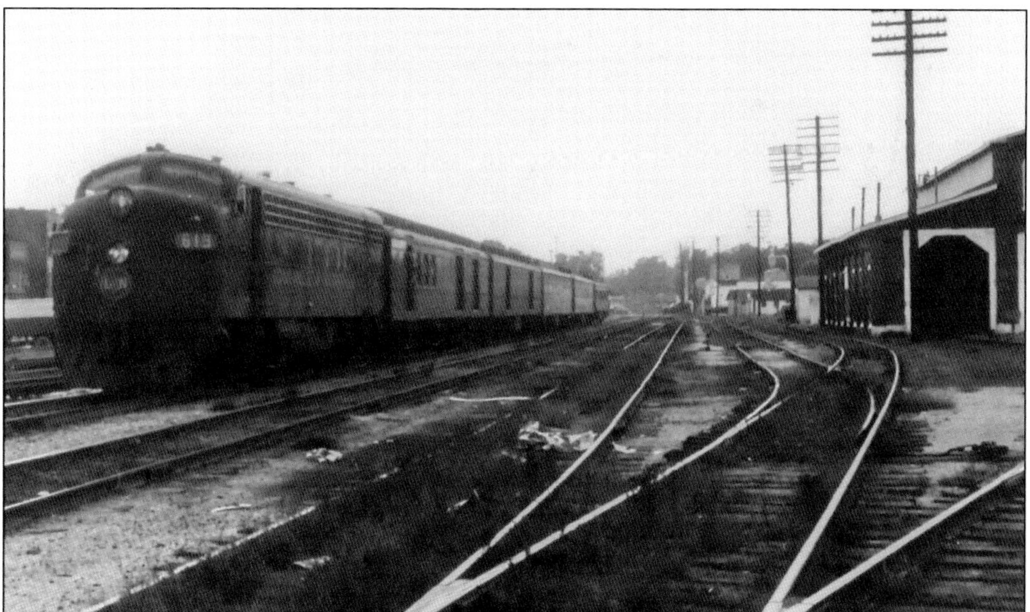

L&N train 198, the northbound Memphis section of the *Pan American*, passes the old shop building in Bowling Green during the early 1960s as it approaches the station. At one time, more than 20 passenger trains made scheduled stops at the Bowling Green Louisville & Nashville Station. During wartime, the movement of troops expanded that number considerably. (Charles B. Castner photograph.)

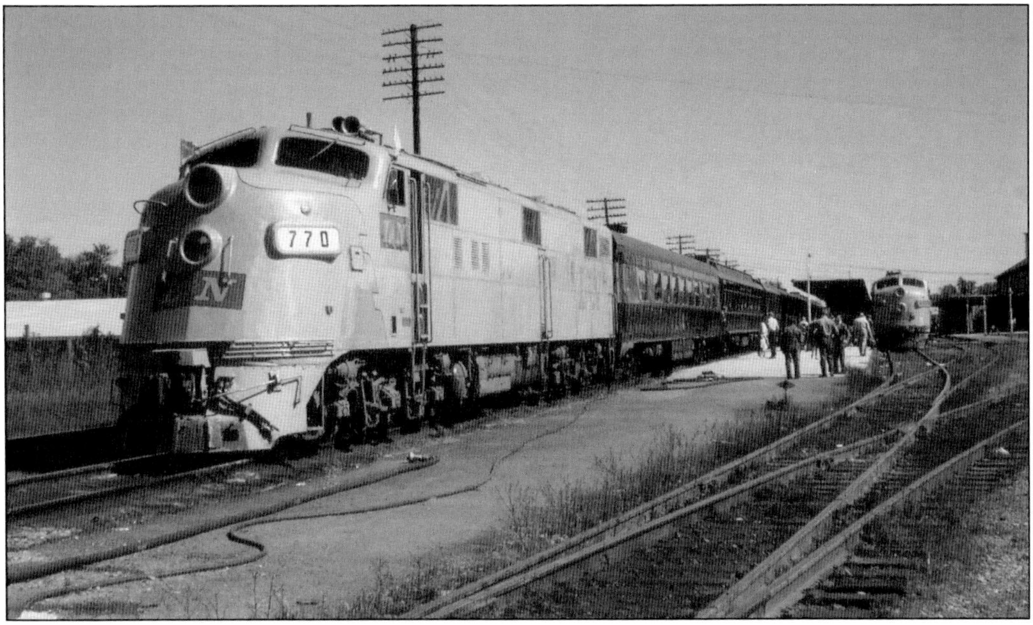

L&N E6 770 is on the point of a Kentucky Railway Museum excursion at Bowling Green in 1970. Donated by the L&N to the museum, the 770 was built in May 1942 as L&N 450B and served the passenger train fleet. Today, it sits in decay on a storage track at Kentucky Railway Museum without prime movers and vandalized. (E.G. Baker photograph, J.R. Herron collection.)

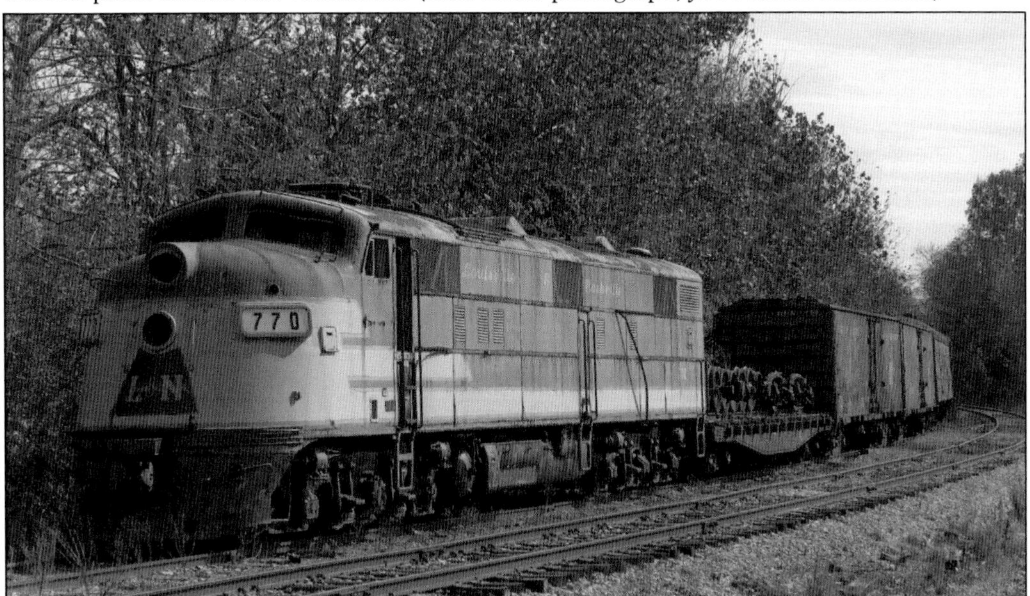

L&N E6 770 is at home on a storage track at the Kentucky Railway Museum in New Haven, Kentucky. With the prime movers and equipment removed, the locomotive would be a very expensive project for restoration. While the 770 deteriorates, the museum does maintain the only operational L&N steam locomotive, using Rogers-built 1905 L&N 4-6-2 Pacific-type 152 to pull excursion trains. In late 2011, the 152 was removed from service for its federally-mandated 15-year boiler inspection, and repairs of worn equipment is estimated at $750,000. (Kevin Comer photograph.)

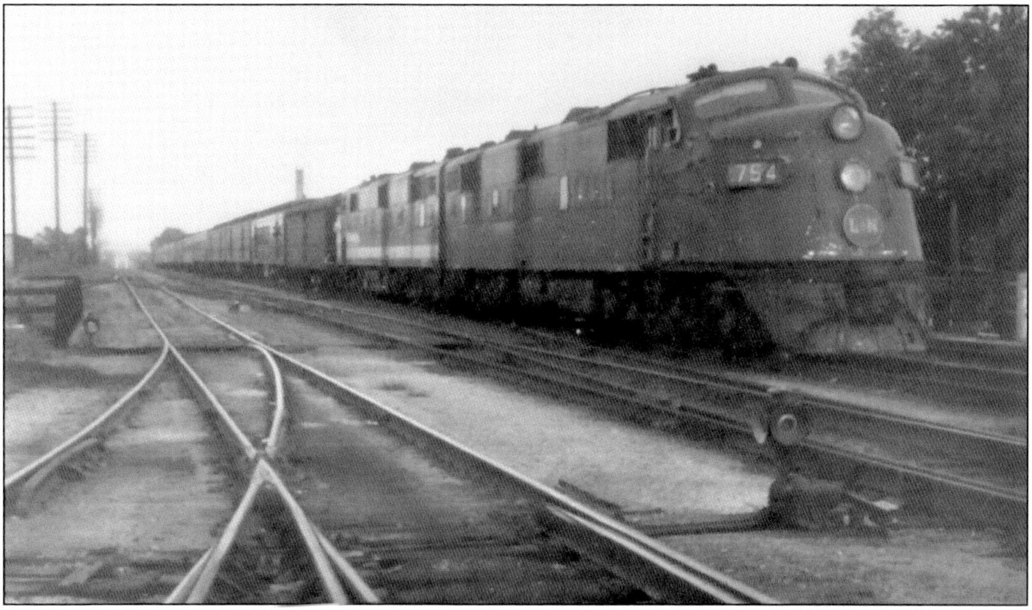

The southbound *Pan American* passes over the old Sixth Street viaduct in Bowling Green near the north end of L&N's downtown yard. The train has an RPO among the four head-end cars, followed by six passenger cars. A pair of E6s are taking the train south in 1962. Car storage tracks begin just behind the camera at left. The Portage wye is just south of the yard tracks. (Dave Englert photograph, Charles Castner collection.)

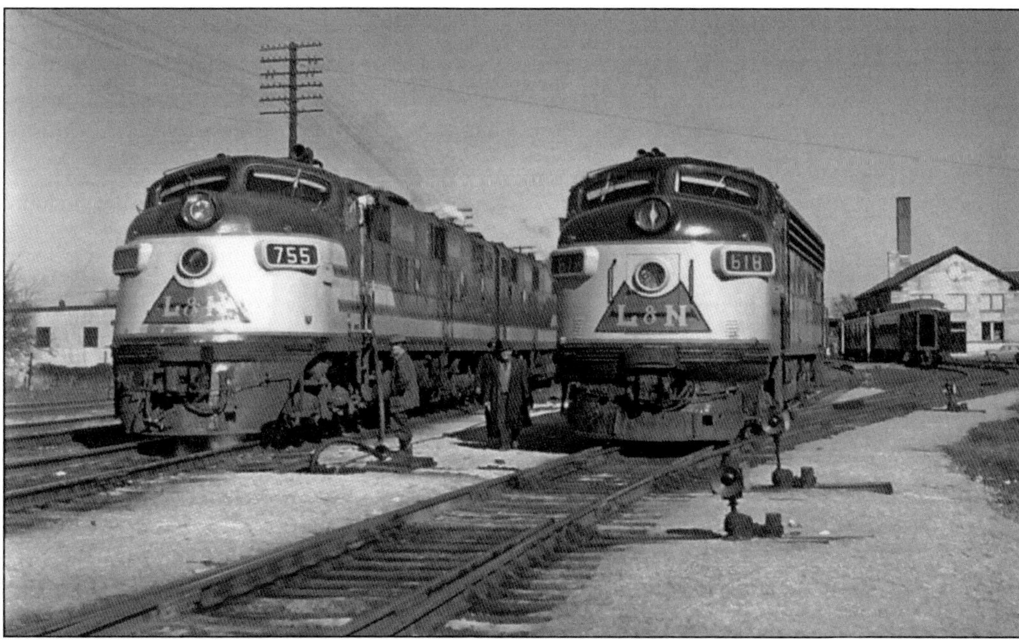

There is much activity around the platforms as Louisville & Nashville cream-and-blue 755 receives attention during a station stop in Bowling Green. At right, also in cream and blue, is L&N FP7A 618, built in March 1951. Today, E8A 796 wears these classic colors and stands near this very spot, representative of L&N passenger locomotives of the past at the Historic RailPark and Train Museum. (Alex Rose photograph.)

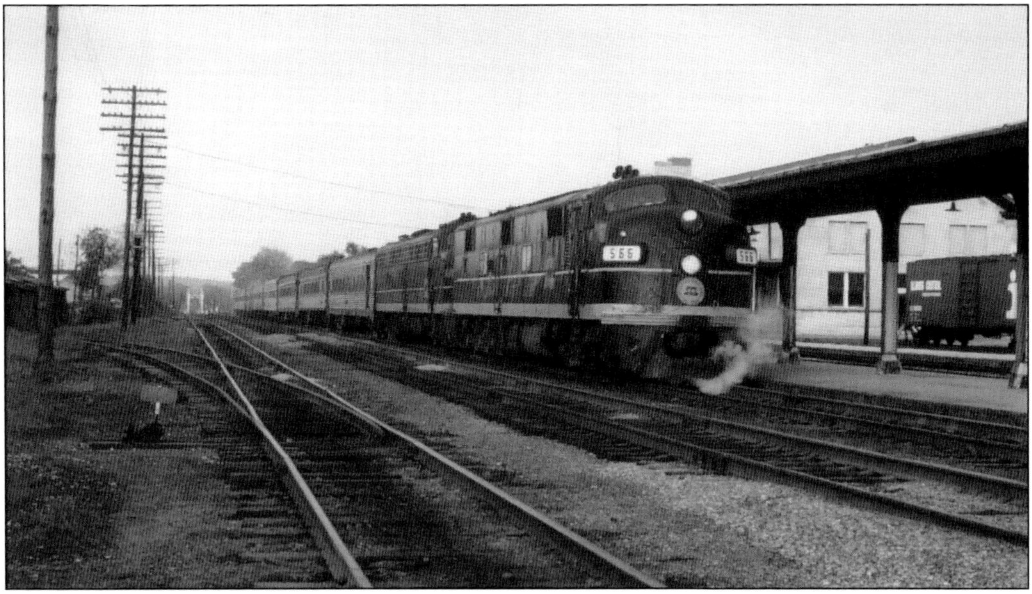

It is May 9, 1971, and the new Amtrak *South Wind* is the only former Louisville & Nashville Railroad passenger train to carry on under the nation's new carrier. With the Barren River Bridge in the distance, Seaboard Coast Line (SCL) E7A 556 makes the stop at Bowling Green's passenger station with the southbound Chicago-to-Florida train. Before long, the *South Wind* would be renamed as the *Floridian*. SCL 556, formerly Seaboard Air Line 3030, built in 1945, was retired by 1974. (Lee Yoder photograph.)

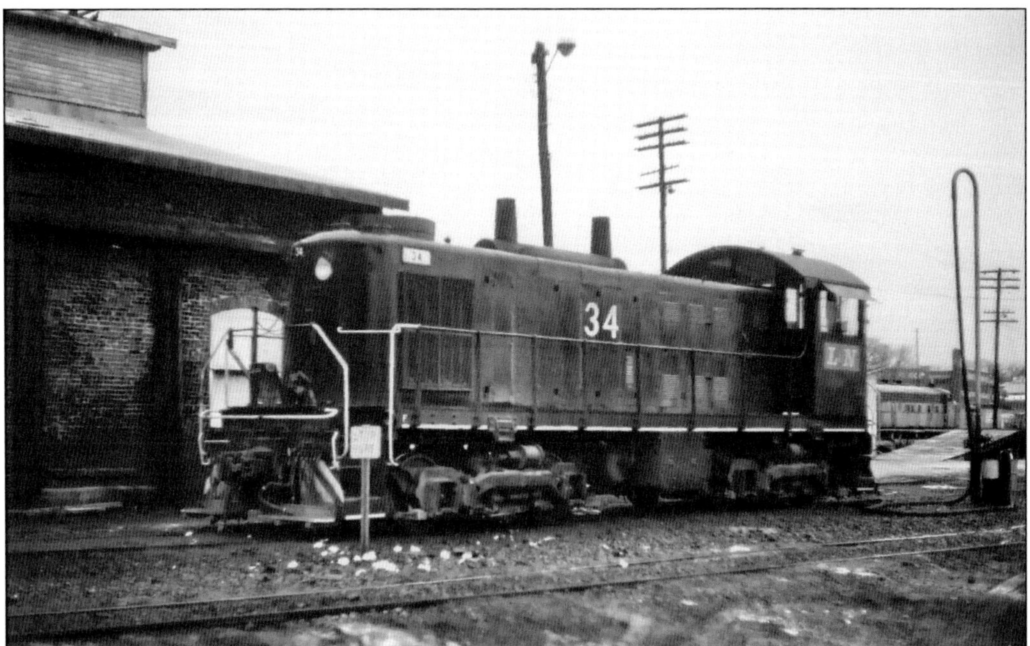

L&N switcher No. 34 sits outside the roundhouse shop building in Bowling Green's downtown yard on December 23, 1971. The rebuilt Alco S1 is idling on the engine track at 8:45 a.m. Looking southeast, one can see a piggyback ramp in the background. (Dennis Mize photograph.)

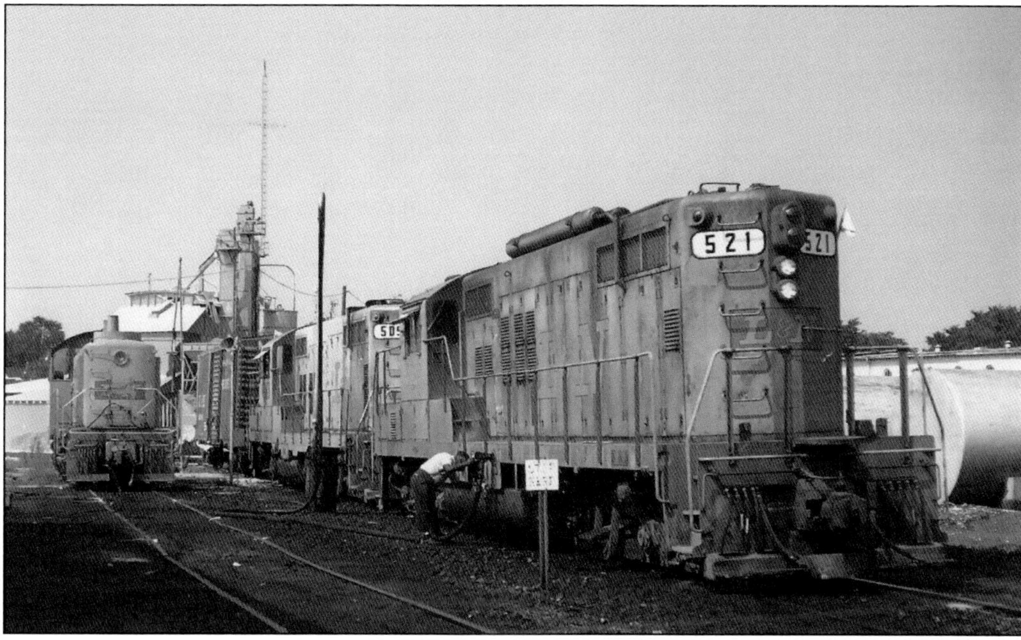

At 10:45 a.m. on August 31, 1972, Dennis Myers services L&N GP9s 521 and 509 at L&N's downtown Bowling Green yard. Switcher No. 37 will be picked up and go dead-in-tow for monthly inspection. The GP9s were built in the mid-1950s and served the L&N and later Seaboard and some lasted into CSX ownership. (Dennis Mize photograph.)

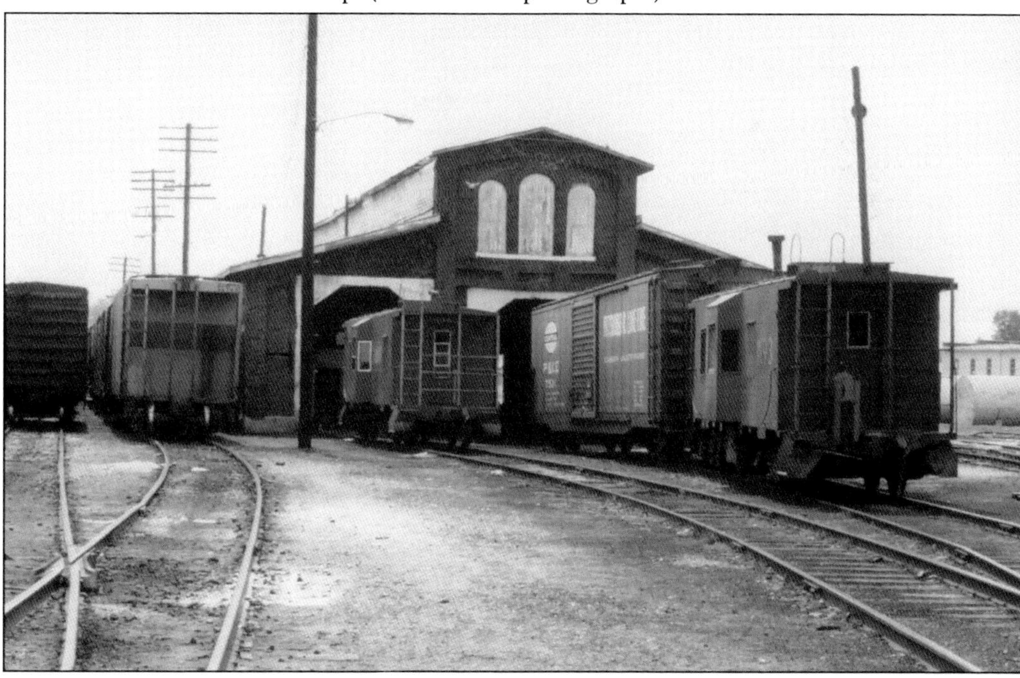

This photograph, taken on June 6, 1971, shows the only remaining structure from the post–Civil War rebuilding of the facilities at Bowling Green. Built in 1870 or before, this building eventually had a partial roundhouse attached to the far side, with an entrance at right. It was being dismantled in the early 1970s when it was set on fire and destroyed. (Lee Yoder photograph.)

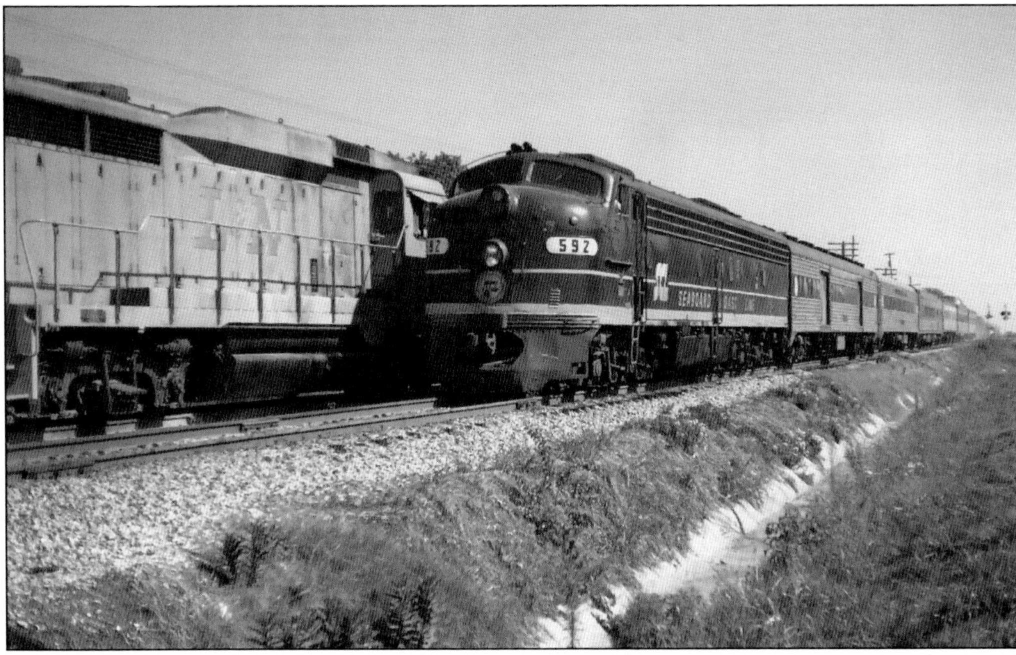

Amtrak's southbound *Floridian* has made a stop at the Bowling Green L&N station and proceeds along University Boulevard at Western Kentucky University at 10:30 a.m. Led by Seaboard Coast Line E8 592 and with six cars in tow, the train meets northbound L&N fast freight No. 78 waiting on the siding near Old Morgantown Road. (Dennis Mize photograph.)

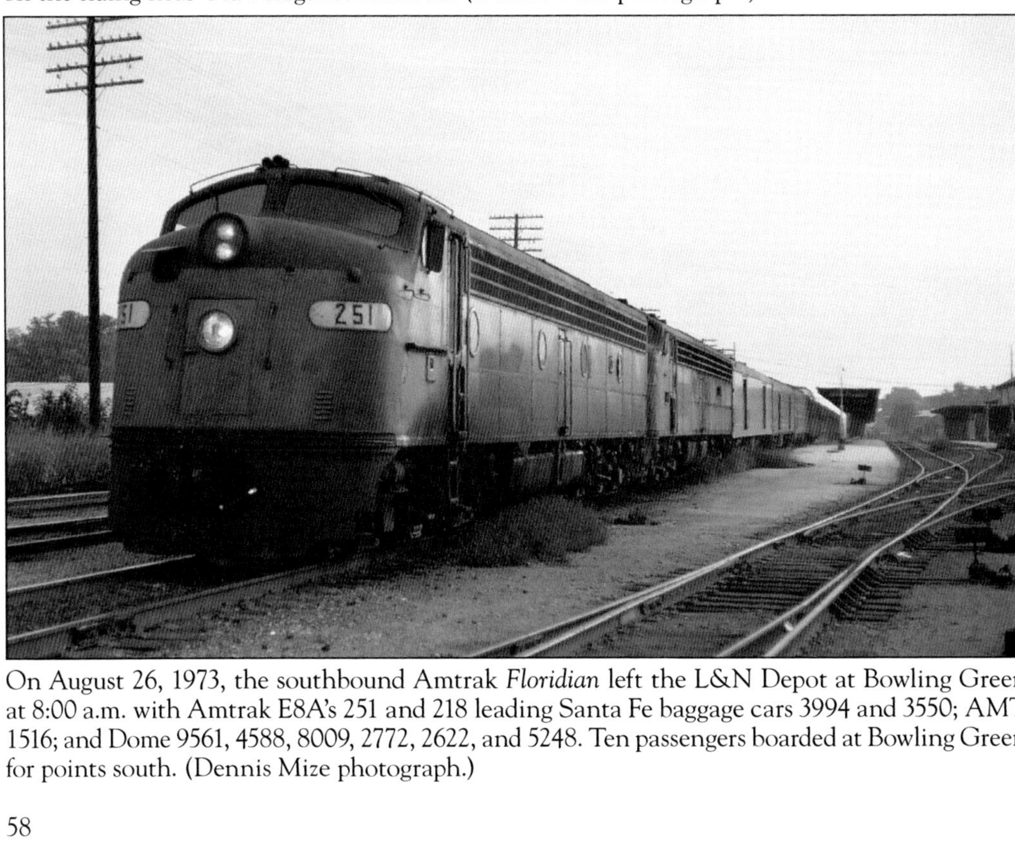

On August 26, 1973, the southbound Amtrak *Floridian* left the L&N Depot at Bowling Green at 8:00 a.m. with Amtrak E8A's 251 and 218 leading Santa Fe baggage cars 3994 and 3550; AMT 1516; and Dome 9561, 4588, 8009, 2772, 2622, and 5248. Ten passengers boarded at Bowling Green for points south. (Dennis Mize photograph.)

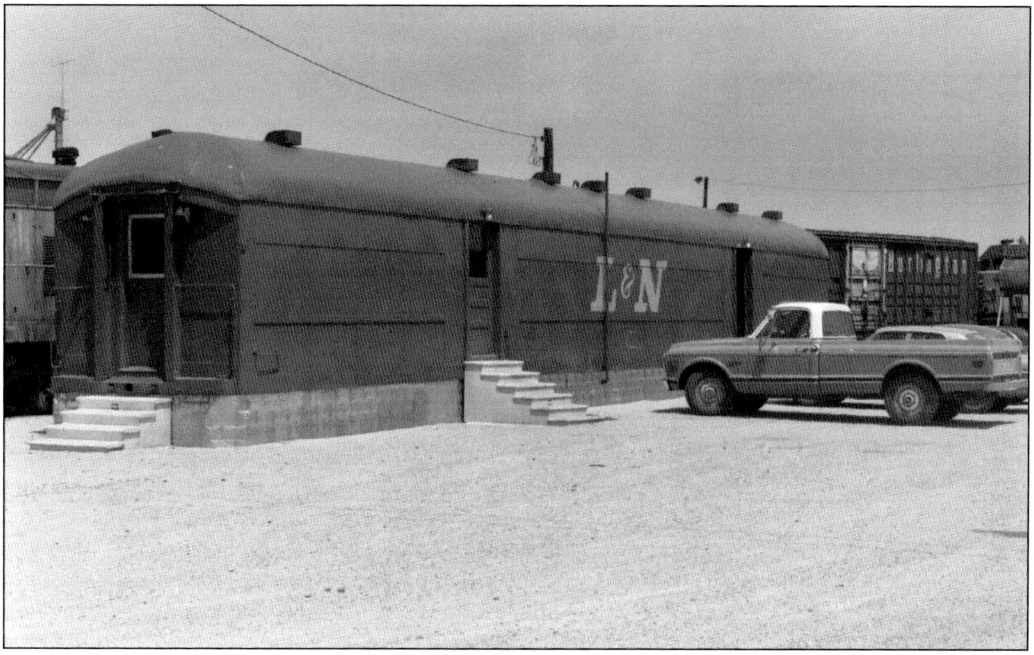

When the ancient shop building was destroyed, a former passenger car became the yard offices, or roundhouse, as the shop building had been known. This structure lasted until the yard moved to Memphis Junction in the early 1980s. When this office was razed, many local L&N records were destroyed with it. (Dennis Mize photograph.)

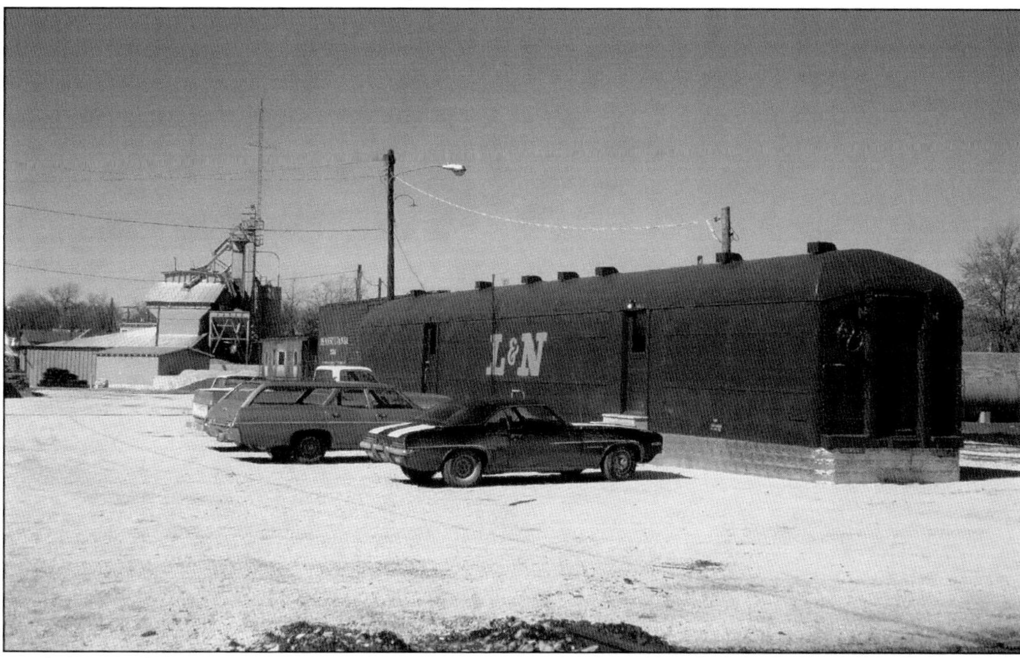

Looking southwest at the makeshift yard office shows the Red "D" Mix Concrete facility in the background. The facility, at the corner of Main and Clay Streets, later became an expensive but seldom used impound lot for the City of Bowling Green. Today, it is part of the Southern Recycling complex that uses most of the block. (Steven D. Johnson photograph.)

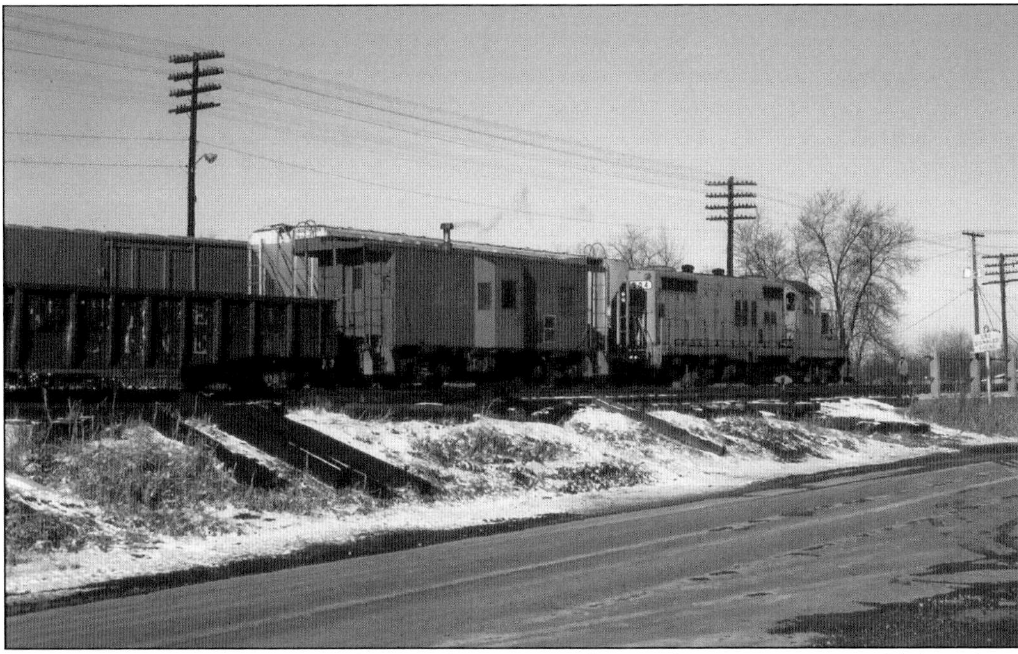

An L&N crew works in the yard at Bowling Green along Adams Street on a cold day after a snowfall. Notice the smoke coming out of the caboose from the hot stove. Adams Street was eventually rerouted and connected into a reconstructed Kentucky Street. The part of old Adams Street pictured here remains as a driveway into a local business. (Rumsie Butler photograph, Rick Williams collection.)

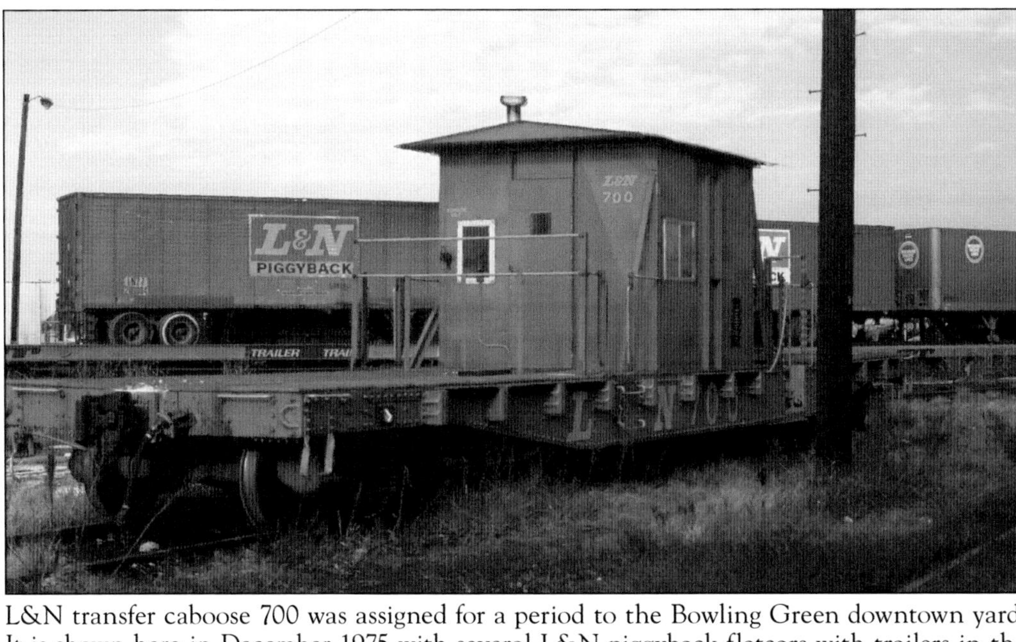

L&N transfer caboose 700 was assigned for a period to the Bowling Green downtown yard. It is shown here in December 1975 with several L&N piggyback flatcars with trailers in the background. The yard had a ramp for loading and unloading the trailers, like many other cities. L&N started the service in the mid-1950s as the TOTE, or Trailer On Train Express. (James L. Paty photograph, Steven Johnson collection.)

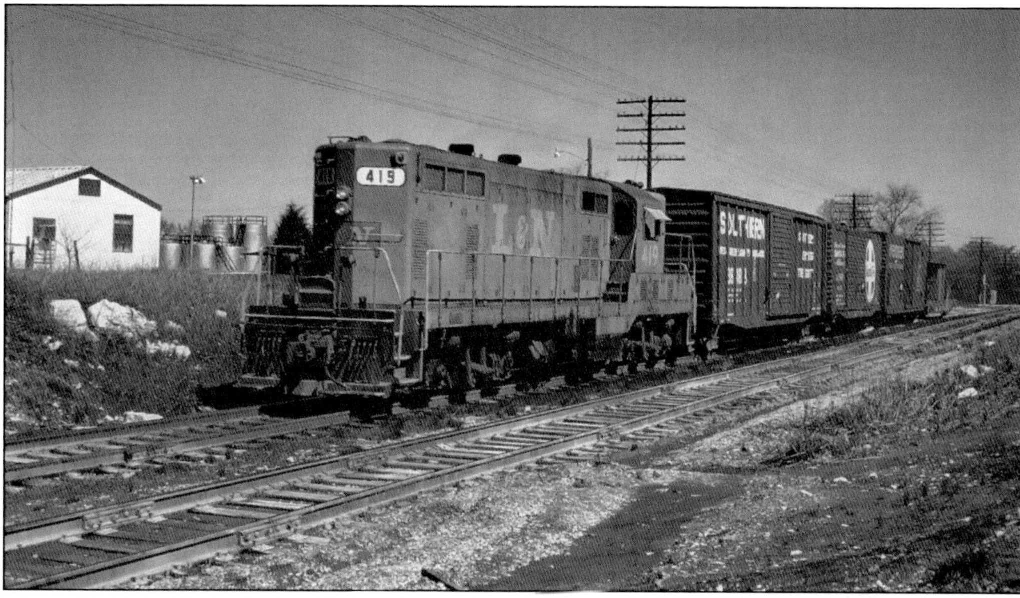

March 18, 1973, finds the local led by four-axle, 1,500-horsepower assigned yard engine L&N GP7 419 taking cars to industries at the south end of Bowing Green. The train has passed Fifteenth Street and is heading for double crossovers at Old Morgantown Road. Note that transfer caboose 700 brings up the rear. (Dennis Mize photograph.)

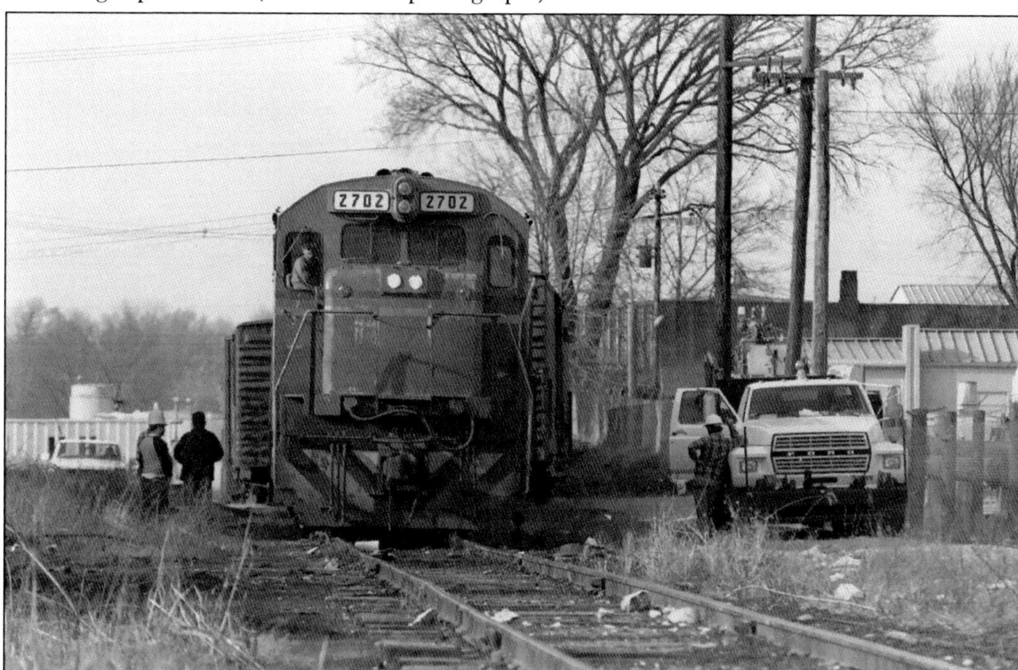

Several bystanders look on as L&N 2702 in Family Lines paint works the Portage Railroad track along Church Street near the Barren River in Bowling Green. This area had been home to the Southern Cut Stone Company, Pet Milk, and Kyrock Asphalt's loading facilities in a more prosperous period. Boxcars are being shuffled around for the scattered businesses along the Portage. (Steven D. Johnson photograph.)

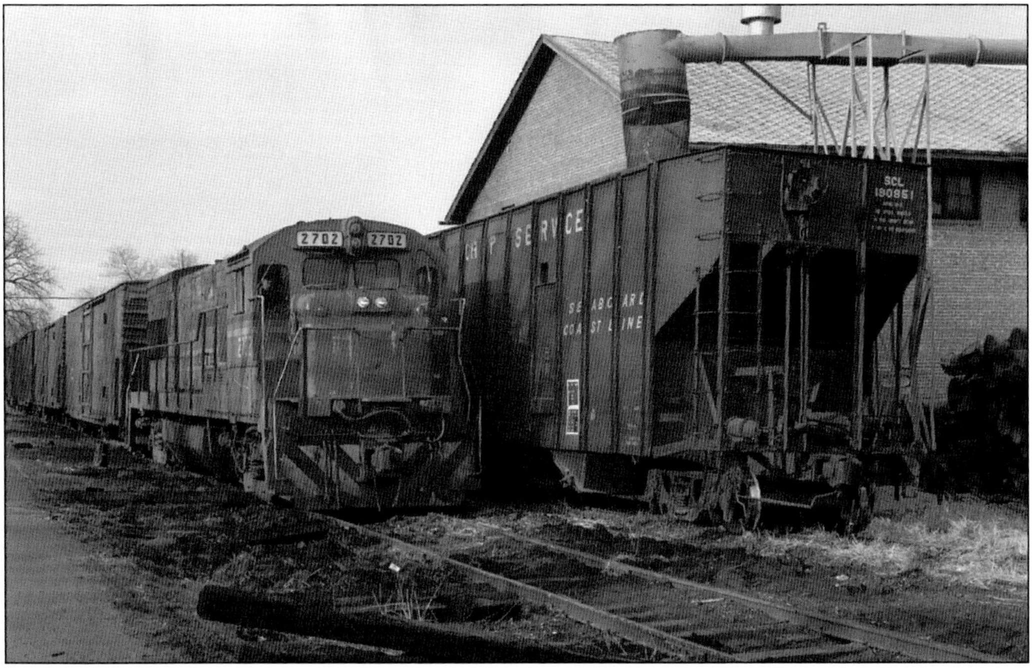

L&N 2702 passes Turner-Day-Woolworth axehandle factory on the Portage Railroad. The factory was one of Bowling Green's first major industries beginning in the early 1850s. The factory closed by the 1980s and the rails are now gone. (Steven D. Johnson photograph.)

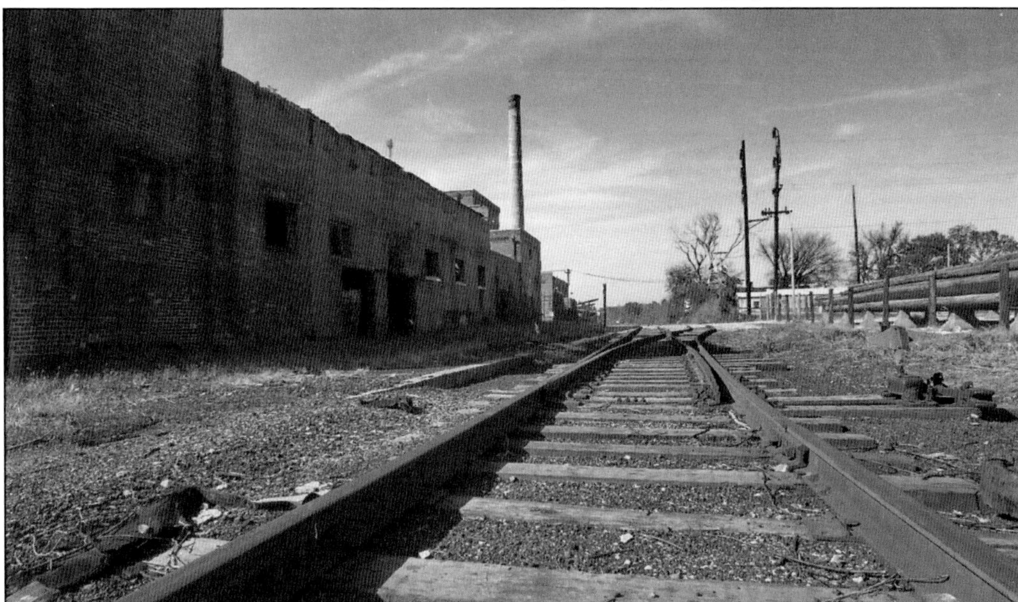

The building at left was one of Bowling Green's early power plant facilities. Across the next street on the left is the old Pet Milk Company. This view shows the abandoned Portage Railroad tracks. The tracks remained intact for a long while before finally being pulled up and sold as scrap. The end of the line is about two blocks farther but extended another block into the Kyrock barge-to-rail transfer facilities on Barren River at one time. (Ben Runner Jr. photograph.)

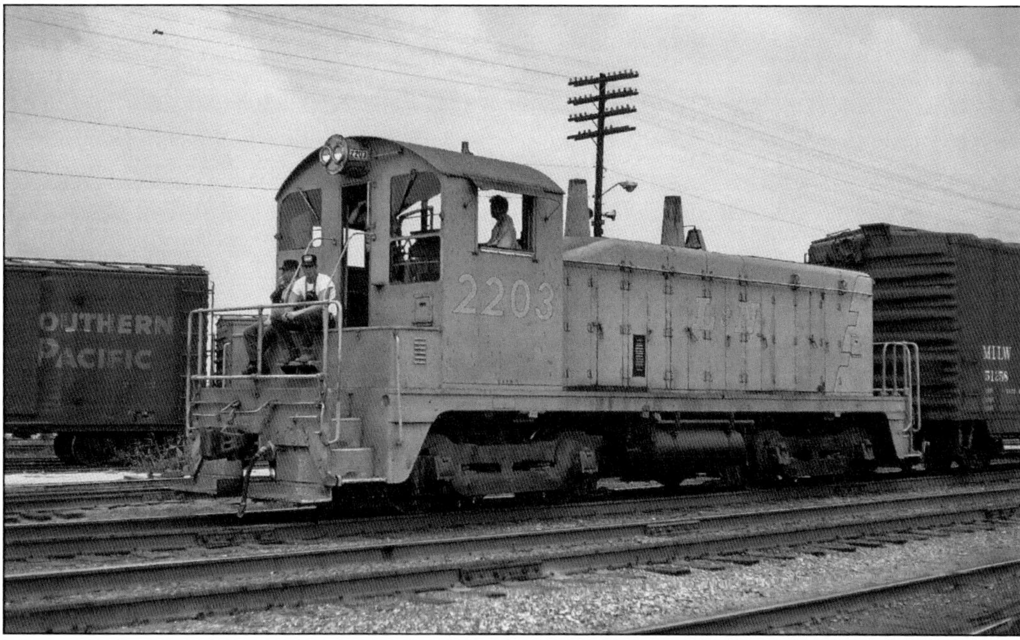

The crew of this L&N switcher is ready to go to work in the Bowling Green yards. Until the late 1960s, cars would be taken off and added to passenger trains stopping at Bowling Green's L&N Station. This required switchers to be on duty around the clock, also working the freight yard. (Dennis Mize photograph.)

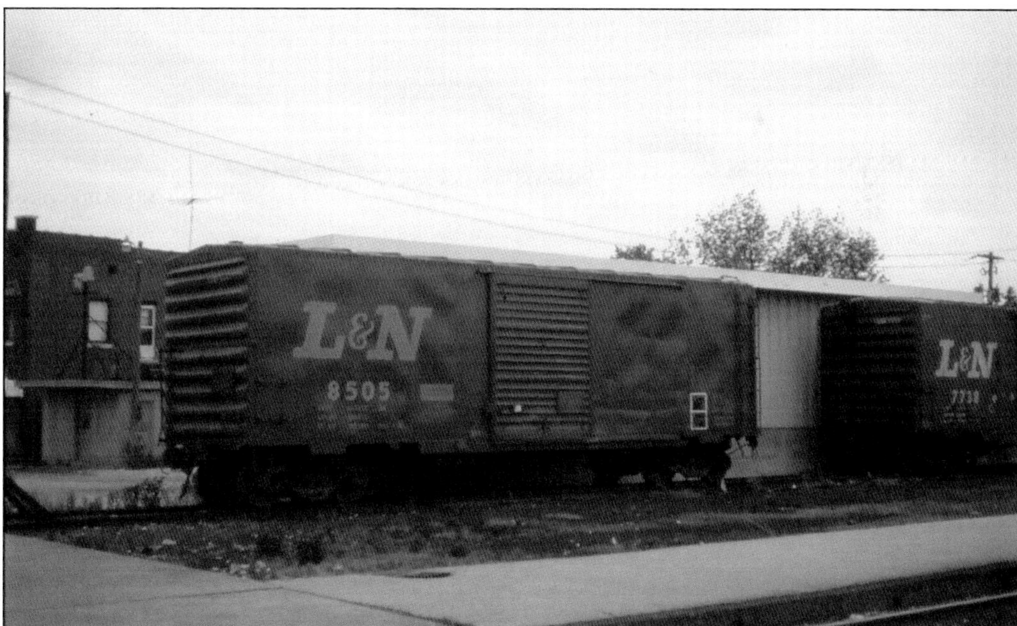

Just to the south of the L&N's passenger station in Bowling Green stood this two bay freight building that was used during the later years of the L&N. Partially visible in the background is the Depot Inn. Many people and crews off of trains would make their way over to eat there, and train men stayed there over the years between runs. (Rumsie Butler photograph, Rick Williams collection.)

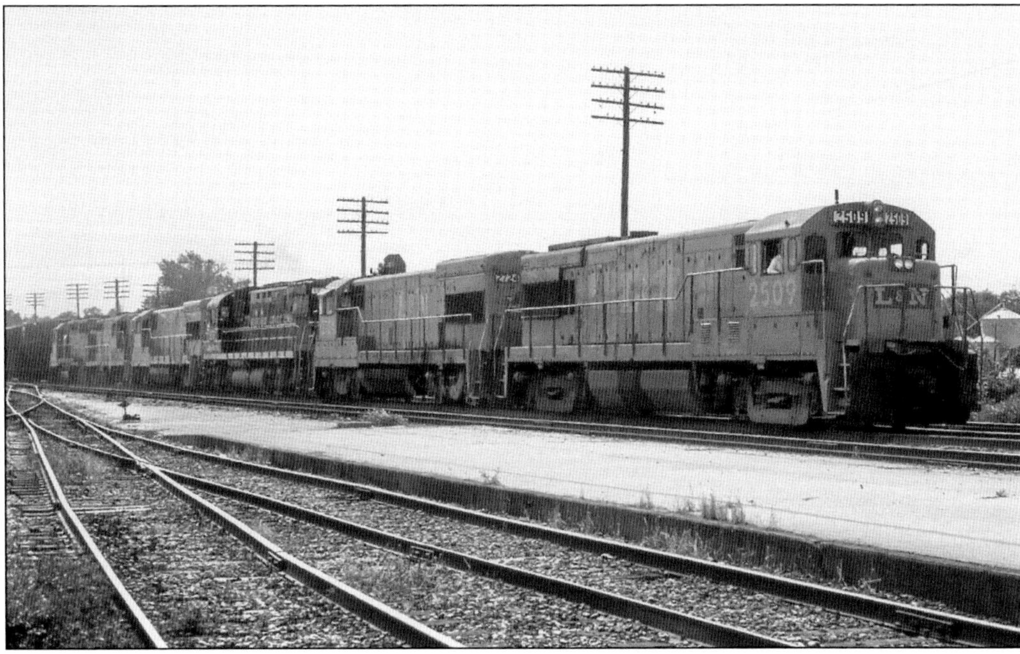

Local railroad enthusiast Rumsie Butler collected several area railroad images, including this photograph taken from the platform at L&N's passenger station in Bowling Green. A nice mixture of power leads a northbound train, including both L&N and Seaboard Coast Line diesels. (Rumsie Butler photograph, Rick Williams collection.)

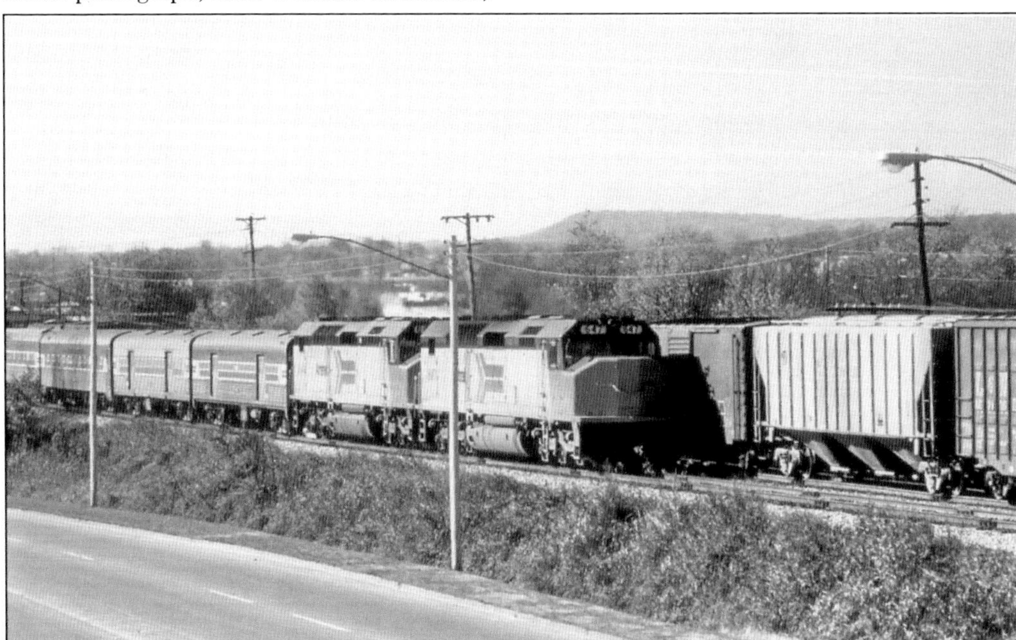

The combined Amtrak *Floridian* and Auto Train are northbound approaching the north end of the Morgantown Road siding at Bowling Green. While the Auto Train was a run-through train with no stops between Louisville, Kentucky, and Sanford, Florida, it did make stops while combined with the *Floridian*. (Rumsie Butler photograph, Rick Williams collection.)

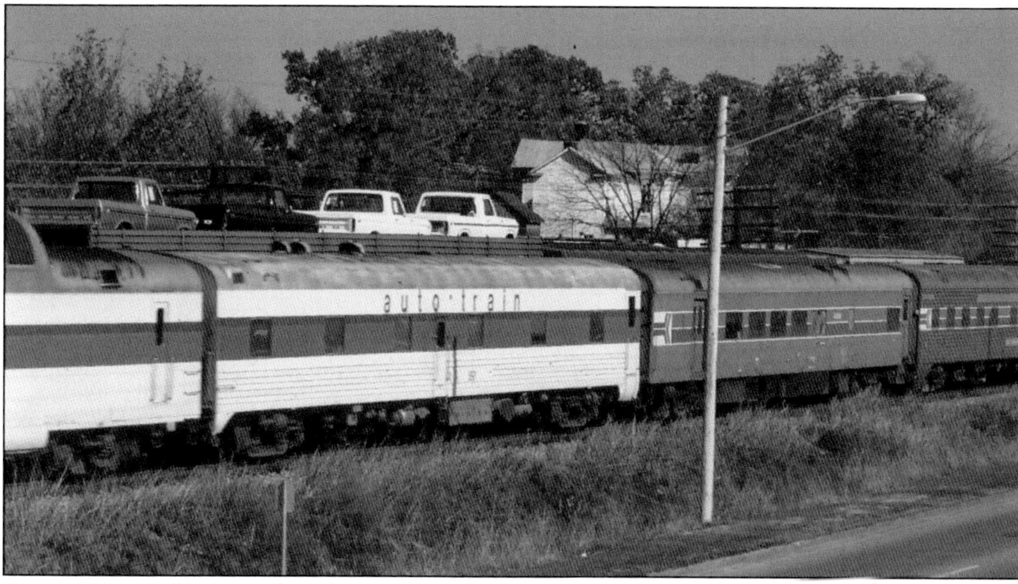

From 1976 to 1978, Amtrak and Auto Train had an agreement in which the trains would combine between Louisville and Florida. The southbound Amtrak *Floridian* consist would make the stop at South Louisville's Auto Train Depot, bypassing Union Station. The Auto Train passenger cars and auto carriers would be added to the *Floridian* for the southbound trip. The Amtrak stops and heavier weight on the long train slowed the schedule, and the train struggled to maintain consistency. Eventually, Auto Train gave up the Louisville-to-Sanford run. (Rumsie Butler photograph, Rick Williams collection.)

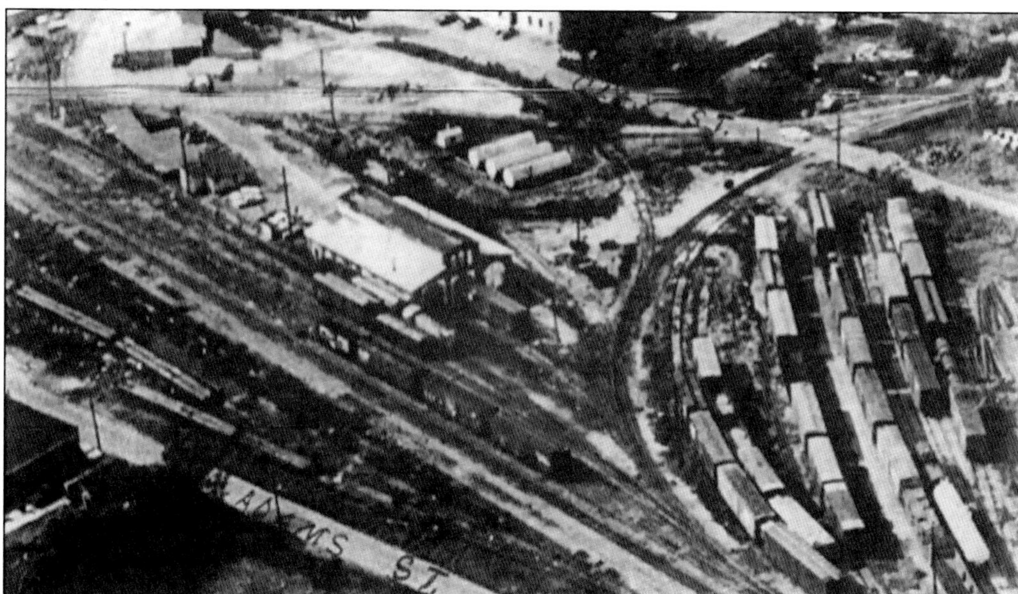

This early-1970s photograph shows the Louisville & Nashville Railroad Bowling Green yard. Railroad employees were on strike at the time. Adams and Clay Streets are marked and Main Street is out of the photograph to the left (south). The 1870s shop building and fuel tanks are in the center of the wye, with car storage tracks to the right. Farther north past Sixth Street is the passenger station. (Paul Hightower photograph.)

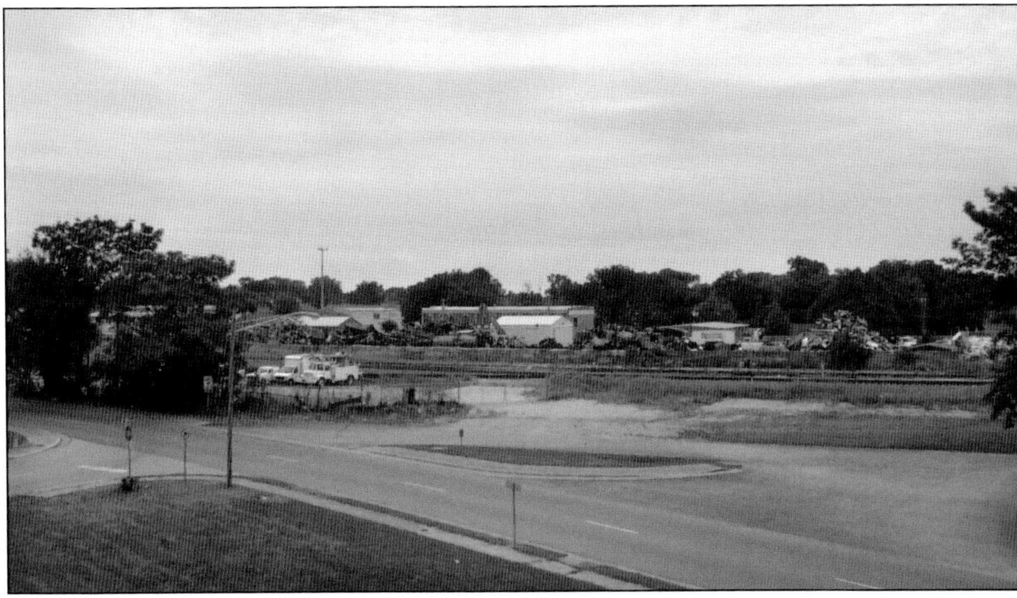

After the L&N yard moved from downtown Bowling Green about five miles south to Dishman Lane, most of the tracks were removed from the area. The Portage Railroad entering the yard, as well as connecting street-running industrial tracks across Main Street, down Brownslock Road, and along Clay Street, have all been removed. Southern Recycling is the remaining customer downtown, but E.H. Harris Lumber still has track in place into their Clay Street location. (Kevin Comer photograph.)

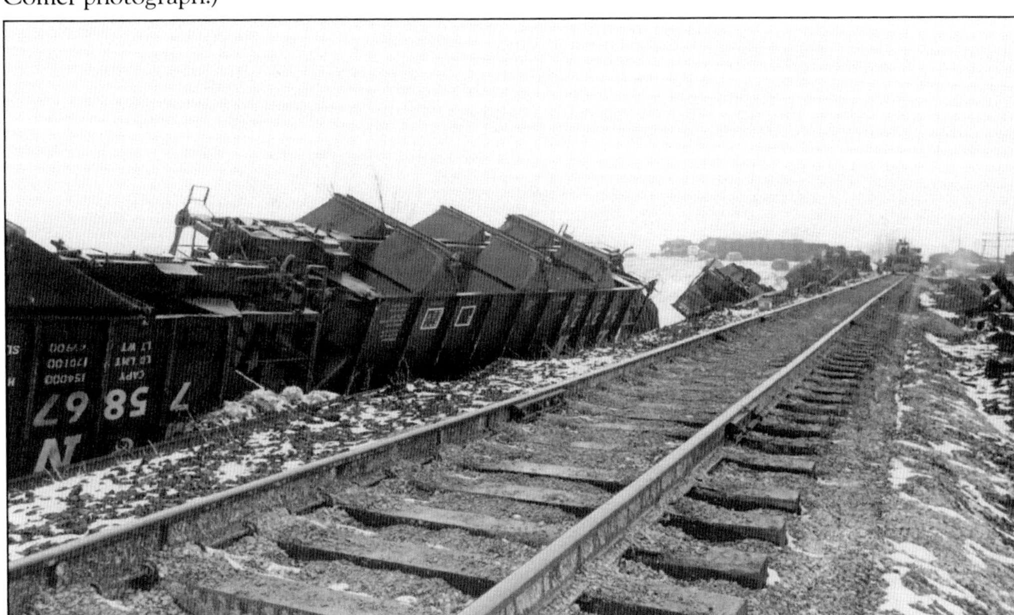

On February 28, 1978, at 1:20 a.m., a 91-car L&N train with three locomotives had 32 cars derail about six miles north of Bowling Green. About 16 of the 32 cars were scattered around, while the others were on their sides along the railroad bed. Fire officials were not notified until 8:52 a.m., state police at 9:30 a.m., and the large Firestone Textiles plant adjoining the site at 9:40 a.m. Two of the cars contained hazardous materials. (Greg Lake photograph.)

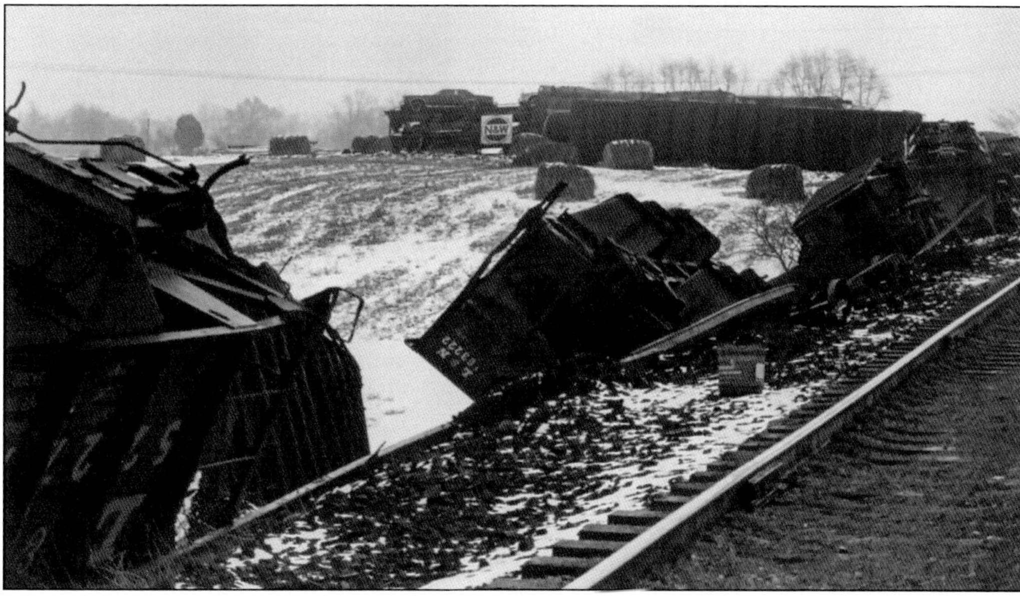

The February 28, 1978, derailment of 16 cars contained two cars with hazardous material—a piggyback trailer with 200 cases of flammable insecticide and a covered hopper car containing titanium dioxide. Titanium dioxide when mixed with water becomes hydrochloric acid. This had been the fourth derailment in recent days and the fifth in Warren County in recent months. Local officials were upset that emergency responders were not immediately notified by the L&N about the derailment. (Greg Lake photograph.)

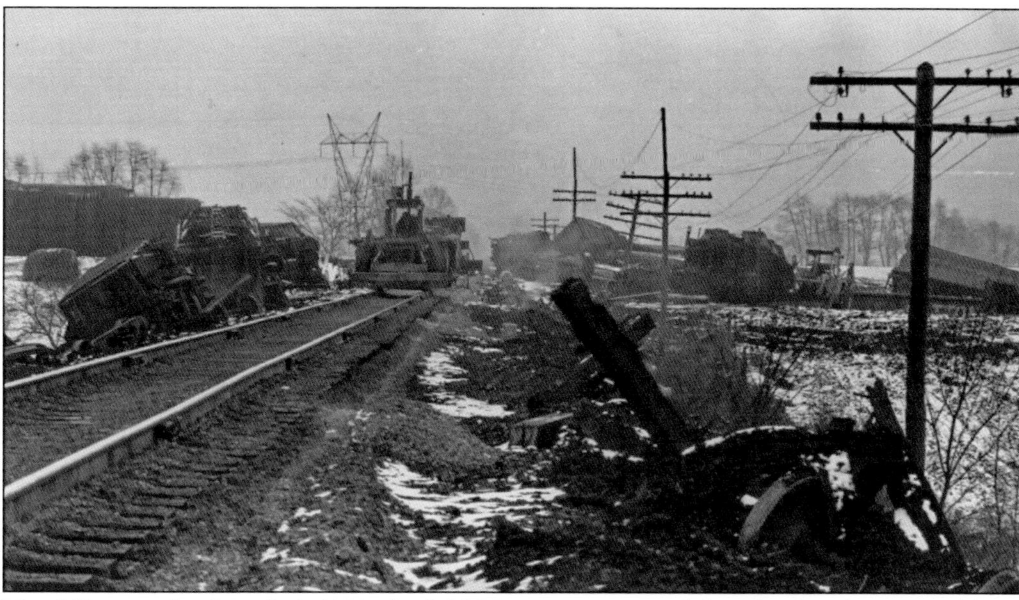

The following day, March 1, 1978, the L&N line was reopened, but the derailment would stay a hot topic. Eventually, the L&N was indicted on charges of first-degree wanton endangerment charging negligence because of faulty wheels and unsafe tracks. Just a few days prior, the Waverly, Tennessee, tank car explosion had killed 16 people, injured 43, destroyed 16 Waverly structures, and heavily damaged 20 others. Both the police chief and fire chief were killed along with L&N wrecker crewmen and bystanders. (Greg Lake photograph.)

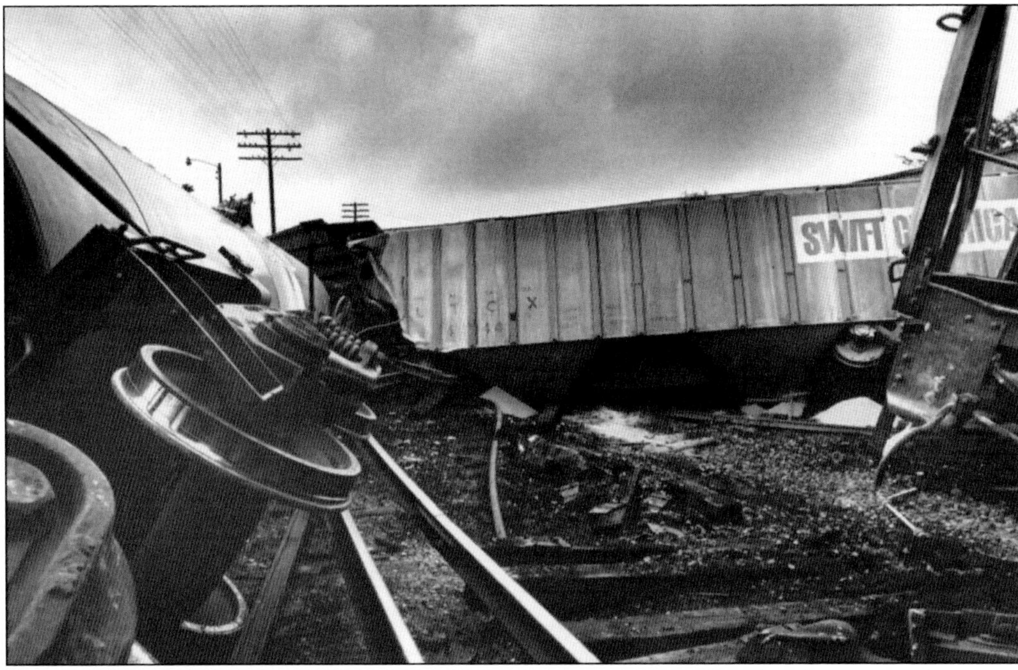

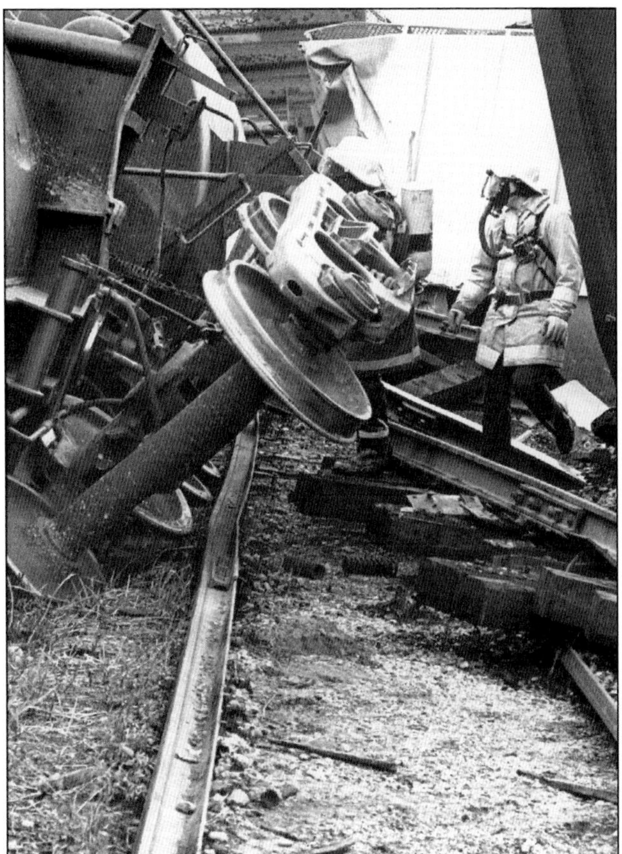

Another derailment at milepost 113 in downtown Bowling Green on April 25, 1978, resulted in the evacuation of nearly 1,000 residents, two schools, and some nearby businesses. Eleven cars of an 87-car northbound train derailed next to a train on a siding, derailing five tank cars. A relief valve leak allowed some poisonous gas to escape, injuring the conductor and one fireman. (Historic RailPark Collection.)

The derailment of April 25, 1978, was the sixth in the local area since October. Those previous derailments occurred at Rich Pond on October 24, 1977, damaging two businesses; Memphis Junction Road on November 5, 1977, where 5 locomotives and 17 cars left the tracks; Franklin, Kentucky, on December 8, 1977, with burning cars and evacuations; December 17, 1977, in downtown Smiths Grove that involved six coal cars and a caboose; and the 32-car derailment six miles north of Bowling Green in late February. (Historic RailPark Collection.)

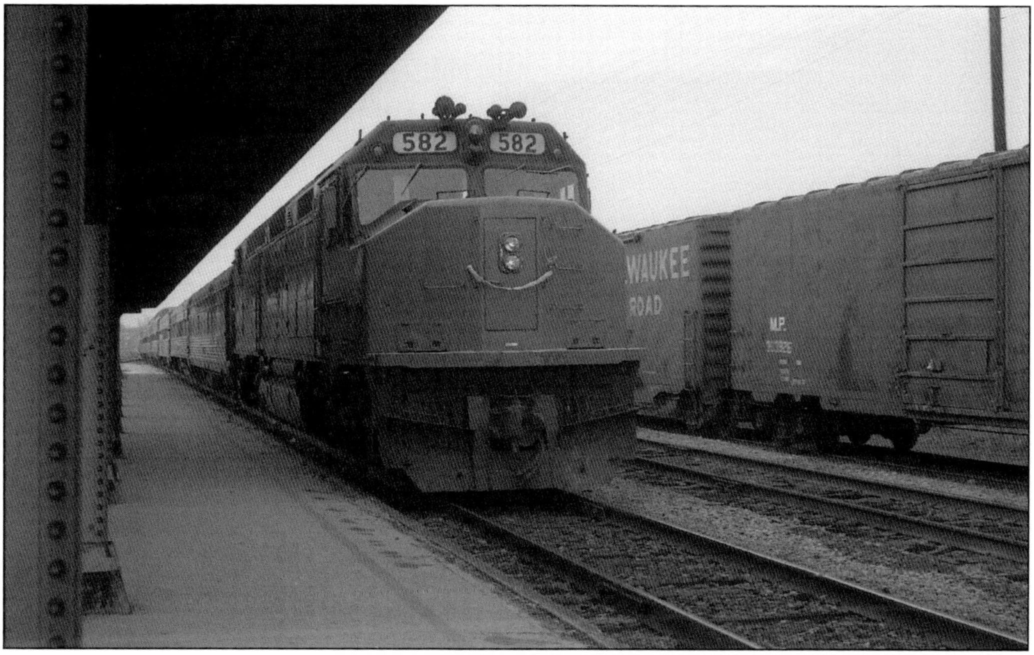

During the final days of Amtrak's *Floridian* in the late 1970s, the stop at Bowling Green would yield few passengers, and there were signs that the end was near. Budget cuts under Pres. Jimmy Carter would eliminate some Amtrak routes, and after having scheduled passenger trains run on the original L&N Main Line since 1859, this would finally end on October 9, 1979. (Ben Runner Jr. Photograph.)

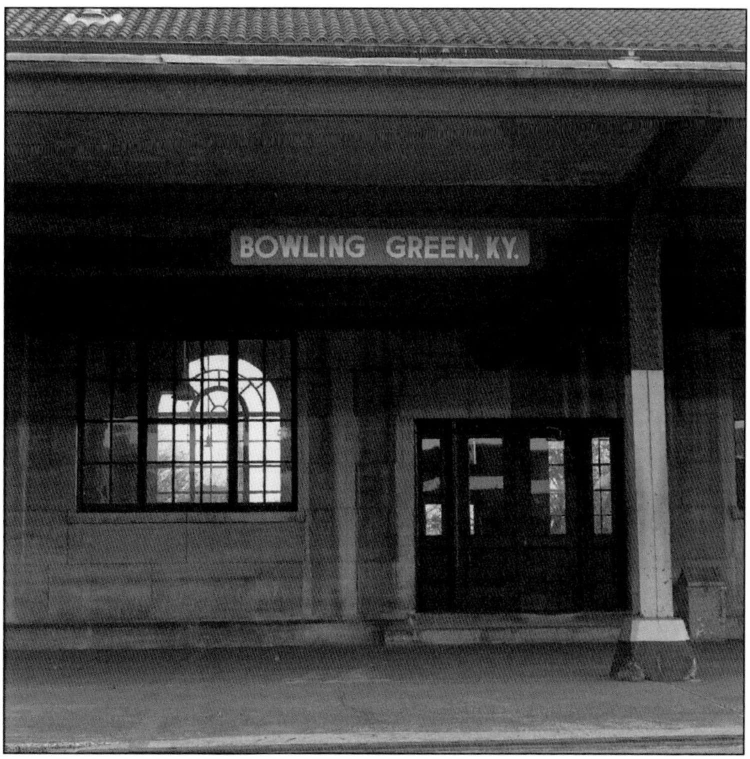

Travelers arriving at Bowling Green's passenger station would see this sign above the back entrance off the platform. Like the butterfly platform's "Bowling Green" signs, this sign also disappeared after the depot closed. There are many who are hopeful that Bowling Green has not seen the last of passenger service. After more than three decades, the outlook is not very promising. (Ben Runner Jr. photograph.)

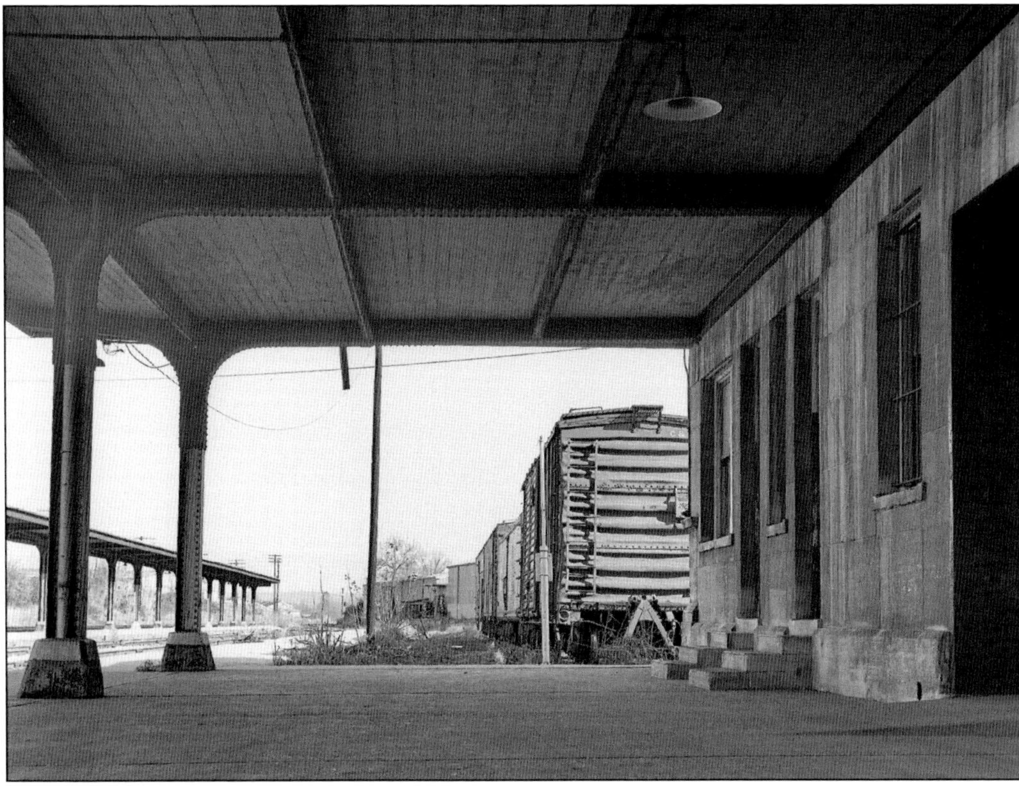

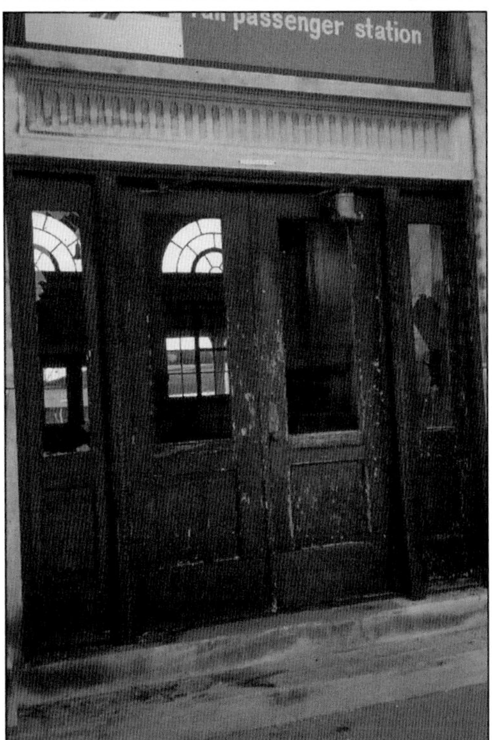

This view looking north from the rear station platform shows a few cars still remaining on the station tracks around 1980. The Sears warehouse and a food service company are along the depot track at right. The tracks converged just north of the butterfly shed. (Ben Runner Jr. photograph.)

It did not take long for the abandoned depot to begin to be vandalized. Broken windows in the front doors below the Amtrak sign make it clear that the Louisville & Nashville Railroad had no further use for the structure. The passenger benches in the main lobby are visible, and some of those were saved and restored as an Eagle Scout project by Ryan Dowell for use in the Historic RailPark and Train Museum. (Ben Runner Jr. photograph.)

As the end of Amtrak passenger service for Bowling Green approached, a letter was posted on the depot door. "To all concerned: Effective October 9, 1979, this station is closed for business because trains 56 & 57, the *Floridian*, are discontinued. For information, tickets, and reservations on other Amtrak trains, please call the telephone number listed in the telephone directory. Thank you for your patronage." (Ben Runner Jr. photograph.)

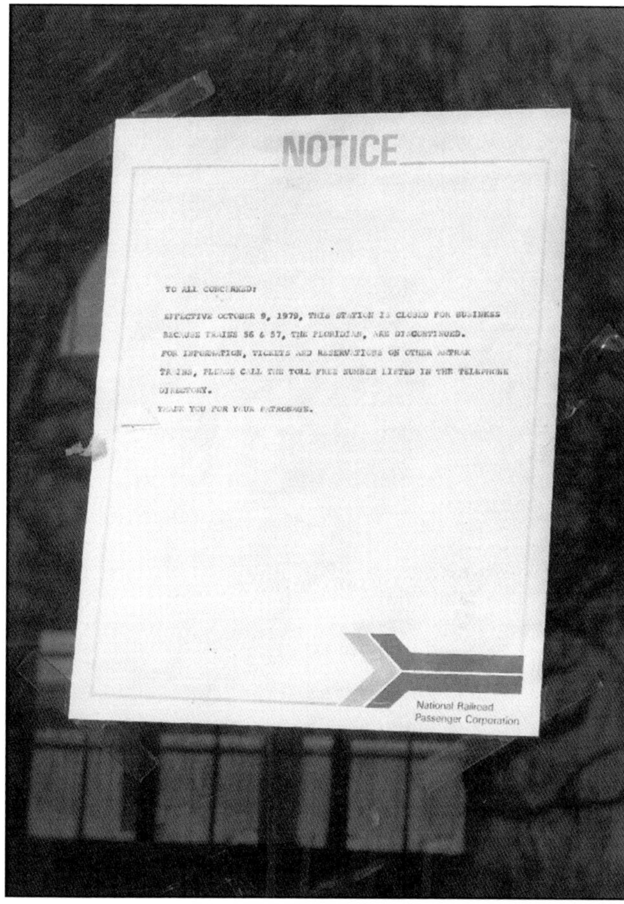

After L&N's passenger station closed, all the station tracks would be pulled up by the railroad. This photograph shows the main line tracks and vacant areas that once were busy with activity along two platforms. As passenger operations ceased, the yard operations soon moved about five miles south to the new L&N Memphis Junction yard. From this point on, the station would begin a rapid decay. (Ben Runner Jr. photograph.)

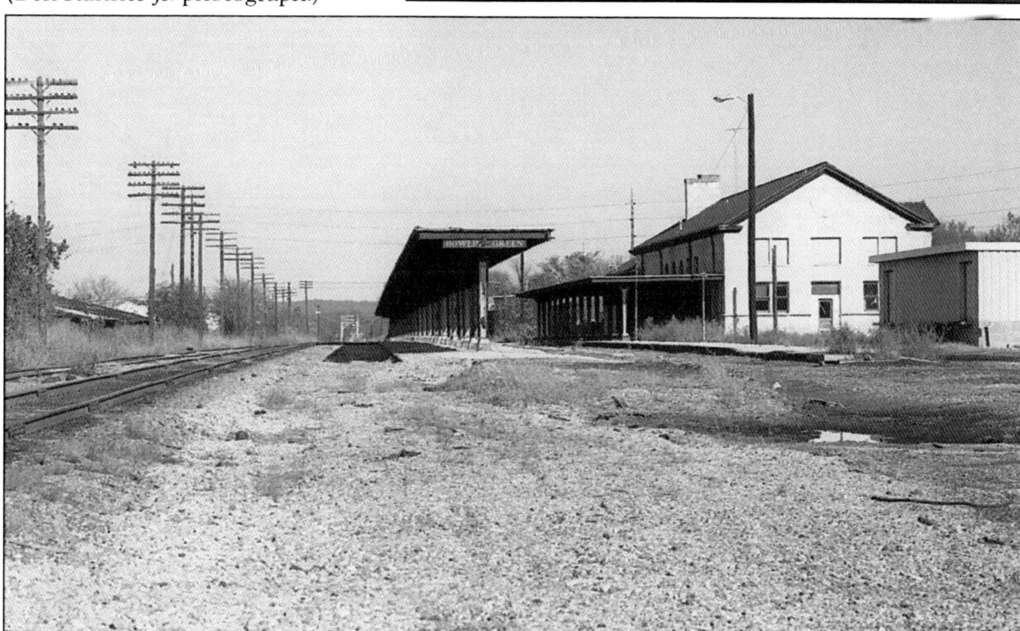

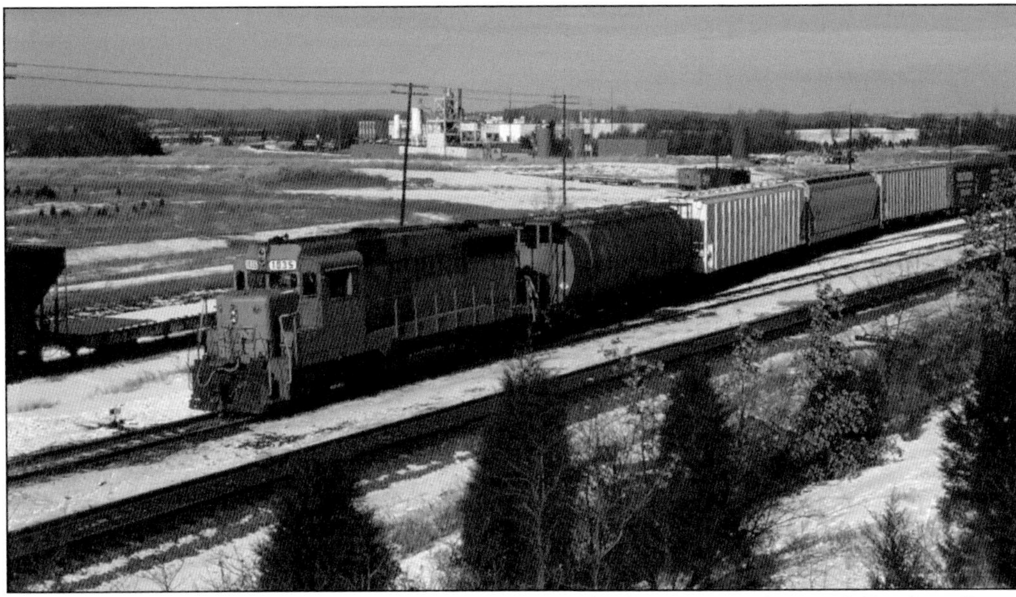

L&N 1035 works switching cuts of cars at the new Memphis Junction yard in south Bowling Green. The nearly mile-long yard stretches between mileposts 117 and 118, just north of the Green River (now William H. Natcher) Parkway. The open space in the background in this photograph from 1981 is now grown up with cedar trees. (Steven D. Johnson photograph.)

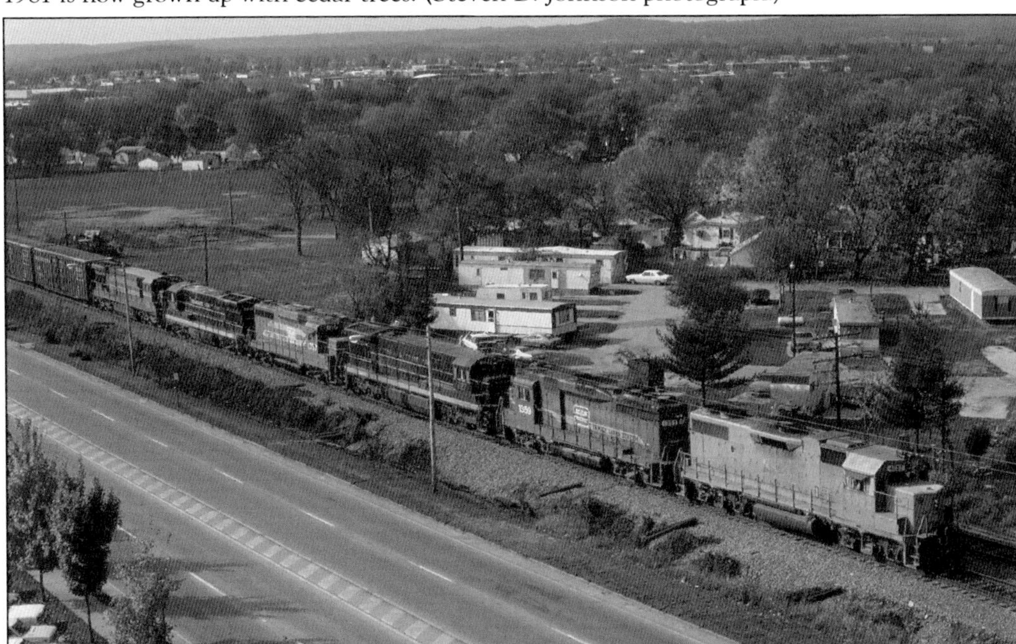

The paint schemes of Louisville & Nashville, Seaboard Coast Line, and SCL-L&N Family Lines are visible in this mixture of power on a northbound train approaching Old Morgantown Road. The Western Kentucky University parking garage provided a great view of the scene. The area between University Boulevard and the railroad was overgrown for a while, but recently it has been cleared of the trees, allowing this shot to be recaptured by current railfans. Miller's Trailer Park has been replaced with multi-story private student housing. (Steven D. Johnson photograph.)

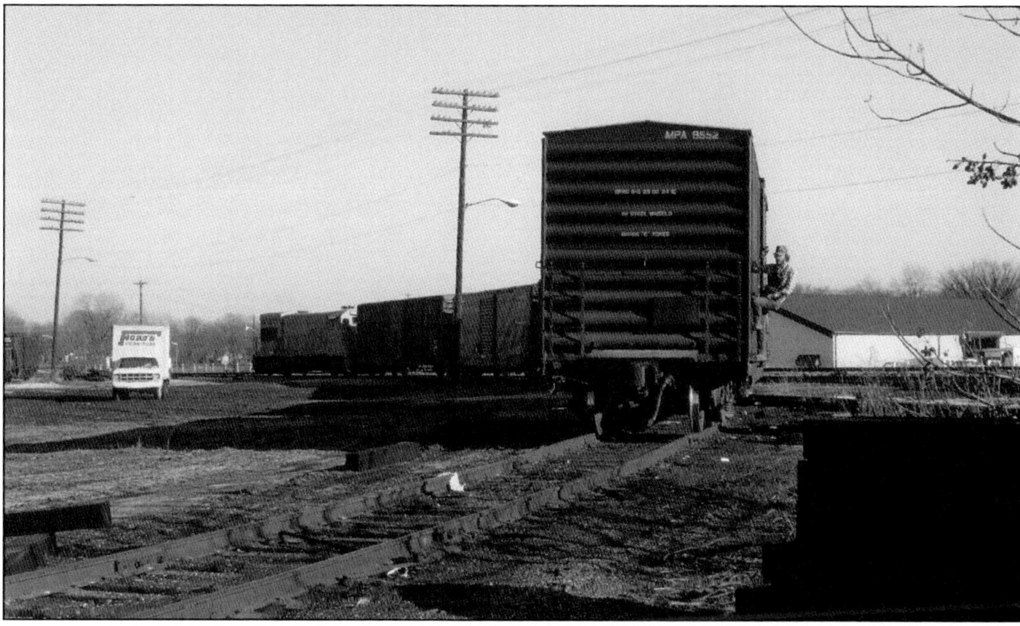

A daily yard job crew was assigned to switch out cars on the L&N's Portage Railroad. Many industries were served throughout the 1970s and into the 1980s. Here, a local crew is shoving down the north leg of the wye from the main to take some cars to industries. The conductor is riding the last car and will open and close the switches at the industries while communicating directions to the engineer. (Steven D. Johnson photograph.)

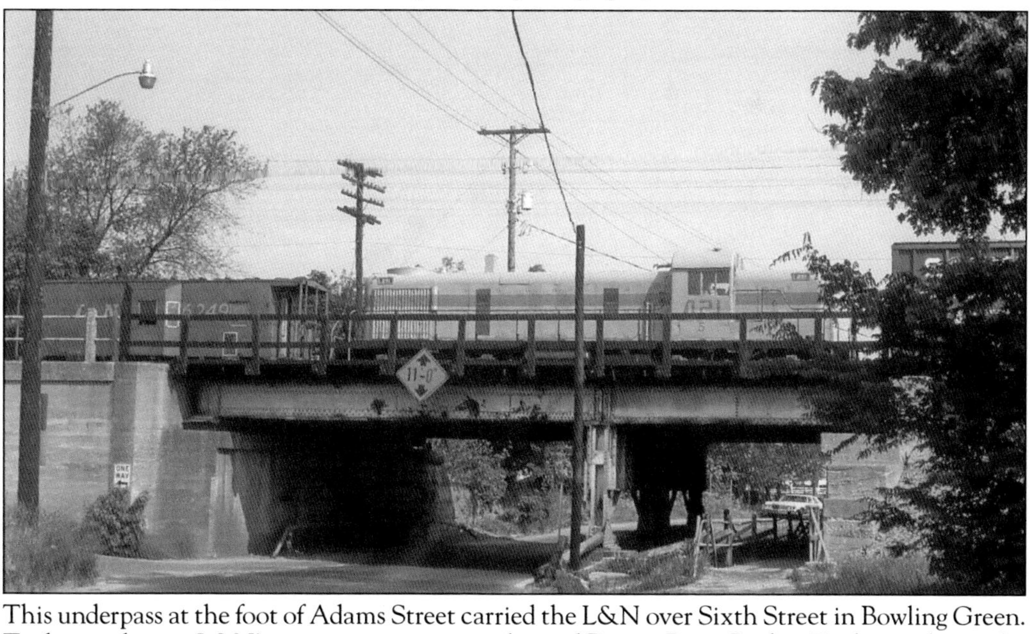

This underpass at the foot of Adams Street carried the L&N over Sixth Street in Bowling Green. To the north were L&N's passenger station, tracks, and Barren River Bridge. To the south was the L&N's downtown Bowling Green yard stretching to Eleventh Street. Urban renewal, along with a major reworking of Adams, Kentucky, Sixth, and Seventh Streets, changed the area forever. A new underpass just to the north replaced this structure in 1977. (Rumsie Butler photograph, Rick Williams collection.)

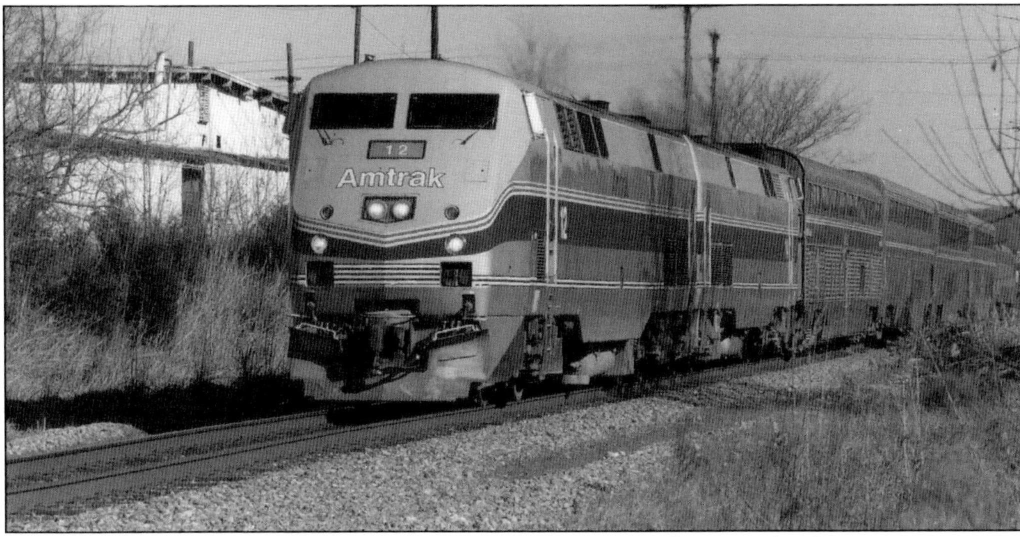

On December 20, 2001, a test run was made between Louisville to Nashville in anticipation of extending Amtrak's *Kentucky Cardinal* into Nashville. The *Kentucky Cardinal* connected with Amtrak's Chicago-to-Washington, DC, *Cardinal* at Indianapolis on the three days a week the *Cardinal* operated but ran as a separate train from Chicago to Jeffersonville and eventually Louisville the other four days. Eventually, the service to Louisville ended, and attempts to establish service between Louisville and Nashville have failed. Here, Amtrak/CSX P934-20 approaches the former L&N Depot near milepost 113 on the southbound trip. (Mike Dowell photograph.)

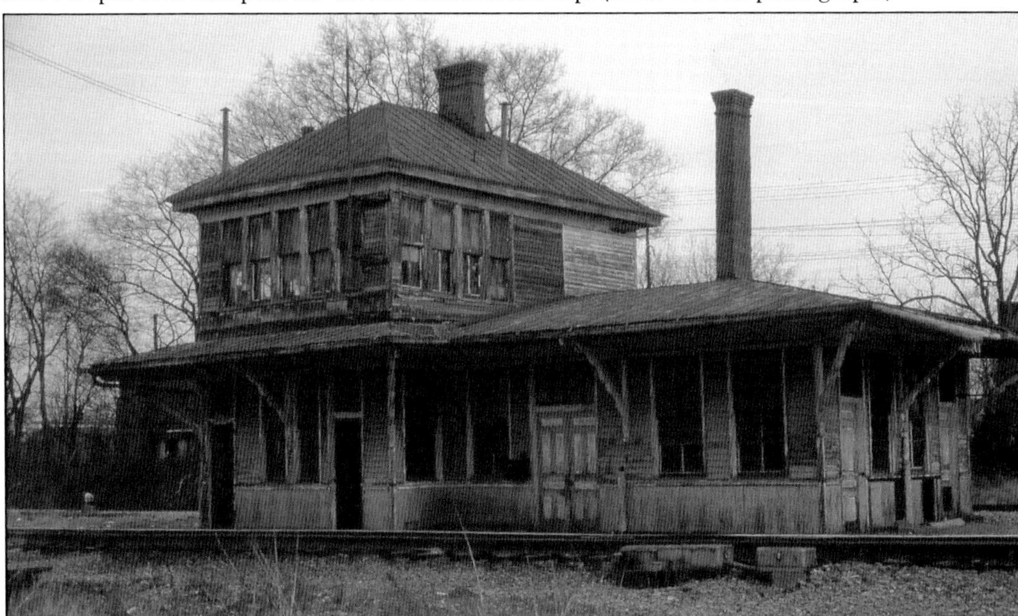

Amqui Station was built in 1910 at the junction of the L&N Louisville to Nashville main and L&N's Evansville to Nashville line. The upper part once housed levers to operate the switches to direct the trains on to the various lines. The lower floor was for passengers. As the building became unnecessary, country music legend Johnny Cash purchased it and moved it ten miles away to Hendersonville to house antiques. Following Cash's death in 2003, the station was relocated to Madison and restored as a museum. (Rumsie Butler photograph, Rick Williams collection.)

Three

Memphis Line

When the Louisville & Nashville Railroad was chartered March 5, 1850, giving the railroad permission to build from Louisville south to the Tennessee state line, two branches were also permitted, one to Lebanon, Kentucky, and the other a branch to Memphis. The Memphis Branch was eventually joined to the main line at a point five miles south of Bowling Green, later called Memphis Junction. The financial support of the building of the L&N by Bowling Green and Warren County citizens, along with citizens of Russellville and Logan County, made this the preferred route chosen by the railroad.

The Memphis Line would be constructed eventually by three different railroads. The L&N constructed 46 miles of it between Memphis Junction and Guthrie, Kentucky, at the state line; the Memphis, Clarksville & Louisville (MC&L) Railroad erected 82 miles of line between Guthrie and Paris, Tennessee; and the Memphis & Ohio (M&O) Railroad completed the largest segment of 132.5 miles between Paris and Memphis. After a series of delays, the M&O completed the section to Paris on May 11, 1860. The MC&L planned to construct track on a 14-mile segment from the Edgefield & Kentucky Railroad to provide service to Clarksville, Tennessee, which had been bypassed by the line from Henderson, Kentucky, to Nashville. Competition with the Nashville & Memphis Railroad, financial concerns, and changes in contractors delayed the construction.

Eventually, the MC&L and M&O were ordered to merge, and the Memphis & Ohio was ordered to assist with construction of the Cumberland River Bridge at Clarksville. This first bridge had been built too low and the channel too narrow under the strong current, resulting in boat accidents. The bridge had to be rebuilt and raised to a higher level. The MC&L portion of the railroad was completed on March 21, 1861, except for the Tennessee River Bridge at Danville, Tennessee.

In the summer of 1860, the L&N had begun to build from both Memphis Junction and State Line (Guthrie). This section was completed on September 13, 1860, and through trains from Louisville to Memphis could begin with the completion of the MC&L section. On April 10, 1861, the Tennessee River Bridge was completed; the line was finally finished from Louisville to Memphis.

Two days later, the Civil War began. On September 18, 1861, Confederate general Simon Bolivar Buckner seized the entire L&N south of Lebanon Junction, including the Memphis Branch. Under Confederate control, the L&N lines were used to move troops and supplies quickly. In February 1862, Union troops advanced into Tennessee taking back most of the railroad, but the Confederates in retreat had damaged or destroyed track, trestles, bridges, and depots. In August 1862, Confederate forces recaptured Clarksville and the Red River Bridge, shutting down the Memphis Branch again. By September 7, the Union had retaken Clarksville and repairs began on the line. During Confederate general Braxton Bragg's invasion of Kentucky, the Union only held about 20 miles of the L&N in the Bowling Green area. Confederate troops again destroyed portions of the Memphis Line, and trains were only able to run between Bowling Green and Russellville. After the Battle of Perryville on October 8, 1862, the Memphis Line was restored to L&N control, but afterward had to deal with bands of guerrillas robbing trains and wreaking havoc on the line. Also, Gen. John Hunt Morgan and his raiders specifically targeted the L&N, periodically shutting down operations. Near the end of the war, in December 1864, a last threat to the L&N occurred when Confederate general Lyon invaded near State Line, eventually moving to Hopkinsville, Kentucky, before damaging the L&N Main Stem near Nolin, Glendale, and Elizabethtown.

After the war's conclusion, repairs and upgrades were completed, and the L&N continued an earlier rerouting of mainline passenger service down the Memphis Line along with the M&O and MC&L, running connecting trains between Bowling Green and Nashville. The L&N had to vastly improve the Memphis & Ohio after leasing it in 1867 to keep service running, and eventually acquired the line in 1872. In 1868, the MC&L, deep in debt, could not meet payroll, and the line was shut down on February 6. The L&N leased the line on February 17 and began improvements. On September 13, 1871, the L&N purchased the MC&L outright. In the early days, four main passenger trains with day coaches ran on the Memphis Line, Nos. 1, 2, 3, and 4. By 1869, Nos. 1 and 2 had sleeping cars added, and later No. 3 had a "palace sleeping car" added that ran between Louisville and New Orleans on a 46-hour schedule via the Mobile & Ohio Railroad at Humbolt, Tennessee. Nos. 1 and 4 became the overnight "Fast Mail" 101 and 104 and connected with the *Azalean* by the 1920s at Bowling Green. Daytime "Fast Line" trains 102 and 103 hit all the stops on the line handling coaches, mail and express, and baggage. From 1921 to 1965, trains 198 and 199, the "Up Pan" and "Down Pan," connected with the main line *Pan American* 98 and 99 at Bowling Green with through sleeping cars from New York and Louisville and a dining car added and removed. During World War II, the Memphis Line "Pans" ran between Cincinnati and Memphis. The Memphis Line towns took great pride in these trains.

To prevent the NC&StL Railway from competing in L&N territory, the L&N was forced to acquire a majority of the stock in 1880, controlling it, but operating as a separate entity, until August 1957.

The merger of the L&N and NC&StL immediately brought changes to the Memphis Line. With both railroads having a parallel route into Memphis south of McKenzie, Tennessee, the extra track was not necessary. Because the Nashville, Chattanooga & St. Louis Route was in better condition and had less operating obstacles, the decision was made to reroute traffic over that track between McKenzie and Nashville. This left the north end of the Memphis Line to local freights and passenger service between McKenzie and Bowling Green. In 1979, the Tennessee River Bridge was abandoned at Danville, Tennessee, reducing the Memphis Line to a branch line. In 1981, the Owensboro & Nashville (O&N) Line between Logan Aluminum and Drakesboro, Kentucky, was abandoned. The eight miles out of Russellville would be used to service the plant. By 1986, L&N successor Seaboard System was operating the 63.5 miles of the Memphis Line as the Clarksville Branch from Bowling Green to a point just west of Clarksville.

In 1987, R.J. Corman Railroad purchased the line between South Union and Clarksville along with the branch to Logan Aluminum. After a proposal to abandon the South Union-to-Bowling Green segment, Corman purchased that section in October 1989. R.J. Corman Railroad purchased six ex-B&O and ex-C&O GP-9s to use on the Memphis Line. Distribution centers were constructed at South Union and Clarksville, and the operation has grown considerably in the past 20 years. Local freights operate between Guthrie and Cumberland City, Guthrie and Russellville, Russellville and Bowling Green, and Logan Aluminum to South Union. An industrial park at Bowling Green has several industries served by R.J. Corman, and there is a daily interchange of several cars at the CSX yard in Bowling Green. Every other day, a train loaded with aluminum ingots arrives via CSX at Bowling Green to be swapped with empty cars from Logan Aluminum.

As of 2011, more improvements are planned to upgrade the track, and some used locomotives arrived for use on the line as some of the older units needed to be replaced. Thanks to R.J. Corman and Logan Aluminum, the north end of the Memphis Line has gone from near abandonment to a busy, productive line once again.

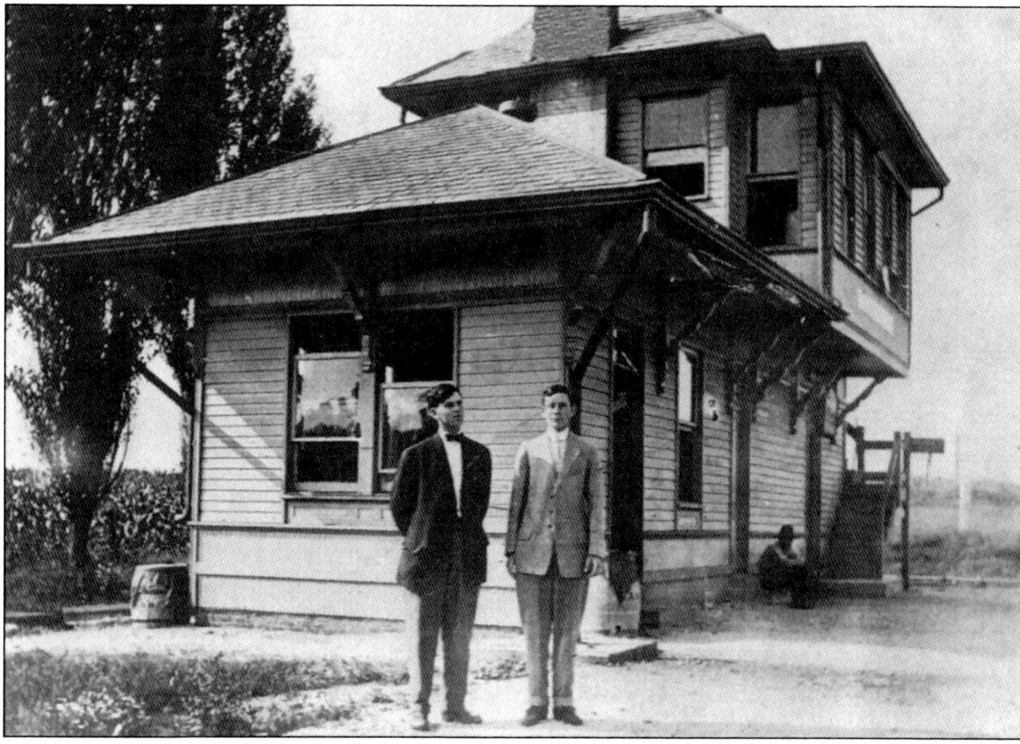

This rare photograph shows the Memphis Junction, Kentucky L&N passenger station. Shown are the agent J. Palmer Brown (left), and his assistant. The community of Memphis Junction once thrived, but today is a part of Bowling Green between R.J. Corman's Memphis Line and the CSX Mainline Subdivison tracks. (Floyd Brown.)

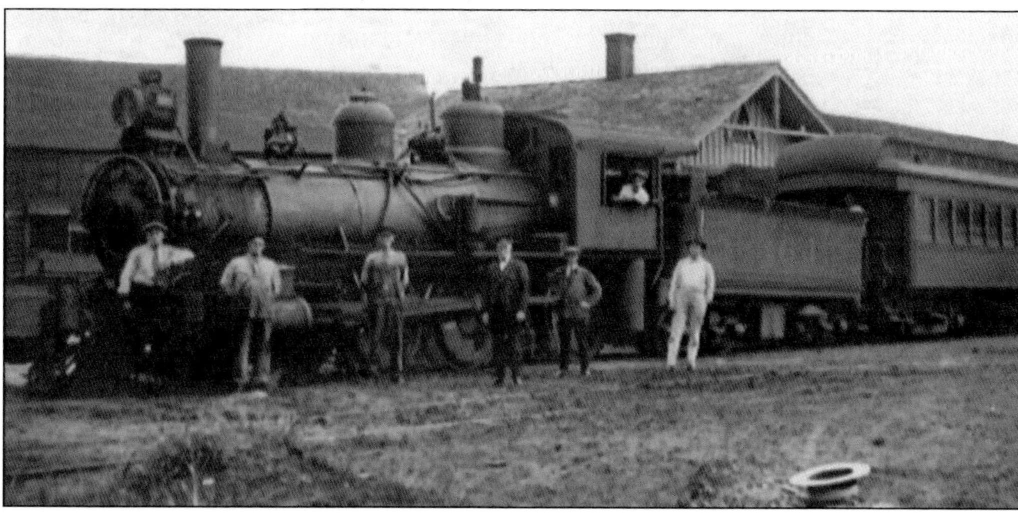

This local train that ran between Russellville, Kentucky, and Adairville, Kentucky, was known as the "Adairville Dinky." The line to Adairville was part of the Owensboro & Nashville, later the L&N O&N Branch. The last train ran on November 30, 1930, and the following year, the track was removed, except for a small section at Russellville. The O&N Between Russellville and Owensboro, Kentucky, served the L&N for many years into the coal region. (Logan County Public Library.)

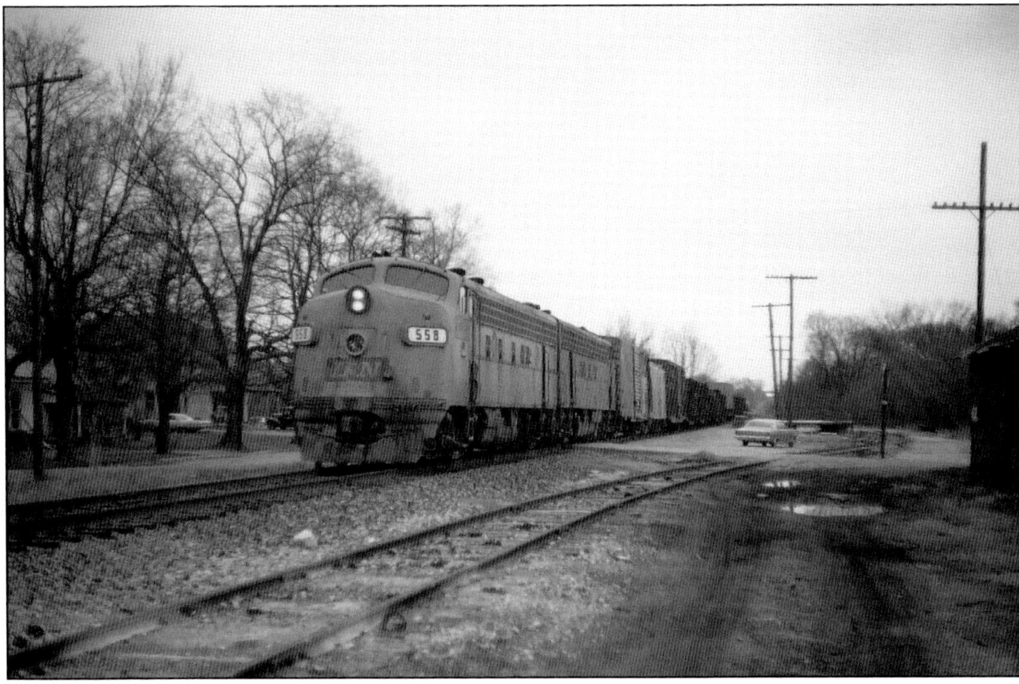

At 9:24 a.m. on Christmas Eve, 1971, the westbound local passes Auburn, Kentucky, on the Memphis Line with L&N F9A 558, FP7A 698, 16 cars, and red caboose 1144. Note the freight platform where the depot was formerly located, just beyond the car. (Dennis Mize photograph.)

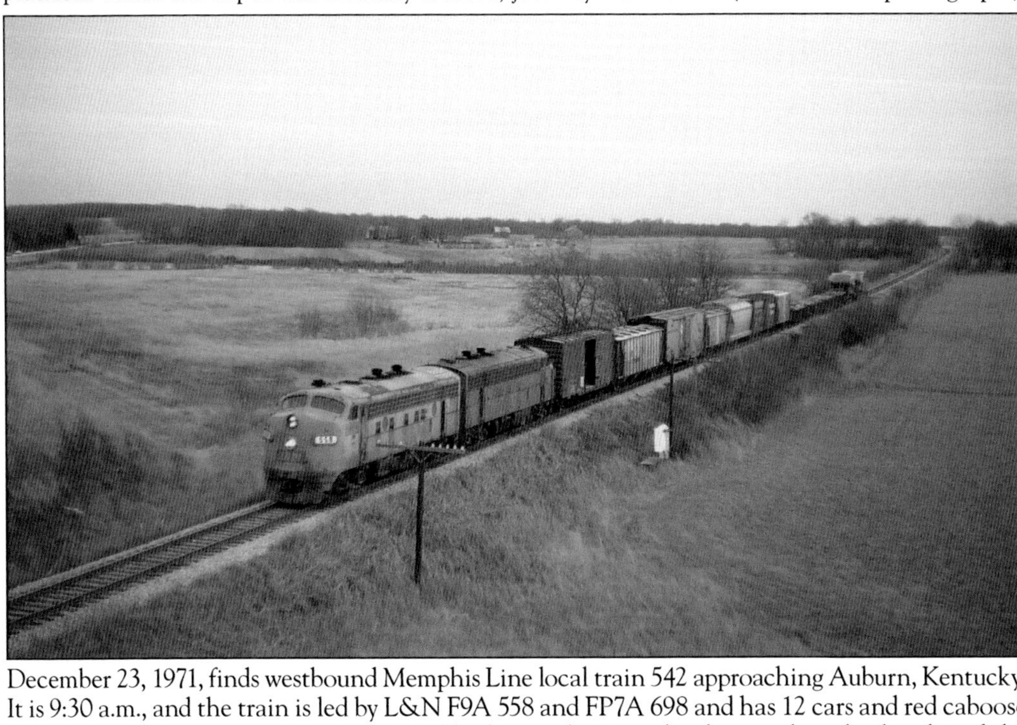

December 23, 1971, finds westbound Memphis Line local train 542 approaching Auburn, Kentucky. It is 9:30 a.m., and the train is led by L&N F9A 558 and FP7A 698 and has 12 cars and red caboose 1347 in tow. Today, this view is impossible due to the growth of trees along both sides of the Memphis Line tracks. (Dennis Mize photograph.)

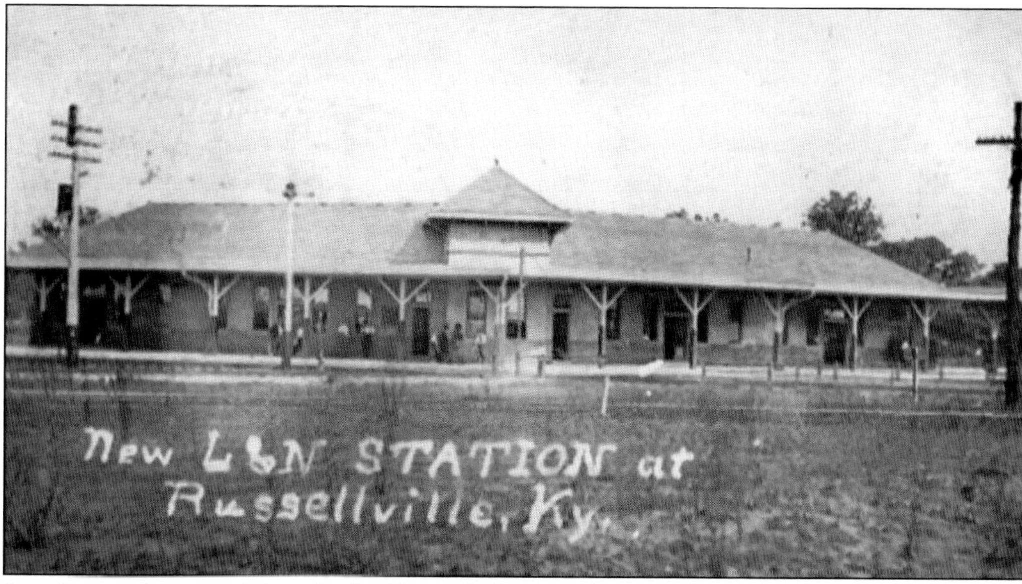

Seen here is the second Russellville, Kentucky Depot, which served both the L&N Memphis Line and the Owensboro & Nashville Railroad (later, acquired by L&N). Opened in 1912, this structure had covered platforms along both the Memphis Line and O&N Main Line. This station burned in 1935 when a 66,000-volt line blew down during a storm. The replacement for this building was smaller and survives today as a Fraternal Order of Police lodge. (Logan County Public Library.)

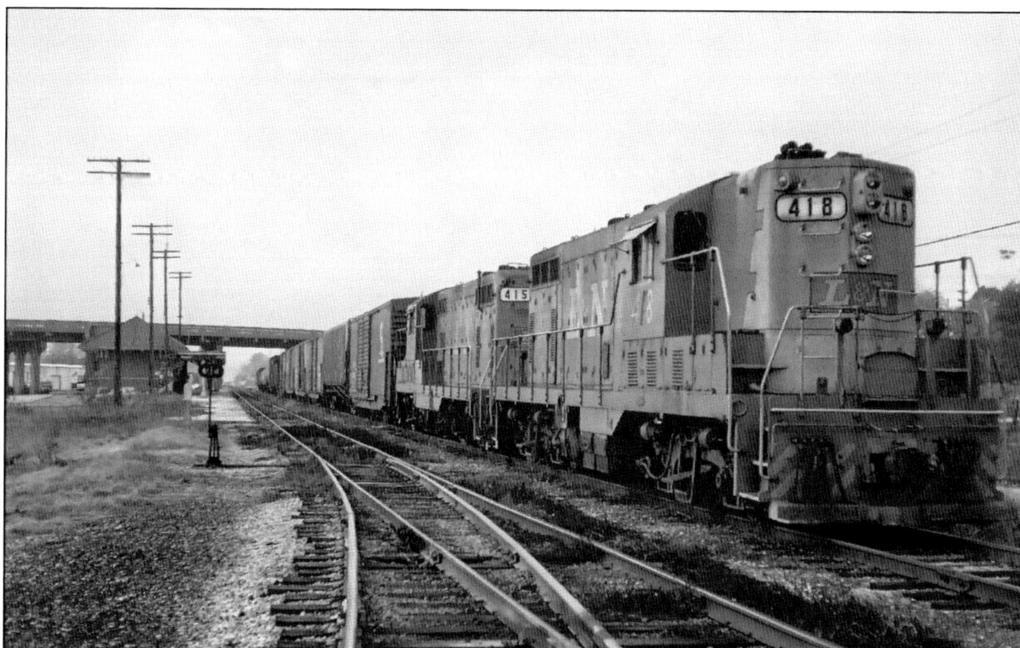

L&N GP7s 418 and 415 are idling at the Russellville Depot with 10 cars and red caboose 1400. These units had brought the Paris, Tennessee turn back to Russellville late the night before. The General Motors Electro-Motive Division–manufactured four-axle 1,500-horsepower GP7s were built between 1949 and 1954. (Dennis Mize photograph.)

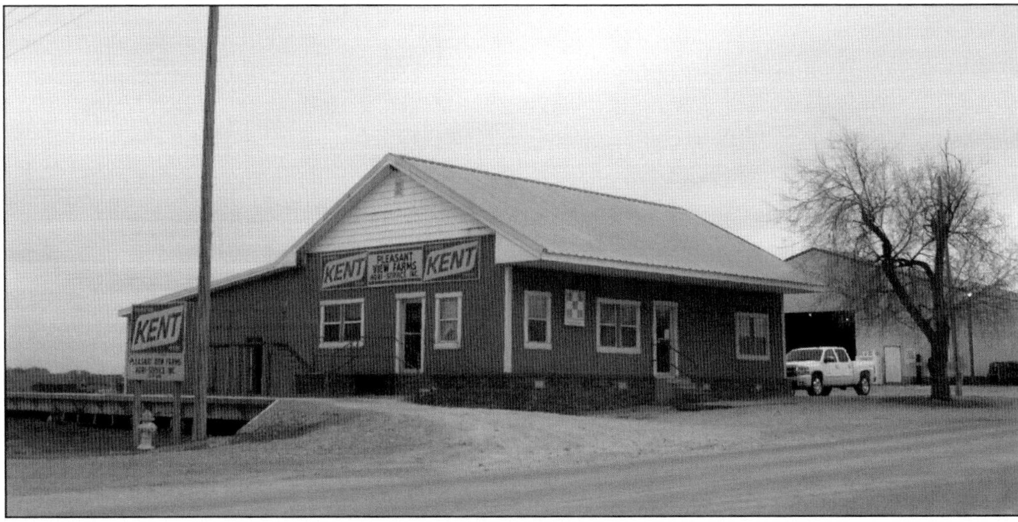

The former Louisville & Nashville Depot at South Union did sit facing the 1869 Shaker Tavern, but the building was moved to face south and became the office of a feed business. It is still in use in 2011. Across the county line to the north, R.J. Corman maintains a distribution facility and small yard serving operations between Bowling Green, Russellville, and Guthrie and also serving the Logan Aluminum plant at Epley's Station. (Kevin Comer photograph.)

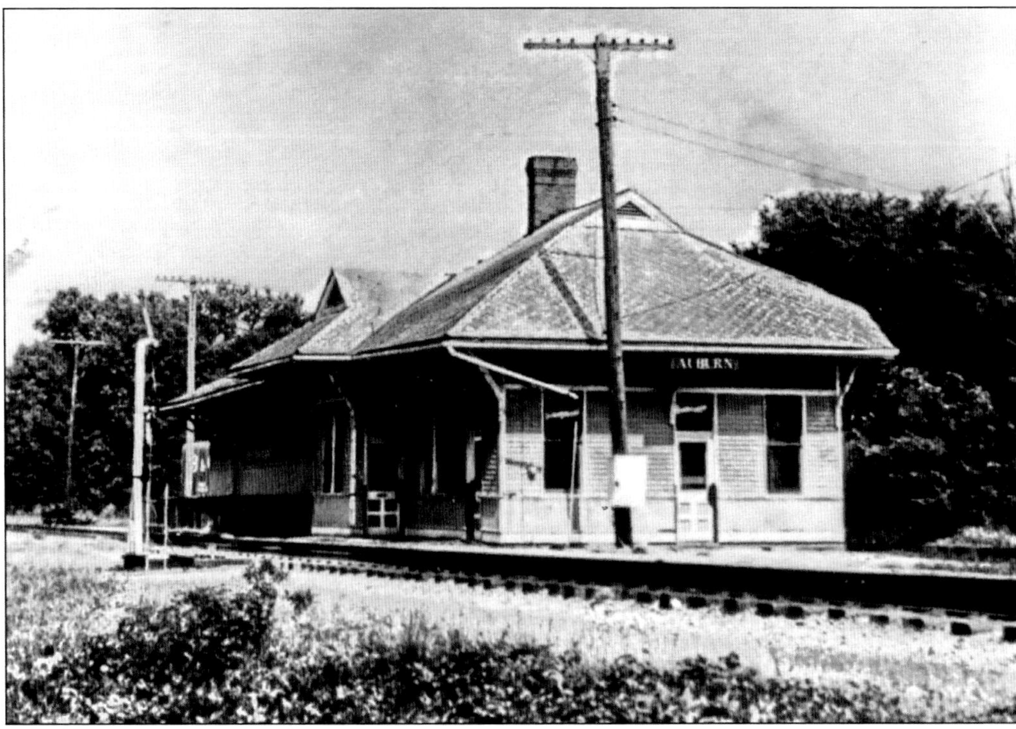

Pictured is the third L&N station at Auburn, Kentucky. Built in 1897, this wood frame depot lasted until the end of passenger service on the Memphis Line in February 1968. After the last passenger trains, night trains 101 and 104 were discontinued, the depot was closed and razed. R.B. Mize was the last station agent, serving from 1938 until the agency closed on April 30, 1959. The "house track" where freight was unloaded survives today. (Auburn Historical Society.)

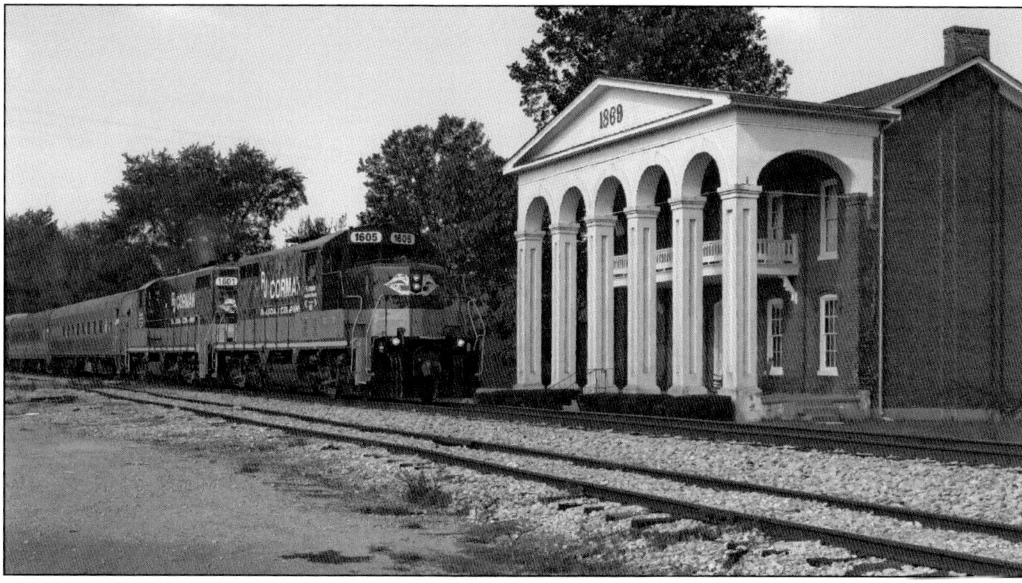

In 2007, Bowling Green had the honor of hosting the Louisville & Nashville Railroad Historical Society at the restored L&N Depot. Activities included a banquet, slide shows, railfanning, exhibits, fellowship, and excursion trips between Bowling Green and Russellville on the former L&N Memphis Line. Current owner R.J. Corman Railroad provided the power, and here the train is seen moving north at the 1869 Shaker Tavern at South Union, Kentucky. (Doyle Massey photograph.)

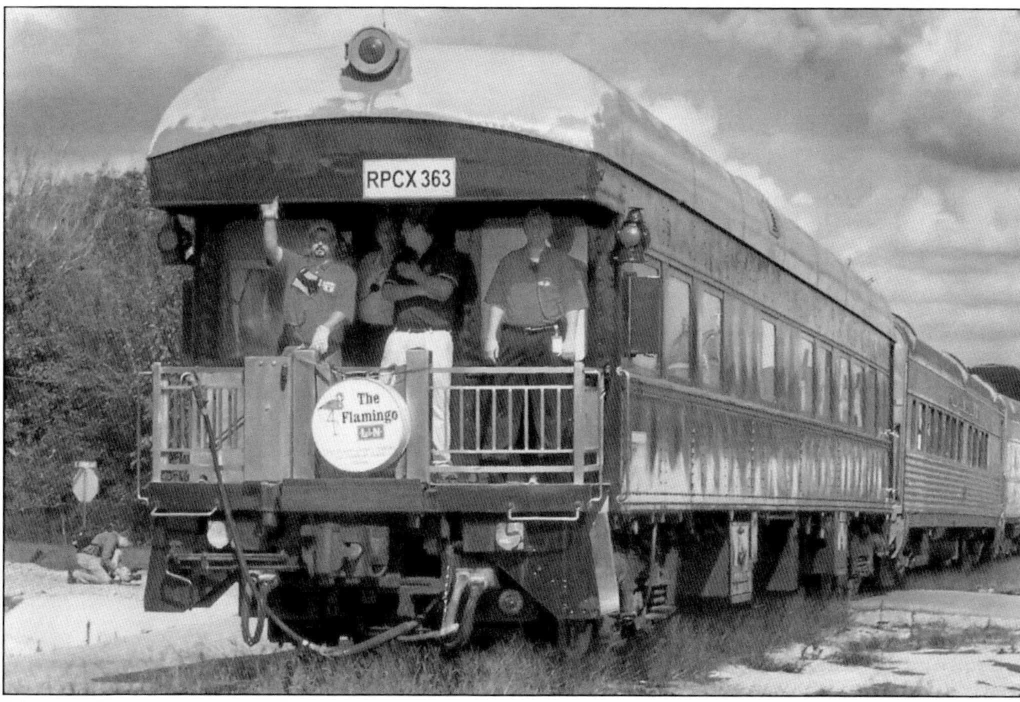

The 2007 L&N Historical Society excursion shoves back into the platform at Russellville. The train had backed around the wye in preparation for the return trip to Bowling Green. L&N office car 363 carried the markers for the trip. Note the drumhead on the rear for the L&N passenger train *Flamingo*. (Kevin Comer photograph.)

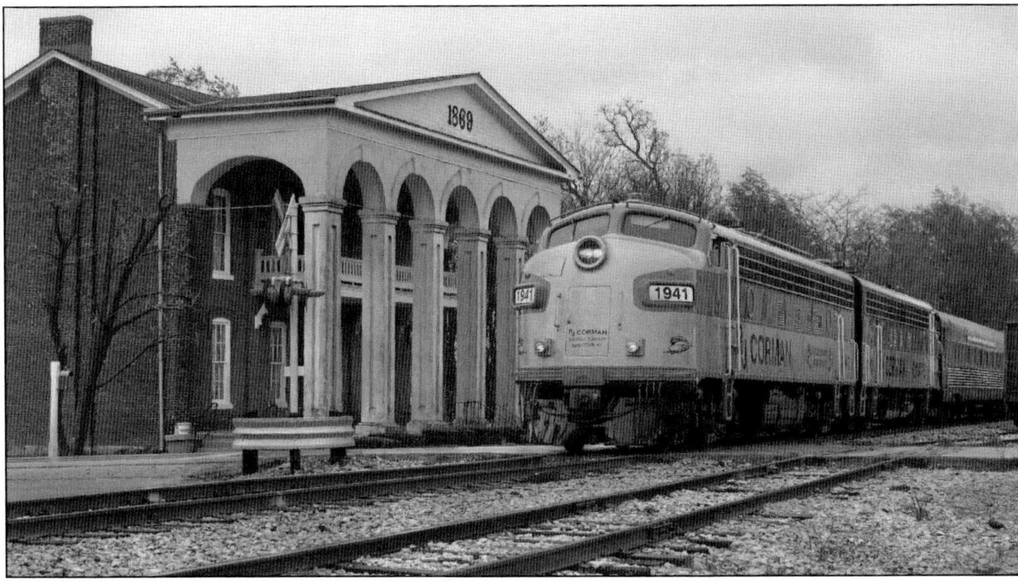

On April 19, 2009, the R.J. Corman Dinner Train, based in Bardstown, Kentucky, made an appearance on the Memphis Line, traveling to Clarksville for a couple of excursion runs for soldiers at Fort Campbell. The train is shown here southbound passing the Shaker Tavern at South Union. Leading are ex-Southern Railroad FP7A units 1941 and 1940, followed by restored 1940s-era dining cars and kitchen car. (Kevin Comer photograph.)

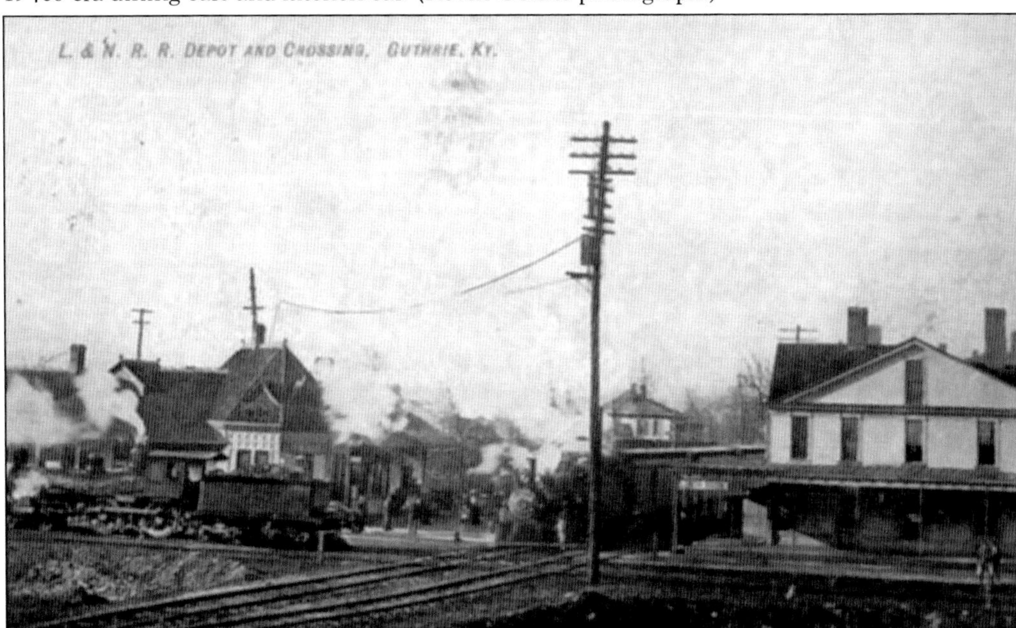

In 1868, the L&N moved the depot from State Line to the crossing of the Evansville, Henderson & Nashville Railroad. This busy junction point on the Memphis Line was named Guthrie and chartered as a town in 1879. A bad collision occurred here June 29, 1957, when southbound Memphis Line freight 121 collided with Henderson Line Chicago-to-Miami passenger train No. 11 *Dixieland*. Three passengers and three employees were killed, and more than 20 were injured. (Greg Hughes collection.)

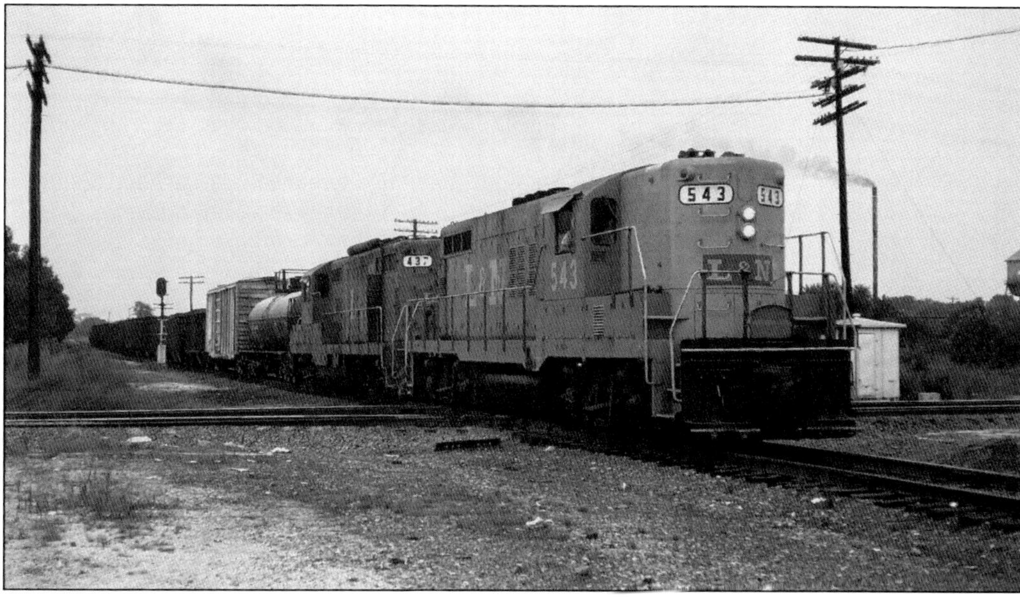

A southbound L&N train on the Memphis line crosses the Evansville-Nashville Line at Guthrie, Kentucky. In September 1980, the crossing diamond was removed. Currently, the R.J. Corman Railroad Guthrie shops sit on the old right-of-way, and Memphis Line trains must use the wye tracks and negotiate the Guthrie CSX yard for movements between Clarksville and Russellville. (Dennis Mize photograph.)

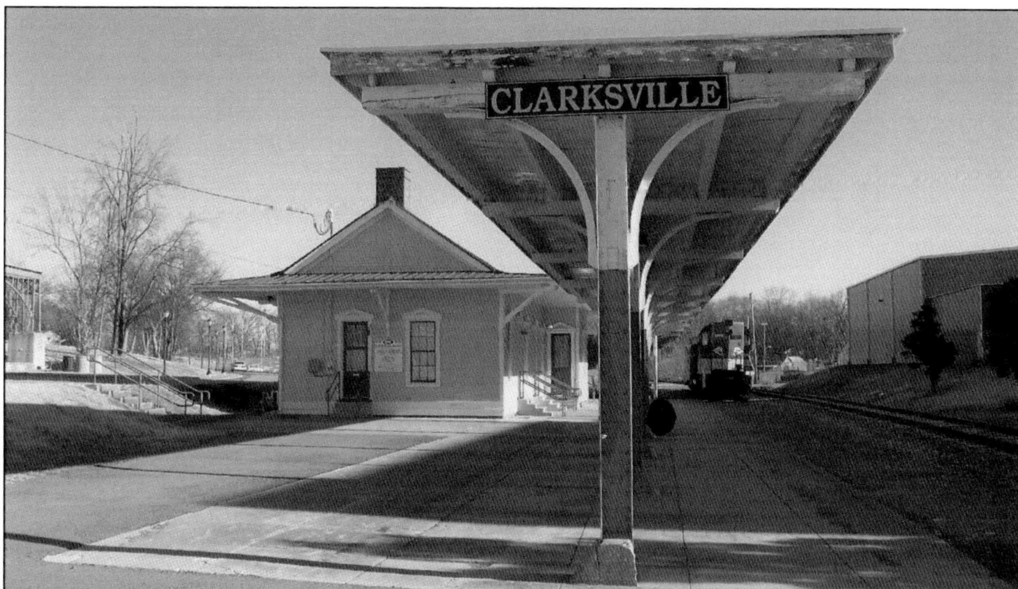

The Clarksville, Tennessee, L&N Depot was restored in 1996 to look as it did when constructed in 1901. It replaced a previous depot on this site at Tenth and Commerce Streets. The first depot in Clarksville had opened in 1860 on Depot Street as part of the Memphis, Clarksville & Louisville Railroad. The depot is home of the Montgomery County Historical Society. On display is retired R.J. Corman locomotive 3501 and a caboose. Corman trains pass the depot just before crossing the Cumberland River Swing Bridge. (Kevin Comer photograph.)

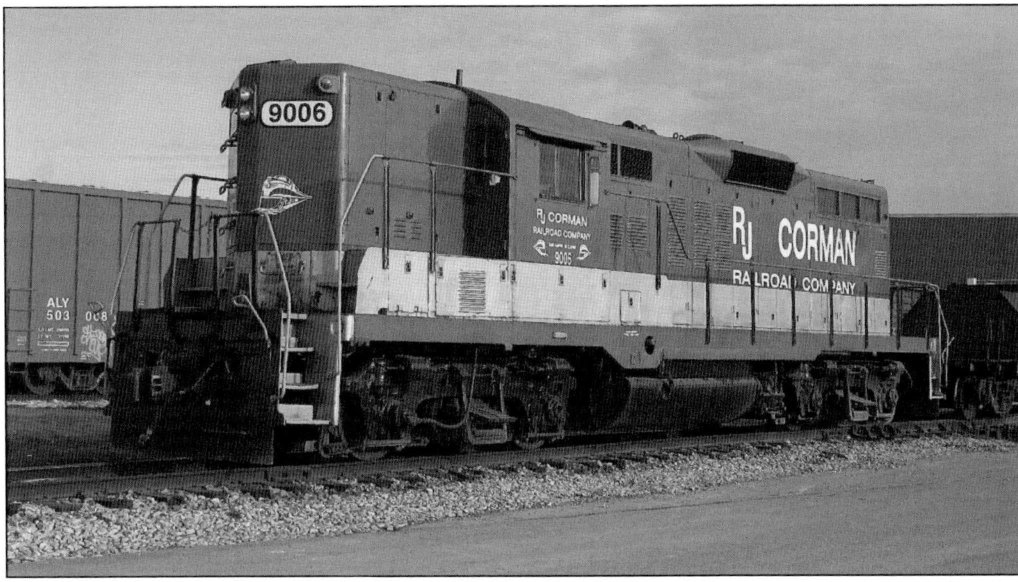

R.J. Corman 9006 was one of the original six GP-9 locomotives (9003-9008) purchased by R.J. Corman for use on the Memphis Line during 1987. Originally Baltimore & Ohio (B&O) 6521, the 9006 is shown here in 2006. Five of the six were still active in 2010, with 9004 being scrapped in 2008. R.J. Corman 9006 usually has the duty as the plant switcher for Logan Aluminum, sometimes bringing cars to Russellville but mostly residing inside the plant confines. (Chris Gadbois photograph.)

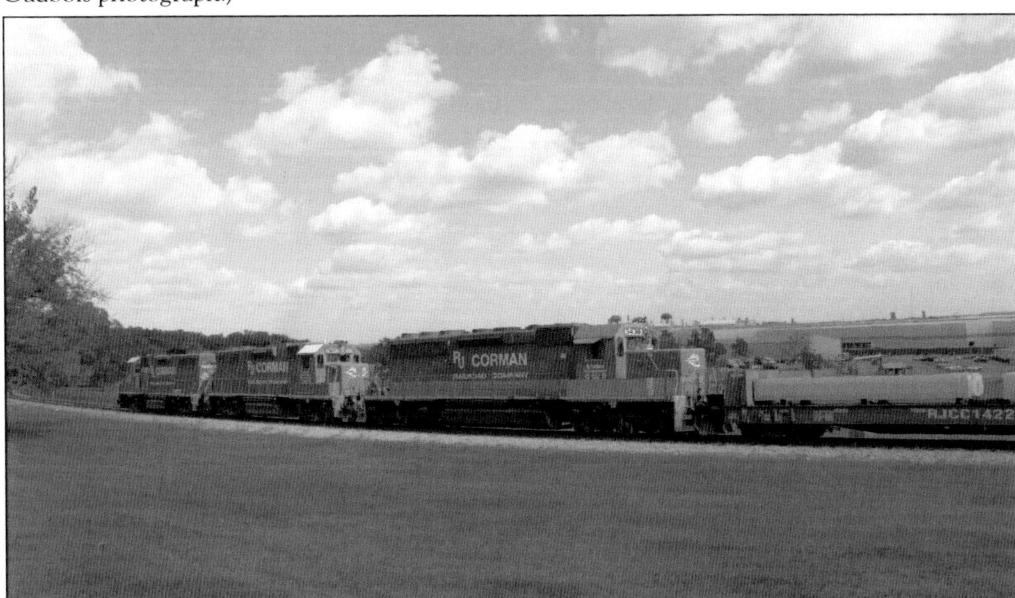

On October 29, 2011, the loaded ingot train arrives at the Logan Aluminum Plant near Epley's Station, Kentucky, on the remaining remnant of the Louisville & Nashville's O&N Line. Former Penn Central and Conrail GP 38s 7710 and 7697, built in 1969, were followed by 1978-built ex–Union Pacific SD40-2 3438, 25 cars of aluminum ingots from Berea, Kentucky, and several boxcars picked up at Russellville. The GP38s arrived on the Memphis Line in 2011 to replace some of the older units in service. (Kevin Comer photograph.)

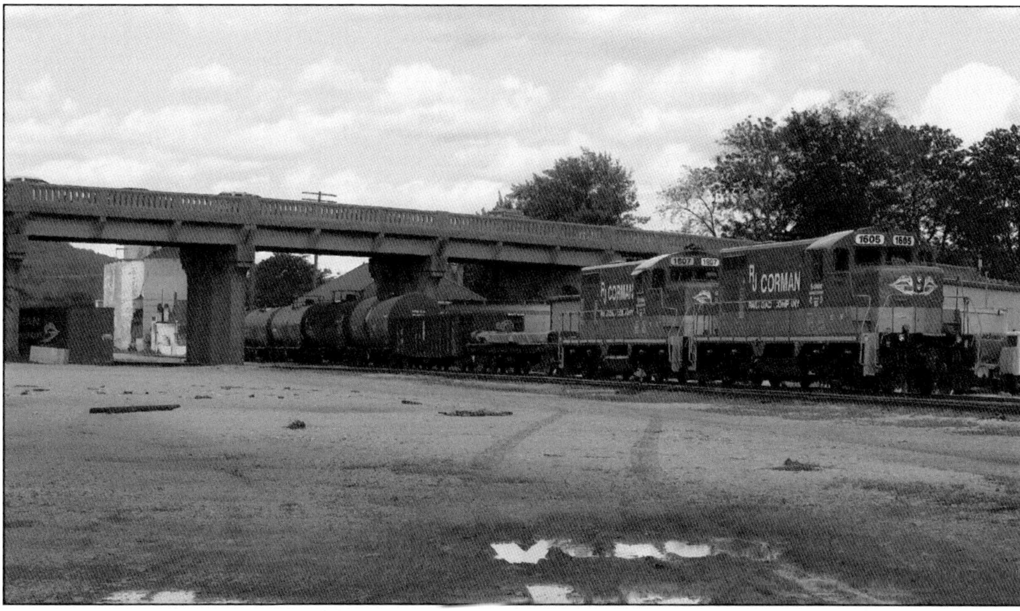

Veteran R.J. Corman GP 16s 1605 and 1807 sit under the US 68/Kentucky 80 overpass near the Russellville, Kentucky Depot in 2011. Several GP 16s are in service on the Memphis Line between Bowling Green and Clarksville, Tennessee. The 1605 was built in November 1951 as Atlantic Coast Line GP7 224, later becoming Seaboard Coast Line 2722, followed by CSX 1768, before becoming R.J. Corman property. (Kevin Comer photograph.)

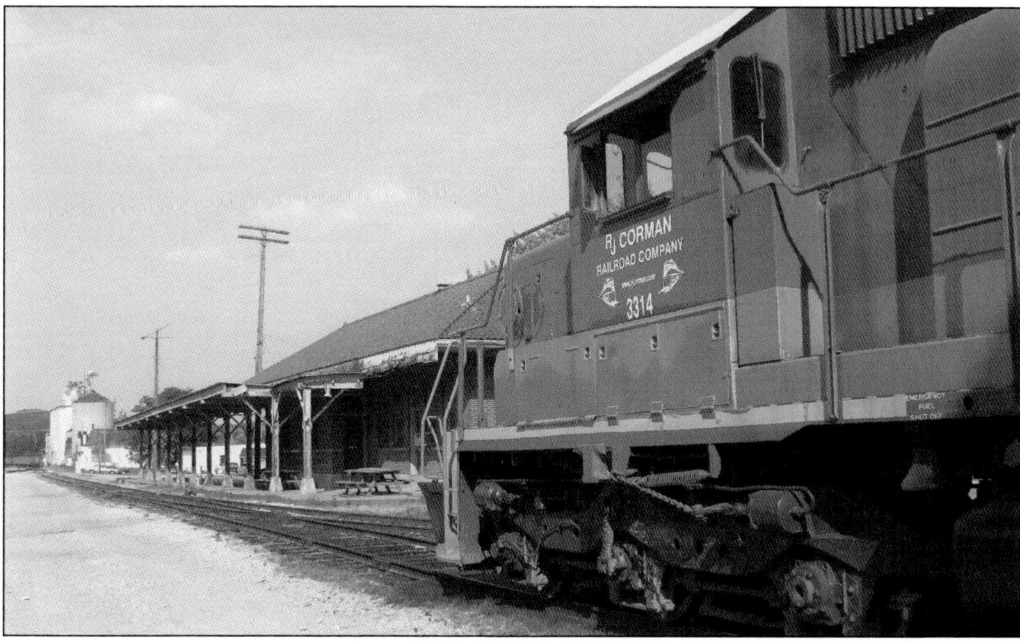

On May 11, 2011, 35-year-old R.J. Corman SD 40 3314 (former Union Pacific) awaits a new assignment next to the historic Russellville, Kentucky L&N Depot. The big six-axle locomotive sits where the Owensboro & Nashville Railroad crossed the L&N Memphis Line and continued to Adairville. The line was purchased by the L&N and never reached Nashville, and the tracks between Russellville and Adairville were removed in 1939. (Kevin Comer photograph.)

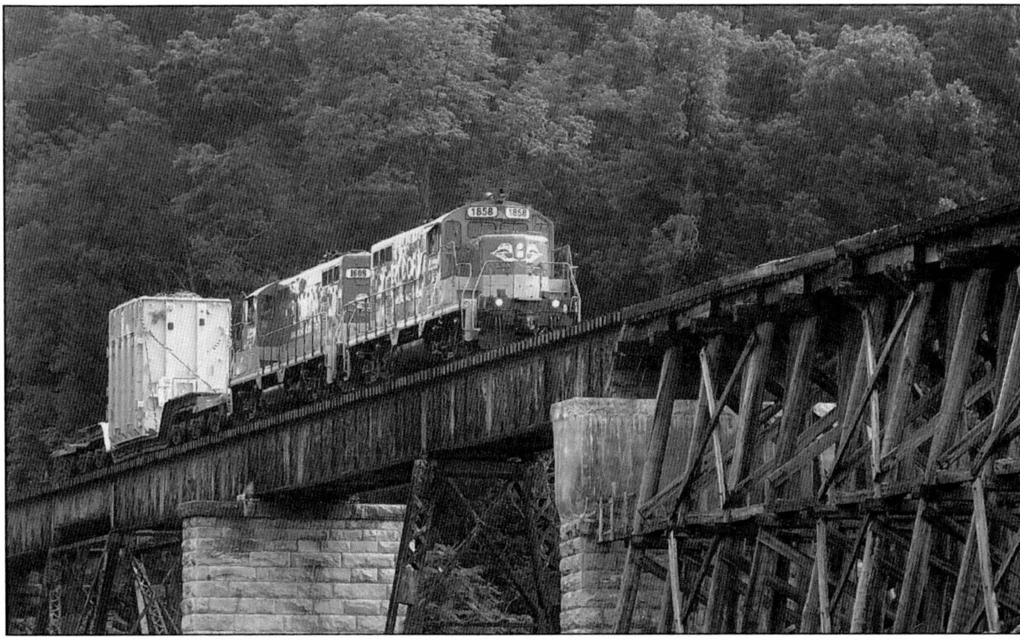

In 2011, a pair of R.J. Corman geeps pull a large load bound for Cumberland City, Tennessee's coal-fired TVA power plant over the Red River trestle at Clarksville, Tennessee. Eventually the trestle will be covered with fill to reduce maintenance costs. (Kevin Comer photograph.)

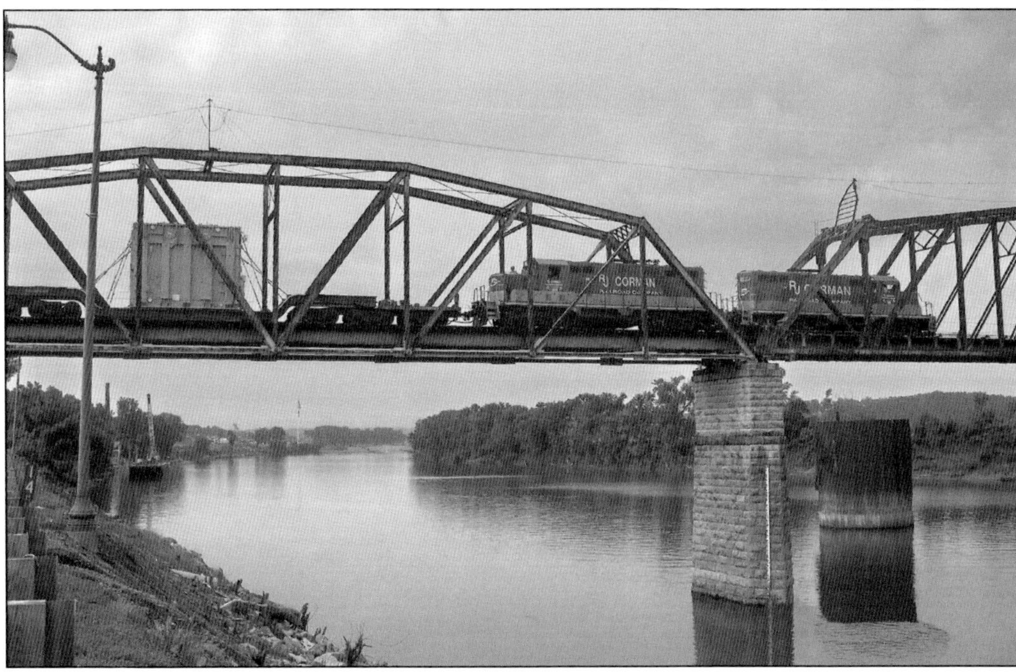

The original Cumberland River Bridge at Clarksville, Tennessee, was built by the Memphis, Clarksville & Louisville Railroad in 1859–1860. Some of the original stone piers still stand supporting L&N's swing bridge, which replaced the original structure. It is now operated by R.J. Corman Railroad. The heavy load is bound for TVA's Cumberland City Power Plant. (Kevin Comer photograph.)

Four

Glasgow Railway and Mammoth Cave Railroad

The Barren County Railroad Company was incorporated on February 9, 1856, and began grading a right-of-way to Three Forks (current Park City) but then suspended operation. On March 6, 1868, the Glasgow Railroad Company was incorporated, having acquired the property and franchises of the defunct Barren County Railroad. The new company continued construction of the line, completing the right-of-way about September 1870. By May 1899, H.C. Trigg and W.L. Porter purchased the rail line, and on December 30, 1899, the road was incorporated as the Glasgow Railway Company, as it still is today. The line has been leased to the Louisville & Nashville Railroad and its successors since September 1, 1870.

H.C. Trigg became the line's first president, with W.L. Porter the vice president; then Porter succeeded Trigg as president. Porter was also a local attorney for the Louisville & Nashville Railroad from 1869 to 1890 and, later, from 1914 until his death in 1937 at the age of 95. At this time, Robert L. Lessenberry became president, later followed by his son Robert A. Lessenberry, the current president.

The Glasgow Railway has never owned a locomotive, and the only piece of rolling stock to grace its roster is Glasgow Railway combine No. 109. All the motor power used on the line has always been provided by L&N and its successors. No. 109, said to have been constructed in 1882, is unique in that it is a three-way coach: the center part for baggage, one end for white passengers, and one end for black passengers, owing its setup to the segregated South and its Jim Crow "separate-but-equal" laws that came about in Kentucky in 1892. This is one of the oldest railcars in existence.

The 10-mile right-of-way to Park City was always contracted out to the leasing railroad but, in recent years, it has been contracted to others. This expense includes rail replacement, ties, ballast, switch maintenance, and labor.

On a typical day of operation in 1955, the Glasgow Railway ran its mixed train between Glasgow and Park City round trip once in the morning and again in the early afternoon. Passenger travel by this time was in severe decline with an average of one or two persons per trip. The train and engine crew in 1955 was composed of G.M. "Captain" Garvin, conductor; Ralph Mochow, engineer; H.G. Tatum, fireman; and R.W. Gillock, flagman. The station crew at that time was F.J. Crain, agent; C.E. Elzy, cashier/clerk; and Thomas Spurgeon Traylor, warehouseman. Stations along the line at that time included Stovall, Carden, and Oil City, with the train stopping for passengers if they were "flagged" to do so.

With Glasgow being the "railhead" for towns such as Tompkinsville, Burkesville, Edmonton, and Gamaliel, freight traffic revenue was good in the 1950s. Passenger traffic had become so sparse in 1955 that the railroad asked to discontinue the mixed service. On August 24, 1955, the coach would make last runs to Park City and return. The car had served since 1899, and more than 65 patrons rode during the last trip, culminating with it being parked in a siding off the Glasgow rail yard. The passenger numbers for this trip had not been seen since the World War II era, when traveling soldiers packed all railroads. The car would sit in Glasgow and deteriorate for 56 more years until being donated by Glasgow Railway president Robert A. Lessenberry to the Historic RailPark and Train Museum in Bowling Green for restoration. The car left Glasgow for the last time in late August 2011 and will eventually join the cars on display at the Bowling Green museum, housed in L&N's former passenger station.

In the summer and fall of 1986, a group of investors from Madison, Indiana, ran an excursion train on the Glasgow Railway called the "Caveland Limited." It consisted of ex–Pennsylvania Railroad 6999 pulling open coaches on two round trips daily, Friday through Monday. Bill Helton, the engineer, also owned the locomotive.

The Glasgow Railway continues to serve many local industries, and CSX, the current leaseholder that followed the L&N and Seaboard companies, runs a daily morning train to Glasgow from Bowling Green. The train drops and picks up cars at R.R. Donnelly printing and scrap metal from shredded automobiles dumped from trucks and loaded onto railcars at the end of the line.

Mammoth Cave had been discovered in 1802, and getting to the cave was not an easy journey, as the trails in the area were rugged at best. Kentucky was very much a part of the Wild West. Eventually, the Louisville & Nashville Railroad reached Glasgow Junction (now Park City) in 1859, making passage to the cave easier. From Cave City or Glasgow Junction, patrons could take a stagecoach ride to Mammoth Cave, now a famous attraction. Col. Larkin Proctor, who ran the stage line from Bells Tavern at Glasgow Junction to the cave, put together investors, mostly from Nashville, to charter the Mammoth Cave Railroad in 1874. Construction on the line did not commence until 1886, with the 8.7-mile line opening in November 1887. It was leased to the Louisville & Nashville Railroad. The line was profitable for the first six years, followed by a couple years of decline. A new company was formed with the same name and took over operations from the L&N completely by 1903. An early beginning to the end of the railroad was foretold in 1904 when an Indianapolis judge drove the first automobile to Mammoth Cave. During the years of operation, 40,000–50,000 visitors rode the railroad annually.

The railroad operated in the rugged cave country and utilized many trestles and curves with grades between three and four percent. The rail was 56 pounds per yard, and the right-of-way was 50 feet. The passengers were transported in two combination coaches, and two passenger coaches were pulled by "dummy" 0-4-2T locomotives, the most famous being No. 3 *Hercules*. The trip to the cave took about 25 minutes and sometimes carried as many as 200 passengers. Before 1892, black passengers rode in the baggage compartments, and after 1892, when the Jim Crow laws took effect, there were two-seat sections separated by partitions that were reserved for blacks but seldom used. The cars contained coal stoves for heat. Engineer Pat Moran and fireman Pete Charlet were longtime fixtures on the railroad, often picking up freight business by shopping for farmers along the line in Glasgow Junction, as well as hauling supplies for Mammoth Cave. Farmers along the line often provided labor for track maintenance.

The Lacey family of Franklin, Kentucky, played a large role in the Mammoth Cave Railroad, with Col. R.H. Lacey being one of the original founders and serving as president from 1904 until his death in 1915. Mrs. I.P. Lacey then served as president from then until 1928, when the railroad was sold to F.L. Gallup of Ypsilanti, Michigan. Gallup had aspirations to extend the line to the asphalt mines along Green River, but this never occurred, and the line was sold again in 1931 to a group called the Mammoth Cave National Park Association, headed by Max B. Nahm of Bowling Green. At a stockholders meeting on June 8, 1931, with the line operating at a loss for several years, it was voted to discontinue operations effective on September 1, 1931. An L&N extra section gang subsequently removed the tracks, and all the equipment and assets were sold except for one of the dummy locomotives, No. 4 (later lettered as *Hercules*, although it had been No. 3), and passenger coach No. 2. These two salvaged pieces were put on display and remain today near the visitor center for Mammoth Cave National Park.

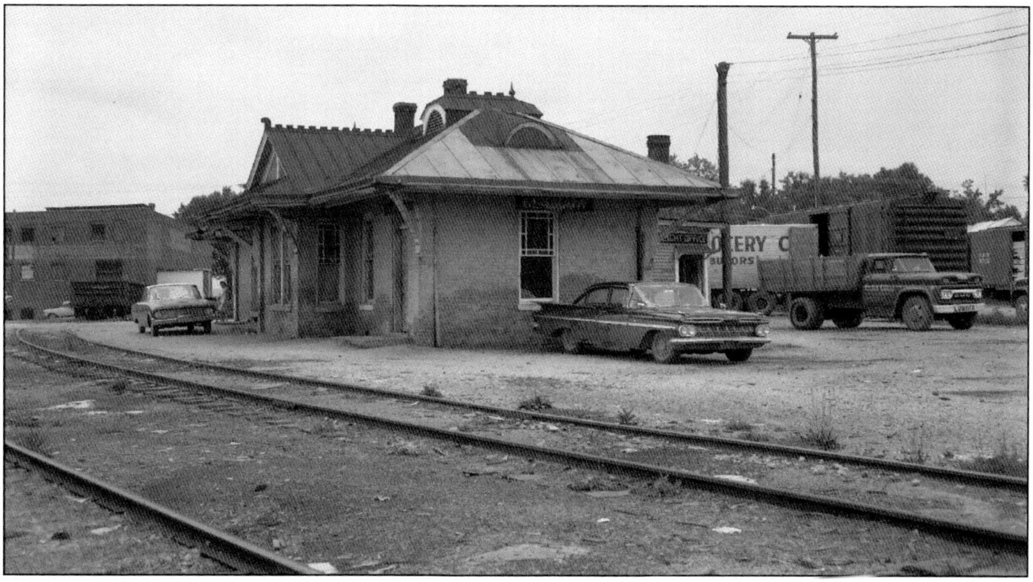

This image shows the passenger depot of Glasgow, Kentucky, that served the Glasgow Railway Company's 10-mile line to Park City, Kentucky, which was a connection with the L&N Main Line and the Mammoth Cave Railroad. The station sat near the end of the line at Leslie Avenue and West Washington Street. Passengers were served by two daily trips to Park City and returned on a mixed train with Glasgow Railway combine No. 109 providing the accommodations. (L&N records, University of Louisville Archives.)

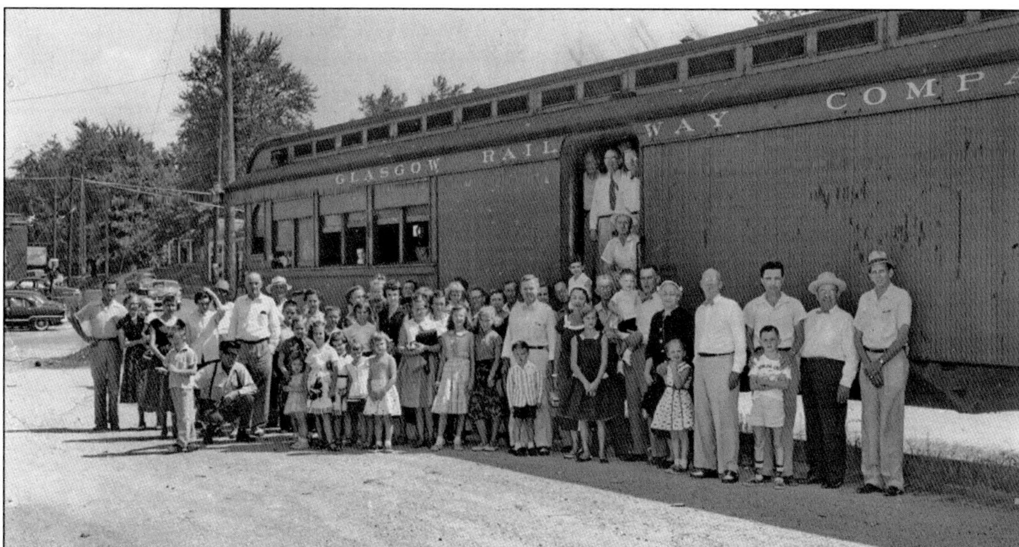

The last passenger trip for the Glasgow Railway Company took place August 24, 1955, and this image captures the large crowd of patrons, railroad personnel, and executives who made the trip. "Jim Crow" combine No. 109 provides the background for the photograph, fittingly taken at the end of the line. Originally L&N 82-seat coach 890, the No. 109 had been rebuilt in 1911 and later converted to a combine. The coach, separated into a section for whites, baggage in the center, and a section for blacks, was the only piece of rolling stock owned by the Glasgow Railway. (Leigh Lessenberry.)

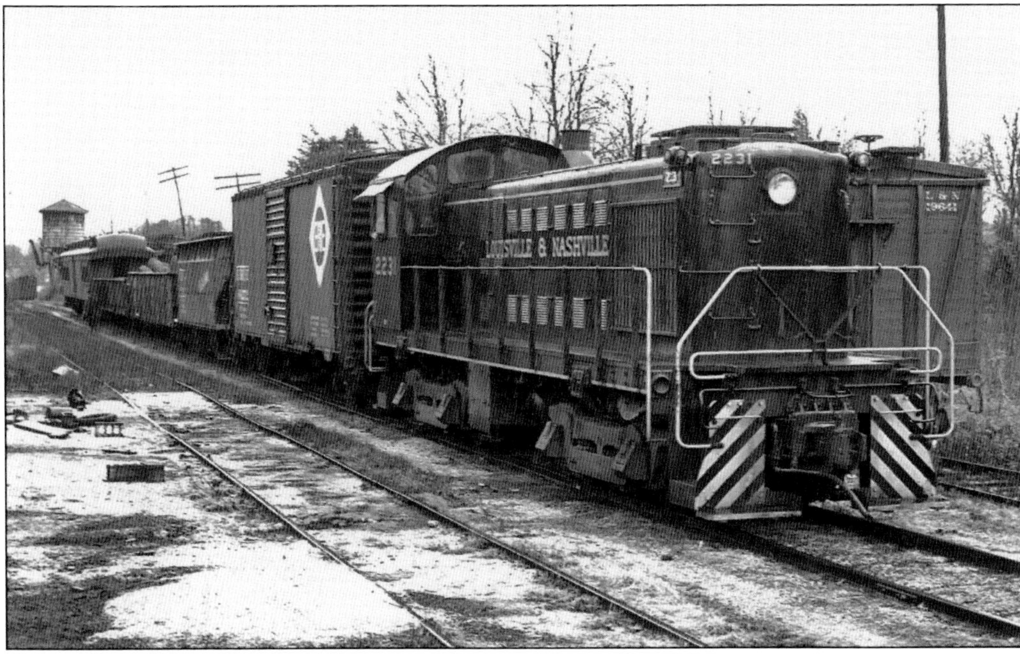

Louisville & Nashville Railroad switcher No. 2231 leads a Glasgow Railway mixed train as the crew prepares to make the run to Park City and interchange cars there with the L&N. A locomotive was always leased from the L&N since Glasgow Railway never owned motive power. (Leigh Lessenberry.)

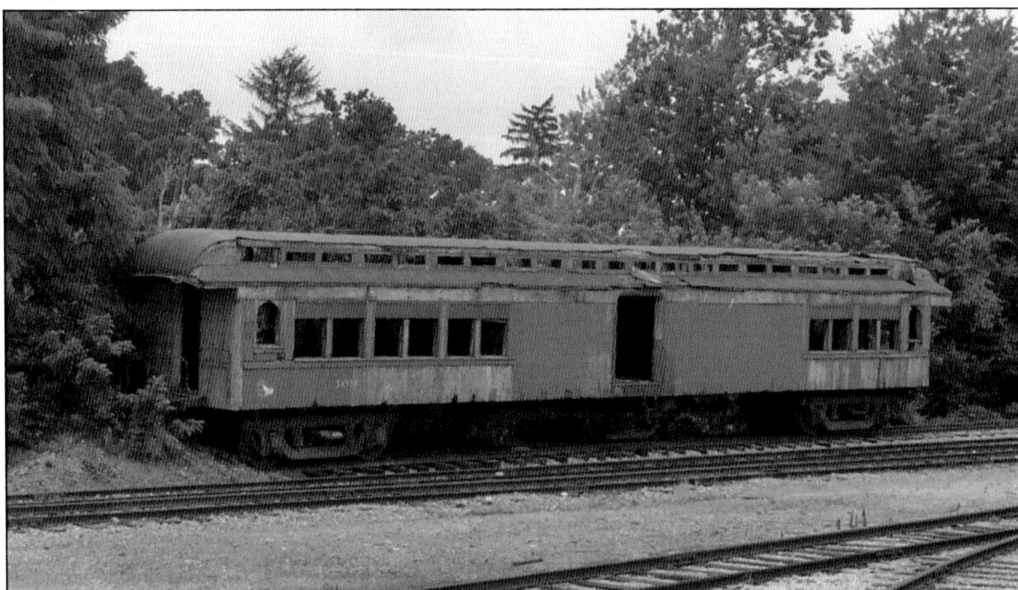

In the summer of 1986, the Glasgow Railway combine No. 109 had been relegated to a spot on an overgrown siding opposite the freight depot of Glasgow for more than 30 years. By this time, age had taken a toll, and many of the furnishings had been stolen, vandalized, or removed to storage. The car would remain here another 25 years before a serious restoration effort would be considered. (Steven D. Johnson photograph.)

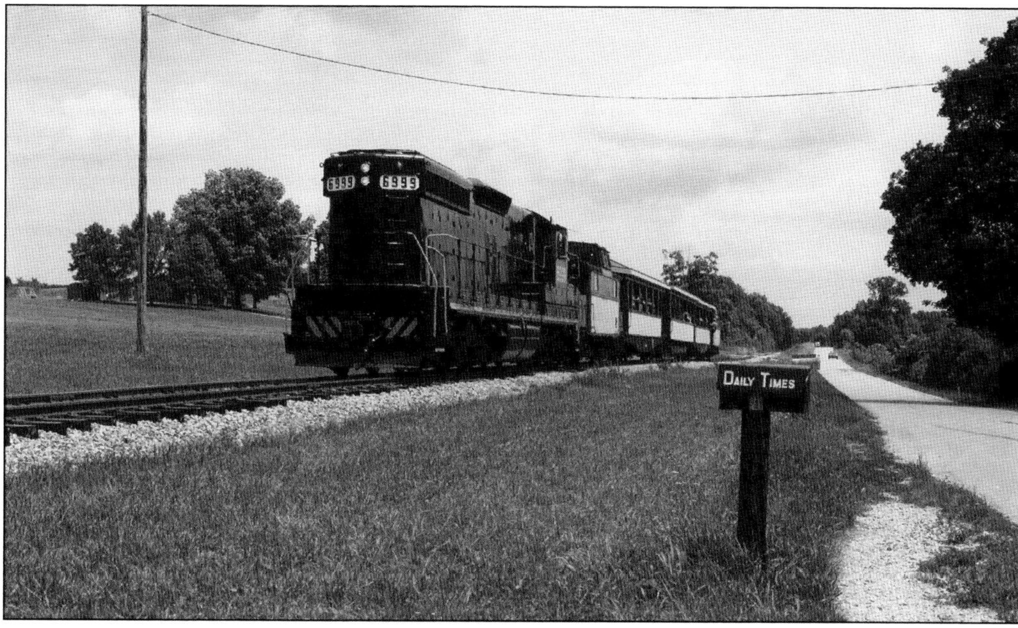

In 1986, an excursion train began to operate on the rails of the Glasgow Railway. The "Caveland Limited" was based at the freight depot in Glasgow and made two round-trip runs daily to Park City, Friday through Sunday, between June and October. The group that operated the excursions was from Madison, Indiana, and brought engine 6999 and several open coaches for the 20-mile round trips. The train is shown near Oil City on July 13, 1986. (Steven D. Johnson photograph.)

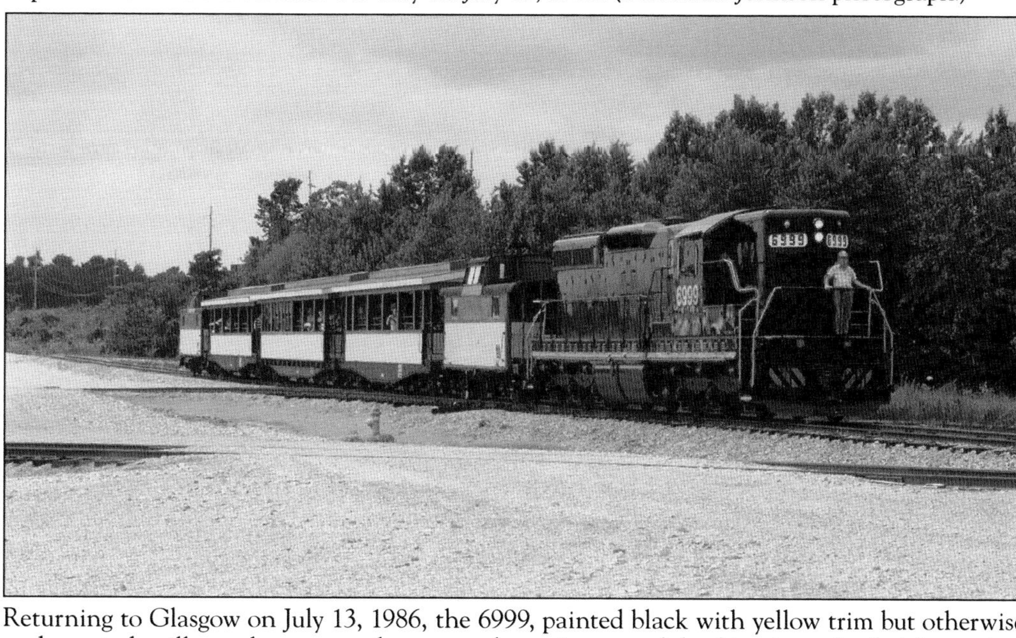

Returning to Glasgow on July 13, 1986, the 6999, painted black with yellow trim but otherwise undecorated, will use the wye track to turn the train around, backing into the freight station. EMD SD-7 6999 is a former Pennsylvania Railroad, Penn Central, and Conrail locomotive, specially ballasted for the grades around Madison, Indiana. The cost of the excursions was $6 for adults and $3.50 for children, but it was not advertised well and did not enjoy heavy ridership. (Steven D. Johnson photograph.)

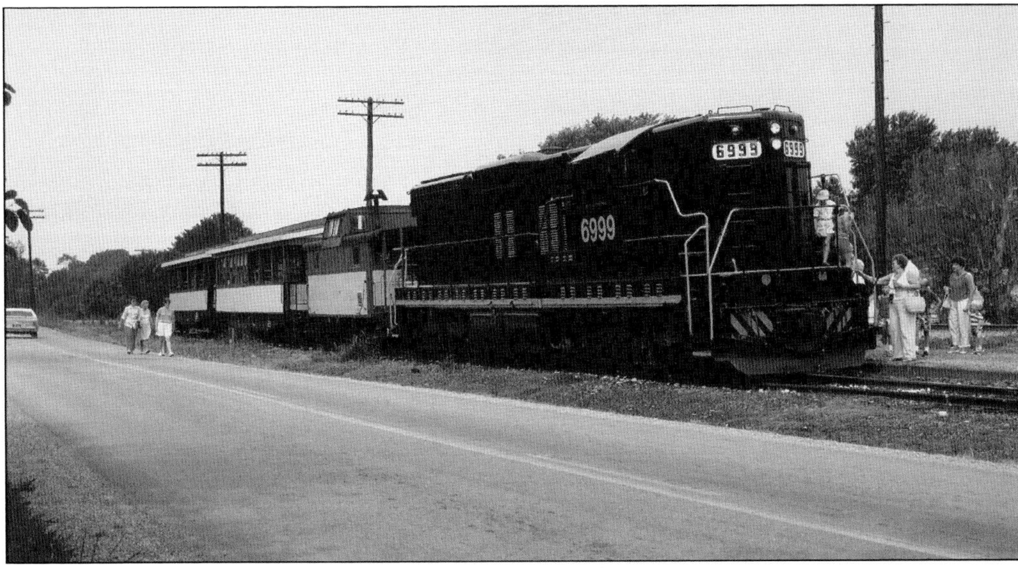

At Park City, Kentucky, on August 15, 1986, the excursion made a stop near the site of the old Park City L&N Station, which had been razed long ago. Historic Bell's Tavern sits across the street, and the large abandoned former Mentz Hotel is also nearby. The locomotive would run around the train before making the return trip to Glasgow. (Steven D. Johnson photograph.)

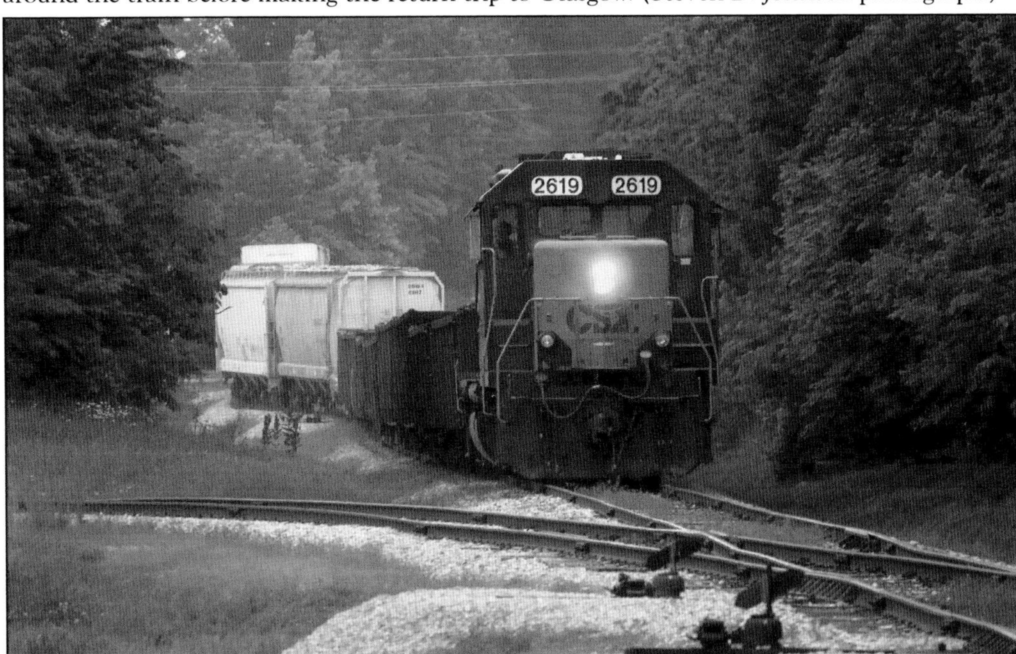

L&N successor CSX Transportation still makes the run to Glasgow out of Bowling Green each weekday. Local J756, the Glasgow turn, is shown working the industrial park in Glasgow on May 18, 2011. The local leaves Bowling Green early for Park City, where the train takes the Glasgow Railway for the 10-mile run. There are several industries to work at Glasgow, taking most of the day, and J756 sometimes works at Park City and north Bowling Green on the return trip to Memphis Junction yard. (Kevin Comer photograph.)

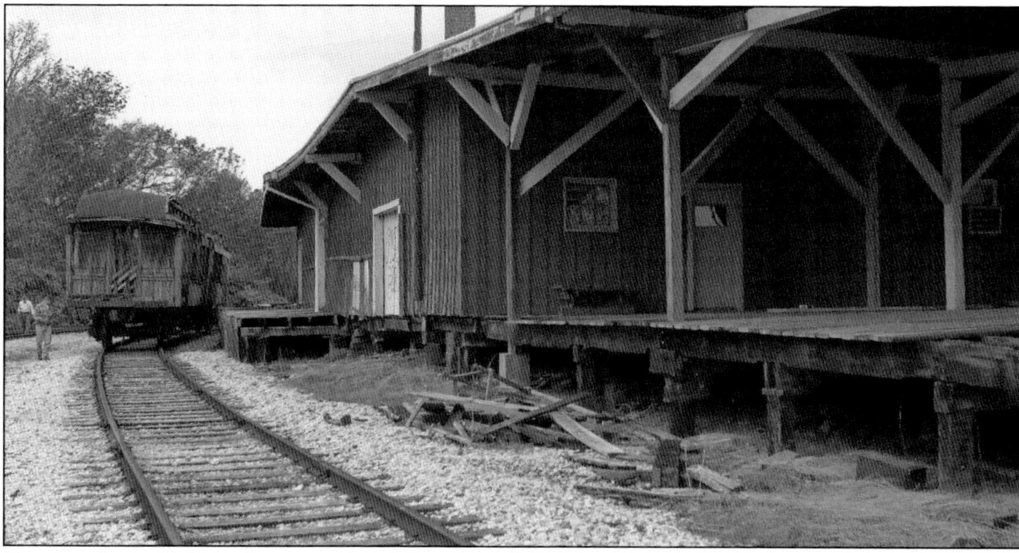

On April 23, 2011, volunteers from the Friends of the L&N Depot and Historic RailPark of Bowling Green freed the Glasgow Railway Company combine No. 109 from its longtime resting spot. With some long hours of coaxing, the car finally rolled from the siding to the main and then back into the house track, making a brief last stop at the freight depot in Glasgow. At the end of the track, the car would be prepared for movement by trailer to Bowling Green for restoration. (Kevin Comer photograph.)

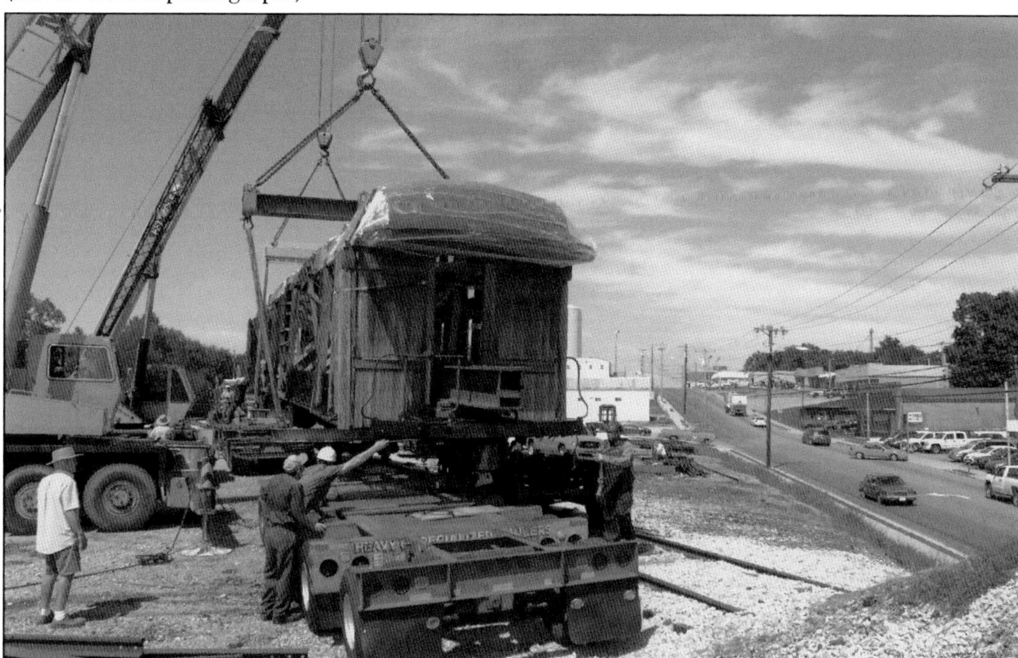

No. 109's last day in Glasgow arrived on August 22, 2011, when cranes from Madison-Smith Machine and Tool Company of Glasgow loaded the car onto the trailer from McCord Heavy and Specialized Haulers for the trip to Bowling Green. The preparation for the move took many hours from several volunteers. The professional crews handled everything with ease, and the loading went smoothly. (Kevin Comer photograph.)

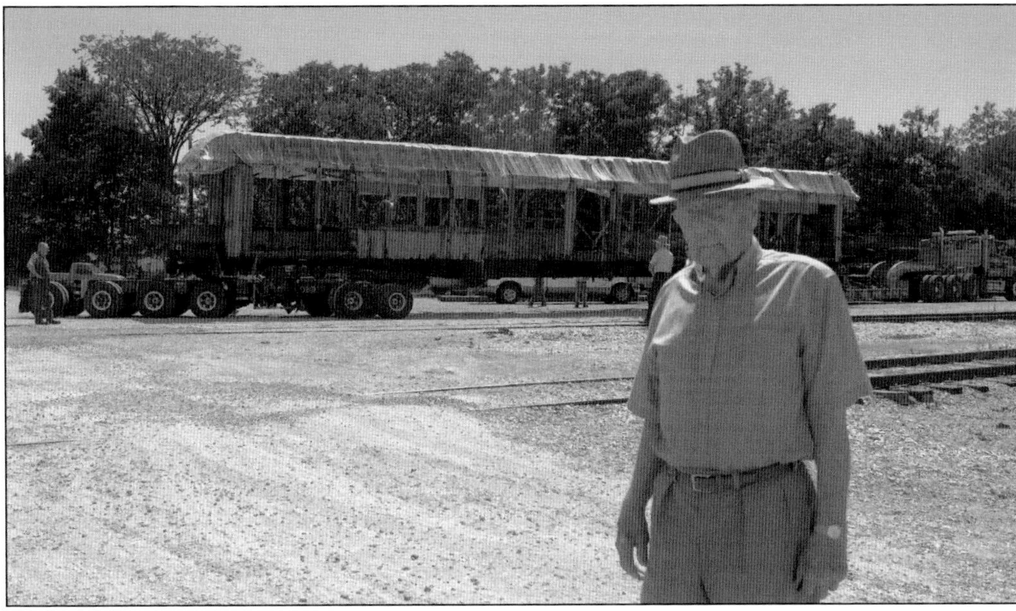

Robert A. Lessenberry, president of the Glasgow Railway Company, was on hand to watch the removal of the passenger car that had been a fixture near the freight depot in Glasgow for more than 50 years. Lessenberry's father Robert L. Lessenberry was the second president of the Glasgow Railway. Glasgow Railway Company owns the 10-mile line from Park City, and the operation has always been leased to the L&N and successors Seaboard and CSX. (Kevin Comer photograph.)

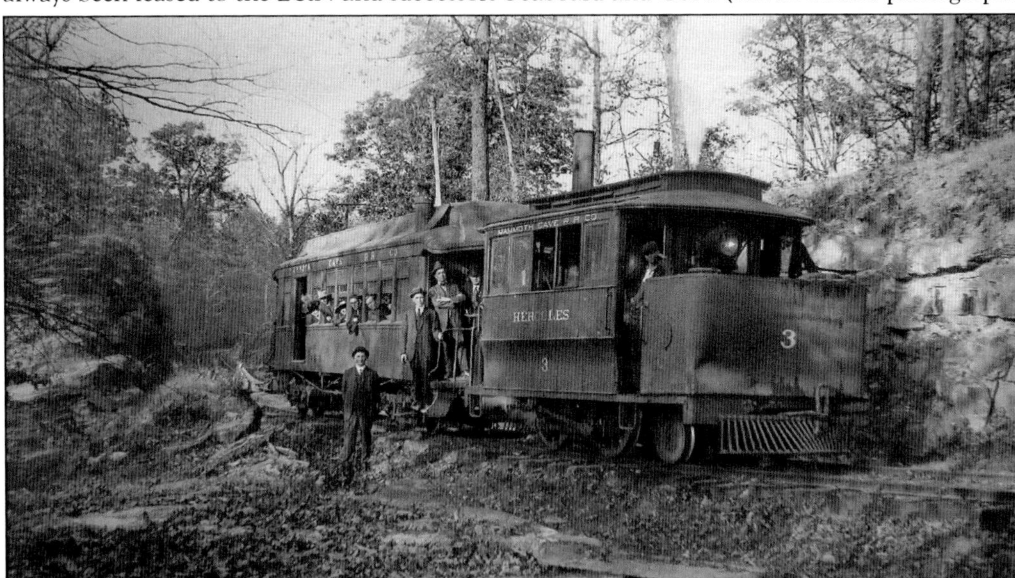

Mammoth Cave Railroad 0-4-2T dummy-type steam locomotive No. 3 *Hercules* is shown here in the early 1900s. The 8.7-mile railroad had opened in 1886 from Park City to the Mammoth Cave Hotel. First leased to the Louisville & Nashville Railroad, the company had financial problems and reorganized under the same name and operated independently in 1903. The railroad owned four of these types of engines along with a handful of baggage/coach combination cars. (James E. Carroll photograph, National Park Service.)

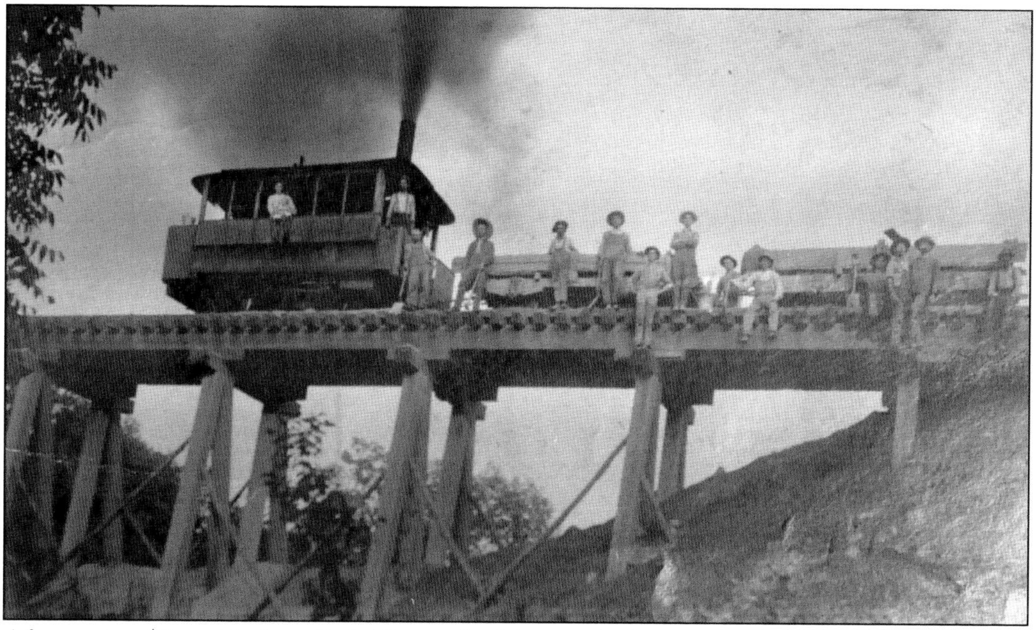

After paying $3 to ride from Park City to the Mammoth Cave estate and hotel, travelers would encounter rolling hills, sinkholes, forest, homes, and farmland during the 8.7-mile trip. Climbing the Chester Escarpment, the railroad gained 200 feet in elevation in less than a mile. Before reaching the hotel, the train crossed the Doyle Valley Trestle. Today, most of this path has been restored as a walking trail through the scenic area. (National Park Service.)

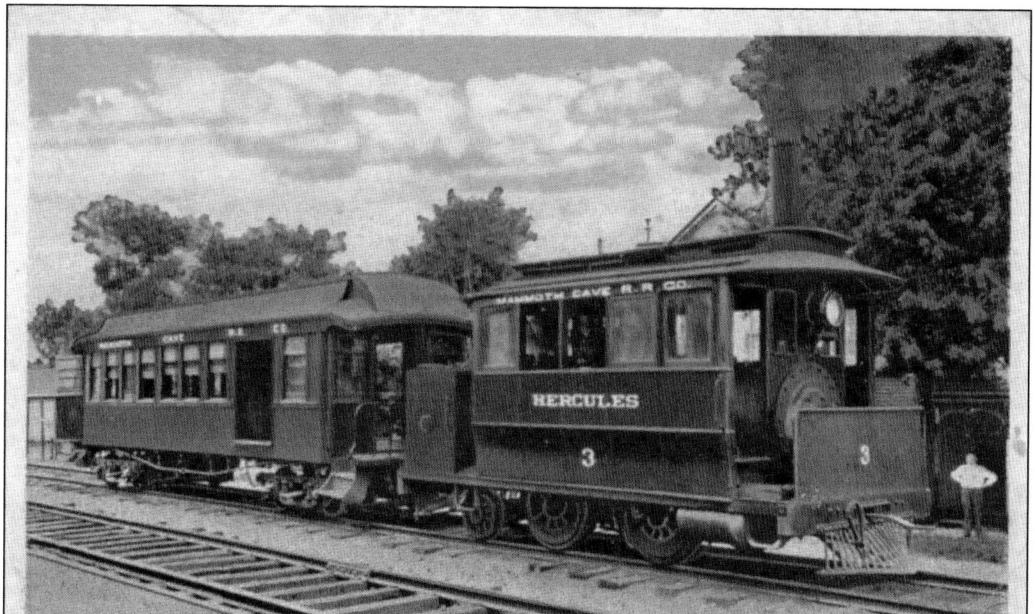

This postcard shows the most famous of the Mammoth Cave Railroad locomotives, *Hercules.* During the trip along the line, visitors had a chance to stop at other local landmarks Diamond Caverns, Grand Avenue Cave, and Procter Cave. Until the automobile came along, followed by improving roads into the area, this was a busy railroad. (Greg Hughes collection.)

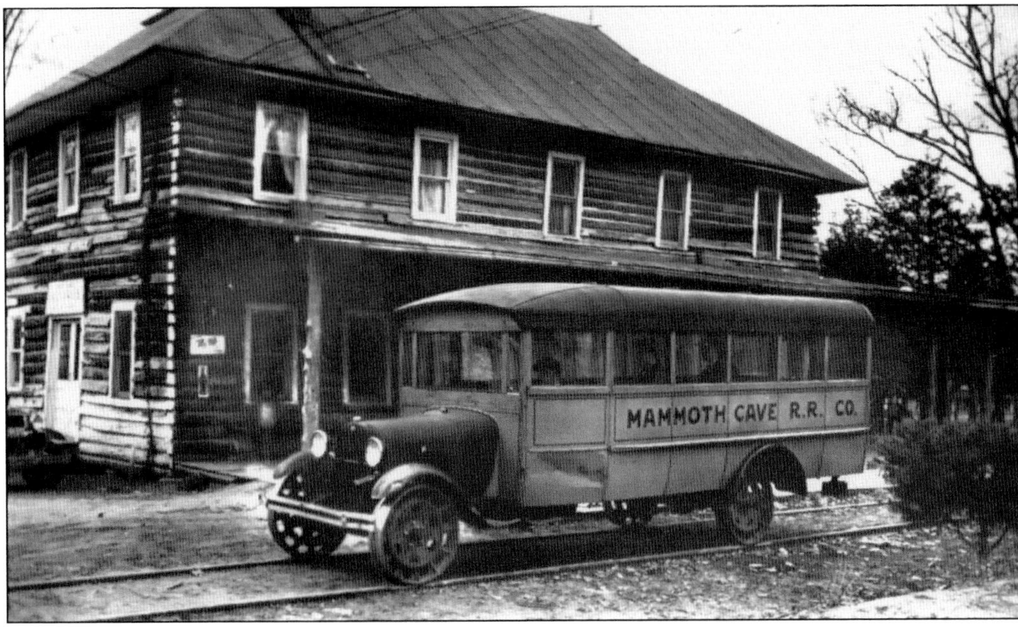

Mammoth Cave Railroad experimented with using a small rail bus to replace the locomotives around 1912. The bus chassis had rail wheels, and small turntables were constructed for turning it around. It proved unable to haul the loaded coaches, and the experiment was discontinued. Pictured is a later version of a rail bus that was used on the railroad. (Kentucky Library and Museum-WKU.)

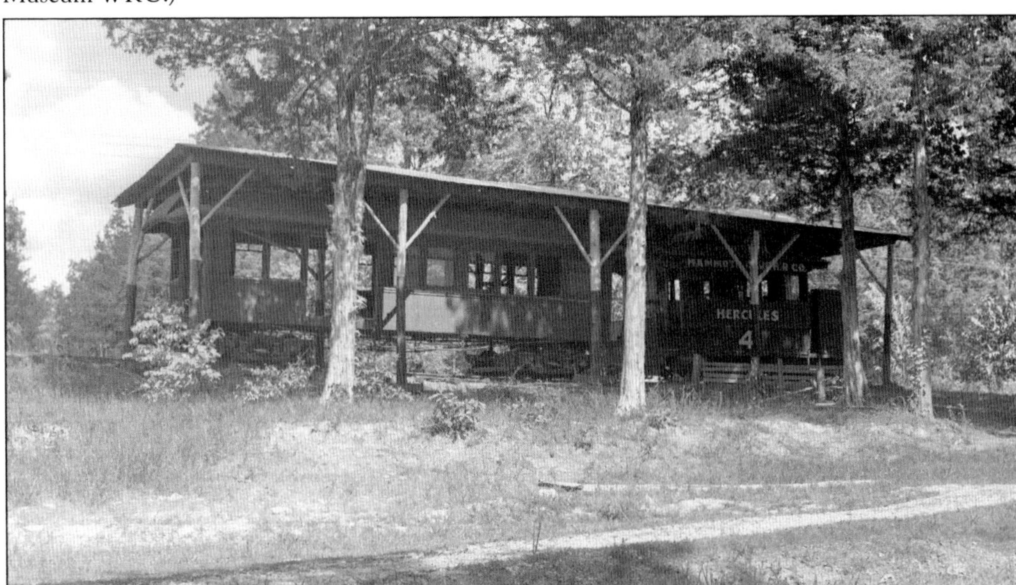

Mammoth Cave Railroad 0-4-2T dummy-type locomotive No. 4 and coach No. 2 are on permanent display near the Mammoth Cave National Park Visitor Venter. No. 4 is named as *Hercules* to represent its more famous sister locomotive. The original *Hercules* was actually No. 3 and was scrapped. The long journey to bring National Park status to Mammoth Cave finally realized success in the 1930s, but that also marked the end of the railroad. An L&N section gang removed the rails, and the equipment was sold. (National Park Service.)

Five

Scottsville Branch

In the 1870s, surveyors from the Cumberland & Ohio (C&O) Railroad Company planned a line from Gallatin, Tennessee, to Scottsville, Kentucky. That company fell apart before completion of the survey. The 35-mile line was completed in the 1880s to Scottsville as the Cincinnati, Green River & Nashville Railroad and connected at Hartsville Junction with the 11-mile Middle & East Tennessee Central Railway to Hartsville. The M&ETC had aspired to reach Knoxville, Tennessee, but never got past Hartsville.

The Gallatin to Scottsville line and the line to Hartsville combined to become the Chesapeake & Nashville Railway in 1898. The traces of the wye at Hartsville Junction are still visible today although the rails are gone. The C&N had intended to build north from Gallatin and Nashville to connect with the Cincinnati Southern Railroad at Danville, Kentucky. Parts of the line north of Scottsville were graded, but never completed.

The town of Westmoreland, Tennessee, was actually laid out by the railroad. Near Westmoreland is a tunnel said to be the shortest in the United States and possibly the world. It measures just 46.5 feet in length. Reportedly, this tunnel came about because the railroad had to make a deep cut in this section, and it would separate the property of George Washington "Wash" Minnick into two pieces. His cattle would not be able to move from one side of his pasture to the other. It is said that the railroad constructed the tunnel to satisfy his needs. Money was allocated in 2004 and used to clear out debris and make the closed tunnel a tourist attraction, but that has not completely materialized. Westmoreland takes pride in having the world's shortest tunnel. A second tunnel south of Westmoreland was called the "big tunnel."

In addition to the tunnels, the line had many trestles, including a huge structure just south of Scottsville spanning a wide valley, two creeks, and U.S. Highway 31 East. The Louisville & Nashville Railroad purchased the line in July 1906 since it connected with their main line at Gallatin. Many such lines were purchased by the L&N to keep competitors from operating in their territory. With the acquisition, the L&N also received Locomotives No. 2, 3, 4, and 5; renumbering them as L&N 140, 458, 2185, and 62. No. 3 was a Mogul, and the others were 4-4-0s.

An L&N timetable from 1907 shows that train 9 left Hartsville at 5:30 a.m., arriving in Gallatin at 6:30 a.m. As soon as Train 9 reached Gallatin, Train 11 would leave Scottsville, stopping at Petroleum at 6:48, Adolphus at 6:59, Turners Station at 7:08, Westmoreland at 7:18, Bransford at 7:32, Bethpage at 7:43, Roganna at 7:52, and finally reaching Gallatin at 8:30 a.m. Afternoon Train 10 would leave Gallatin at 4:30 p.m. and make the same stops northbound, reaching Scottsville at 6:30 p.m. The equipment would remain in Scottsville overnight and begin the next morning as Train 11. Train 9, which had reached Gallatin at 6:30 a.m., would run back to Hartsville as Train 12 at 6:30 p.m., leaving as soon as Train 10 reached Scottsville. Train 12 would arrive at Hartsville at 7:30 p.m. and tie down for the evening, then leave Hartsville the next morning as Train 9.

An article in the Scottsville *Times-Messenger* in 1907 noted that "the town has been free from the sale of intoxicating liquors for the past forty years." However, in reality, the daily train from Tennessee had many jugs, barrels, and bottles addressed to unfamiliar names in Scottsville, usually claimed by local residents.

In the line's best times, eight trains per day traveled the line carrying passengers, strawberries, tobacco, fertilizer, cloth goods, sand, lumber, livestock, timber, oil, and general freight and mail. Oil was a big part of the line's commerce, since there were large oil fields in the area.

The 170-room Epperson Springs Hotel near Westmoreland became famous for the implied medicinal value of the sulfur water in a nearby spring. Travelers would come to Westmoreland by train and be transported to the hotel. The hotel was destroyed by fire in the 1920s and never rebuilt, eliminating most passenger service.

There were reports that the L&N might convert the line into an electric trolley line at one point, but that never materialized. With the small tunnel and many trestles, the L&N eventually used a 70-ton switch engine, usually No. 98 or 99, which was assigned to Gallatin to handle the infrequent trains on the line. No. 98 was eventually sold to Tropicana for switching refrigerated cars of orange juice, and now resides at the Tennessee Central Railway Museum in Nashville.

Near the end, the line saw a couple of trains out of Gallatin a week at best. The maintenance cost of the line with all the trestles eventually outweighed the revenue, and the L&N abandoned it on December 10, 1976. Not long after, the rails were pulled up, and the large trestle near Scottsville eventually came down. All that is left today are the large concrete piers that supported the bridge over US 31 East near Scottsville. Depots remain at Scottsville and Hartsville, and traces of the right-of-way are very visible in several areas.

In tracing the former line, one might find whistle posts, a few stray rails, crossing signs, culverts, bridge piers, and even an intact bridge or two. With no railroad serving the area, and very few reminders, the one-time importance of rail service to Scottsville and Hartsville is easily forgotten.

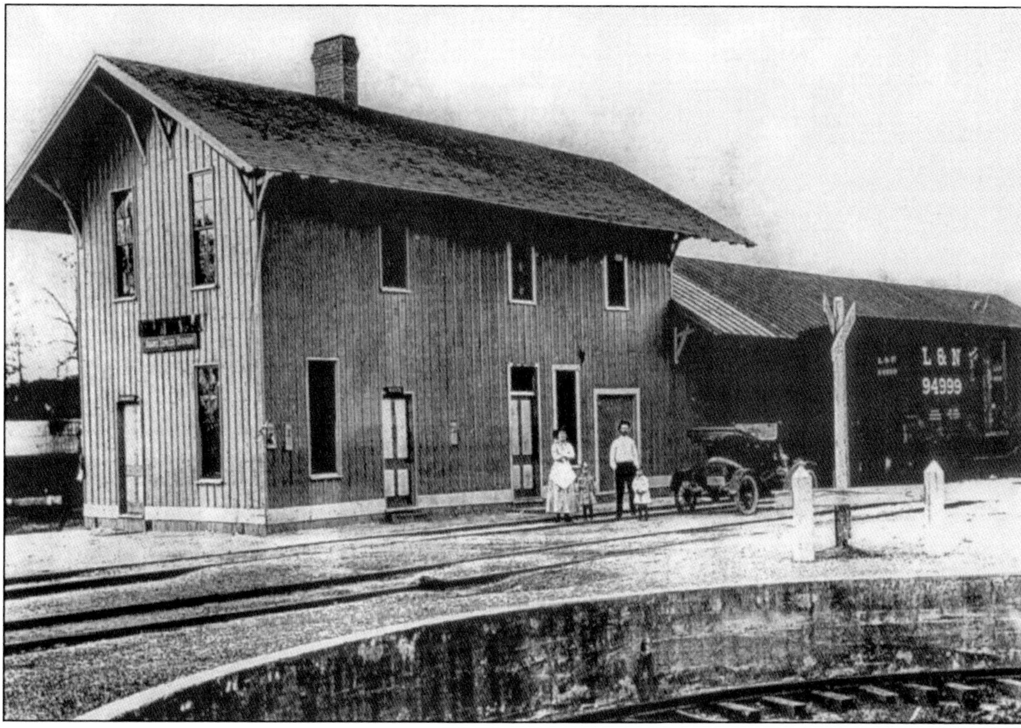

At Scottsville, Kentucky, a depot had been constructed on the Chesapeake & Nashville Railroad, with plans to extend the line farther, but those plans never materialized. A turntable was used at Scottsville to turn the locomotives back toward Gallatin, Tennessee. Shown here is the original Scottsville Depot with the two-story tower on one end. Scottsville also had a small yard and some industrial tracks near the depot. (Allen County Historical Society.)

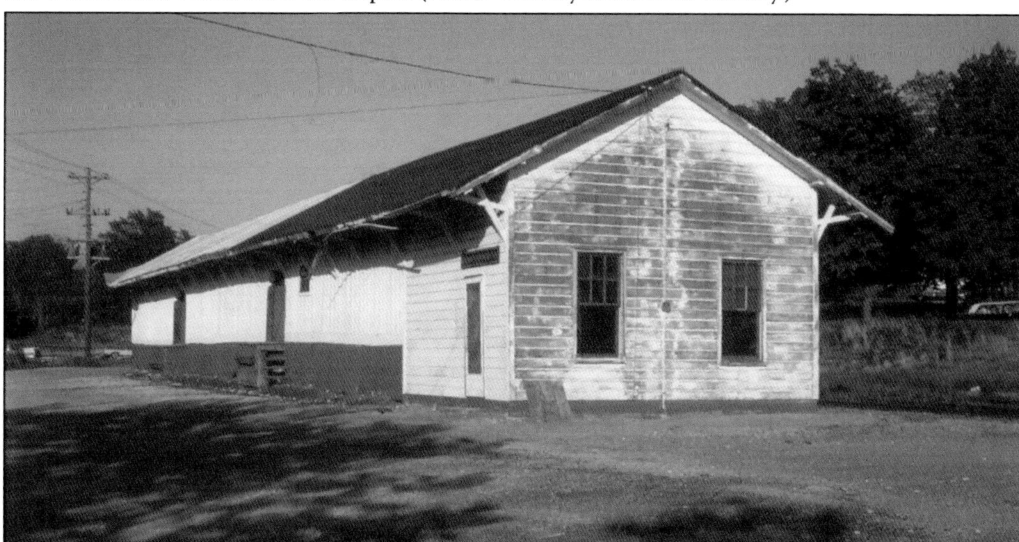

This mid-1970s view of the Scottsville, Kentucky Depot shows the Railway Express sign still on the building and the remaining track still in place. Shortly afterward, the track was removed when the line was abandoned. In many cases of abandonment, depots are torn down. A few, like this one, survive to serve other uses. (Rumsie Butler photograph, Rick Williams collection.)

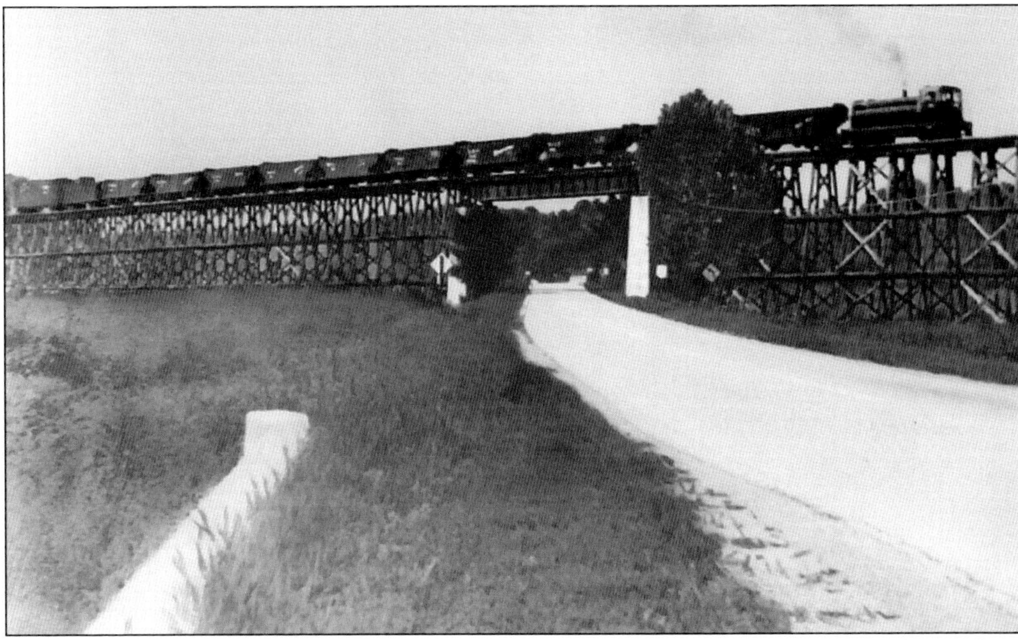

One of the switchers out of Gallatin heads across the long trestle to Scottsville in this undated view. The train is crossing over US 31 East and will reach the end of the line in a few miles. L&N switchers Nos. 98 and 99 were assigned to Gallatin, and one of them made the run to Hartsville and Scottsville. The trestles on the line dictated that lighter power be used. Some cars were also restricted due to the tunnels. (Robert Carter photograph.)

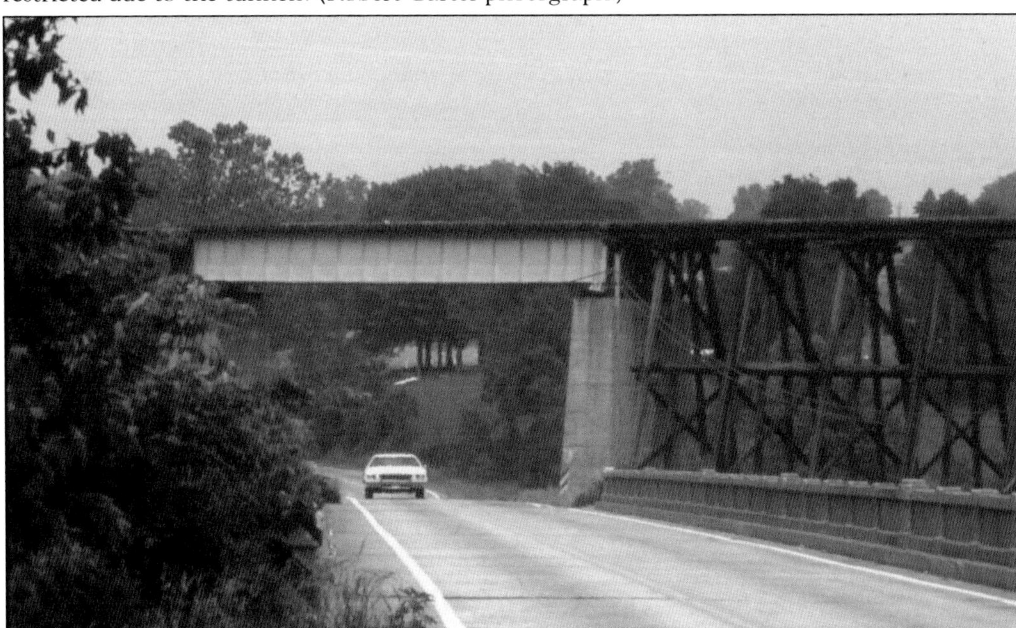

A mid-1970s view of US 31 East shows a car passing under the Scottsville Branch Bridge and trestle near Petroleum, Kentucky, before crossing the highway bridge over Drakes Creek. Today, a new US 31 East/US 231 runs west of the original route, with the old US 31 East becoming state highway 3500 Old Gallatin Road. (Rumsie Butler photograph, Rick Williams collection.)

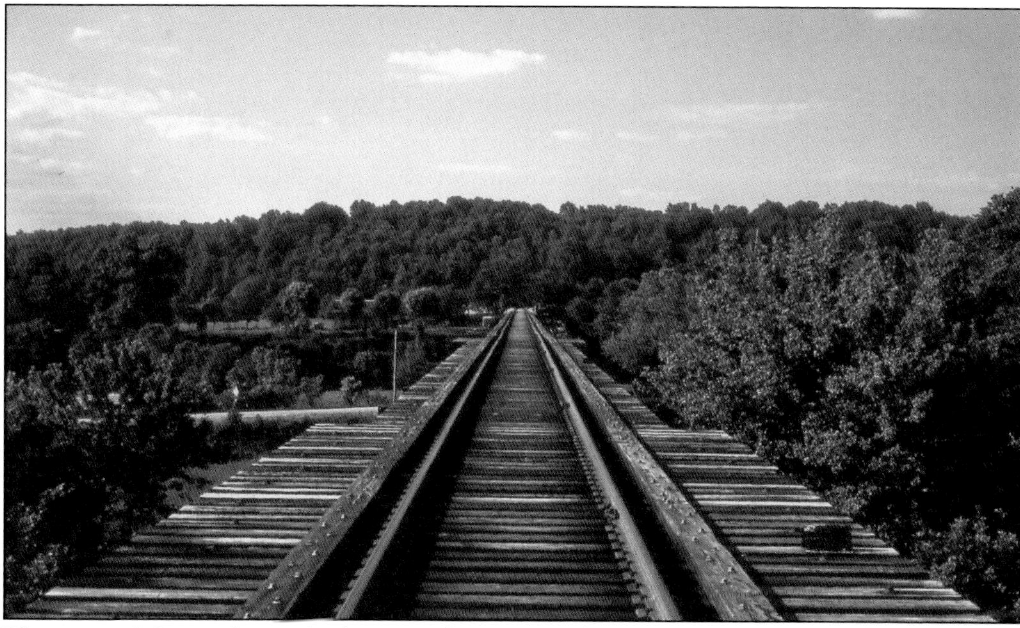

This view of the tracks on the long trestle near Petroleum, just south of Scottsville, Kentucky, provides a sense of the trestle's massive size. After abandonment, the long trestle stood for a while before finally being destroyed. Trains had a very slow speed restriction over the trestle in its final years of use. Maintenance of this type of structure versus the sparse revenue from the line led to its abandonment. (Lee Yoder photograph.)

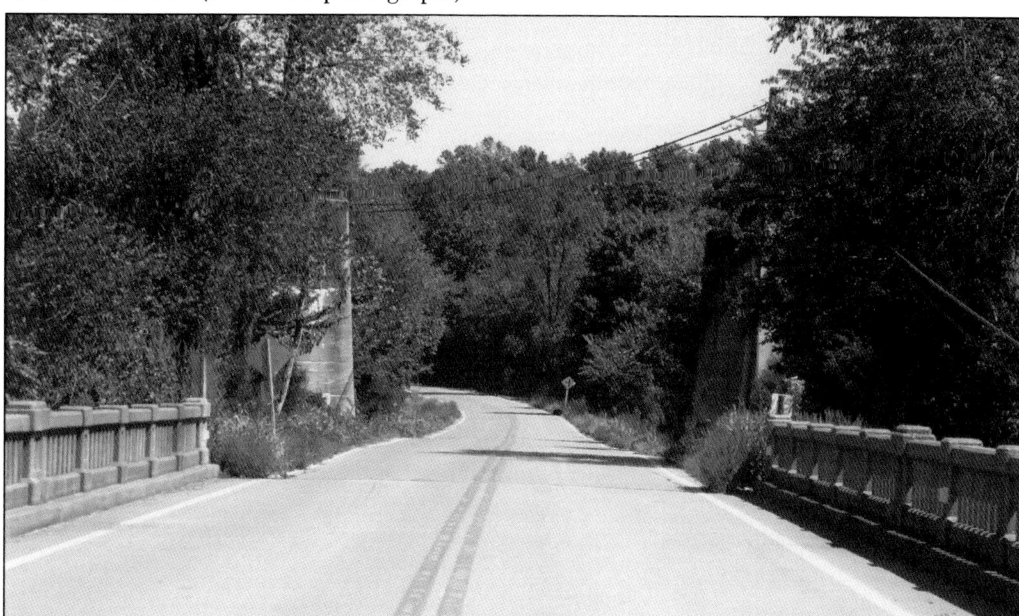

In 2010, a trip along the remnants of the old L&N Scottville branch still revealed many traces of the line. The bridge supports, shown here, at US 31 East and the surrounding terrain give an idea of the size of the long trestle. On other parts of the line, there are whistle posts, roadbed, bridge supports, a few rails still in place, crossing signs, and, of course, the two tunnels. (Kevin Comer photograph.)

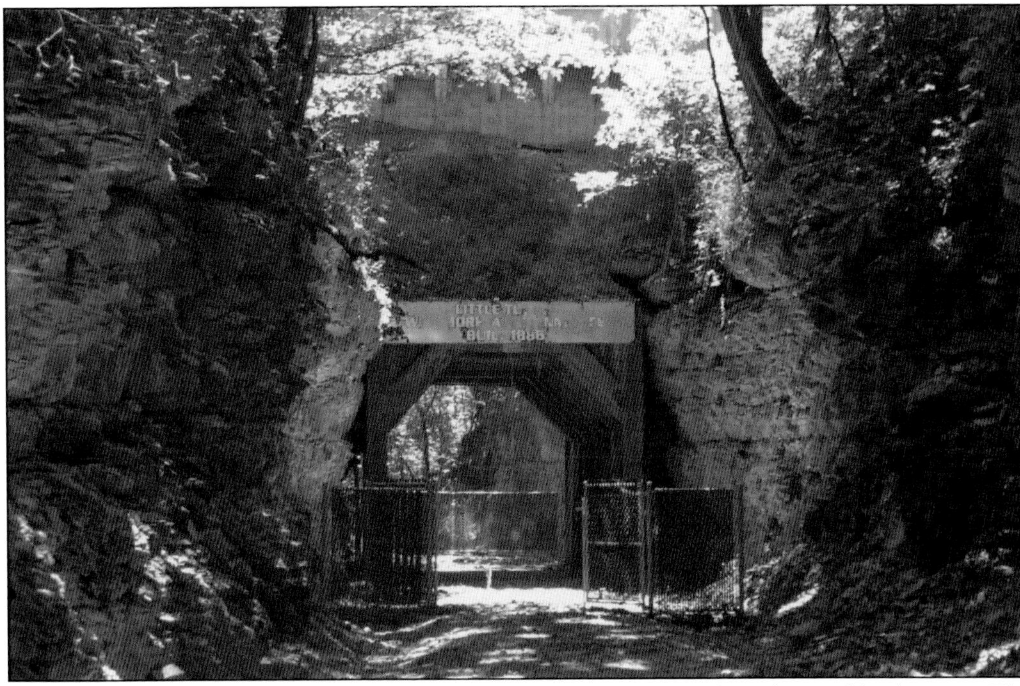

This tunnel just south of Westmoreland, Tennessee, is advertised as the world's shortest. The popular story is that it was originally constructed to provide a farmer access to both sides of his property over the railroad. In recent years, funds were spent to stabilize and rehabilitate the tunnel. If it is to be a tourist attraction, better access will need to be provided. A much larger tunnel is located south of Westmoreland. (Kevin Comer photograph.)

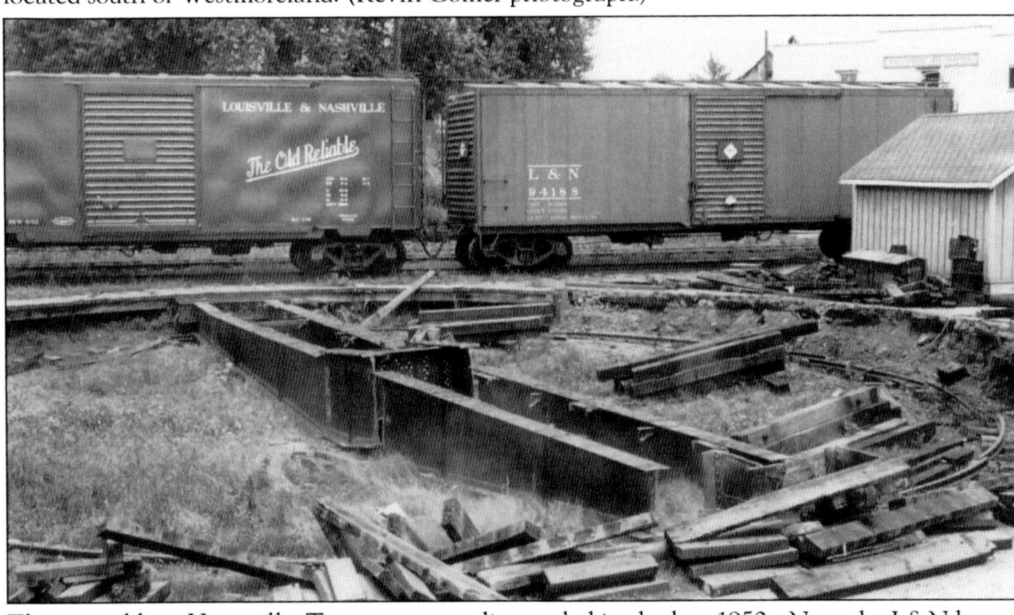

The turntable at Hartsville, Tennessee, was dismantled in the late 1950s. Note the L&N boxcar at left with famous "the Old Reliable" slogan on the side. Also, a stencil reports that the car was new in April 1952. After merging the Nashville, Chattanooga & St. Louis into the L&N system in 1957, the L&N began to use "the Dixie Line" slogan also. (Allen Haynes collection.)

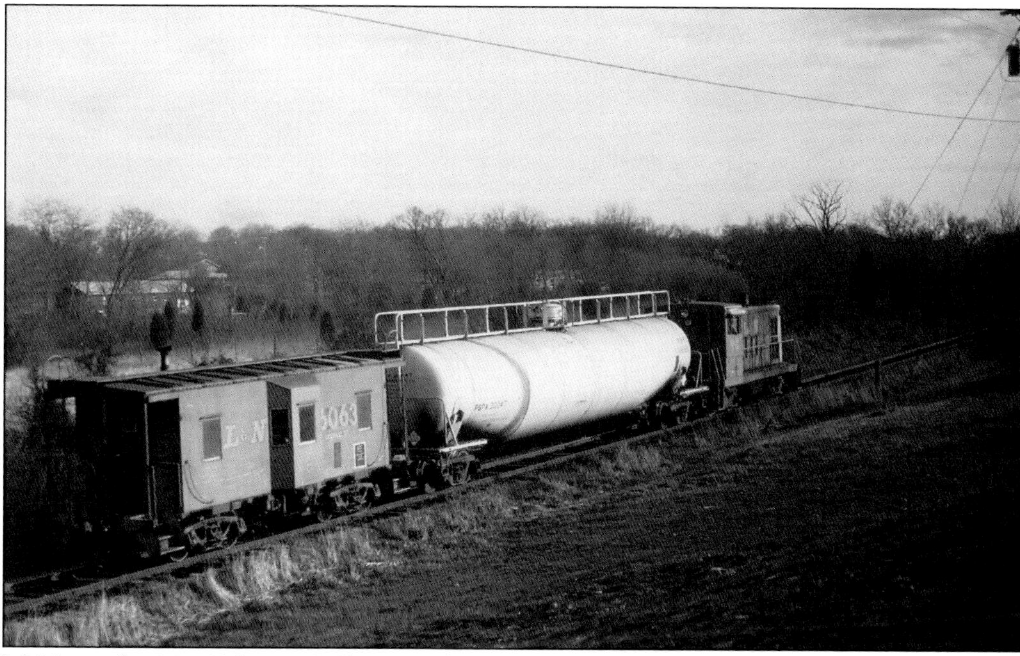

L&N switcher No. 98 leaves Gallatin on the Scottsville Branch with a short consist that includes only a large tank car and L&N caboose 6063. A part of the Scottsville Branch remains in use to serve some industries in Gallatin, including a propane dealer. (Lee Yoder photograph.)

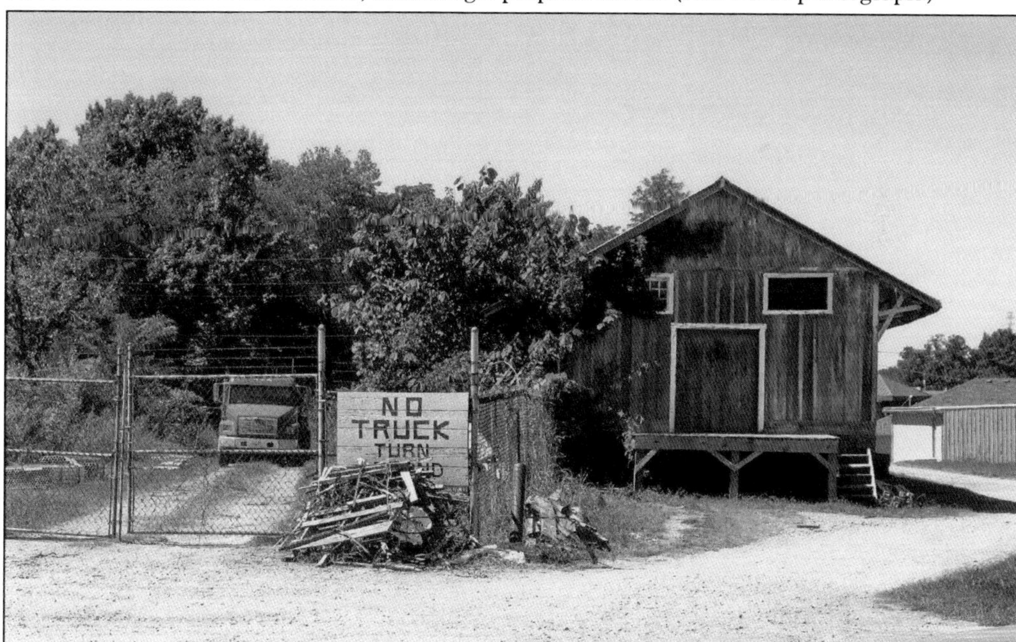

At Scottsville, Kentucky, the former L&N Depot is used as a storage facility for the lumber company next door. The turntable and tracks are long gone; however, parts of the former right-of-way can be found with relative ease. The two-story passenger portion of the station was removed long before the station saw the last train, leaving only the freight portion in later years. (Kevin Comer photograph.)

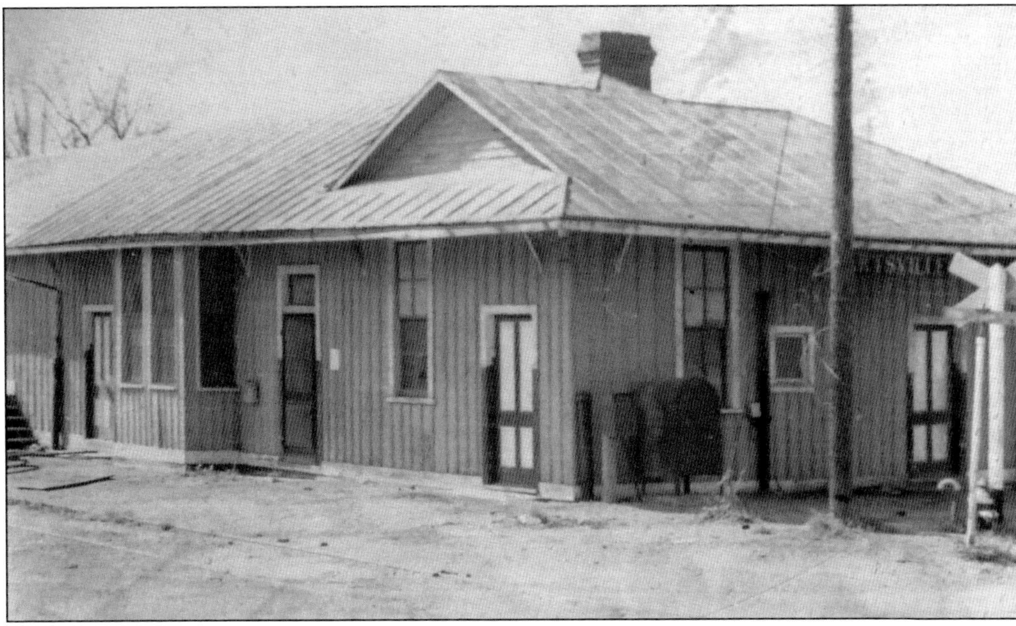

The Middle & East Tennessee Central Railway was chartered in 1883 and completed 11.38 miles between Roganna (Hartsville Junction) and Hartsville in 1892. The Battle of Hartsville on December 7, 1862, occurred when Col. John Hunt Morgan and 1,300 men engaged a much larger Federal force and scored a decisive victory, killing 2,096 and capturing 1,800, while losing only 139. After this battle, Morgan was promoted to brigadier general. (Allen Haynes collection.)

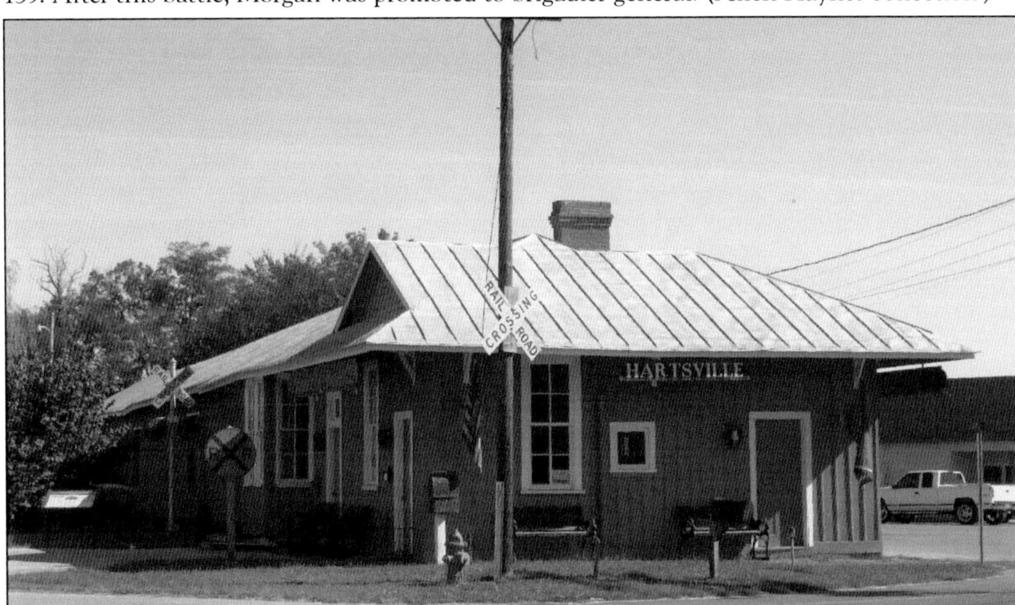

After the rails to Hartsville had been merged into the Chesapeake & Nashville Railway, the L&N took over operation in July 1906, becoming owner in January 1907. After the rails were removed in the 1970s, a plea to the L&N from locals saved the station from destruction. Today, it proudly serves as the Hartsville Chamber of Commerce and contains a nice museum and gift shop. (Kevin Comer photograph.)

Six

Family Lines, Seaboard, and CSX

The original Louisville & Nashville Railroad Main Line between the namesake cities was operated by the company from 1859 until 1983, when the L&N name finally gave way to Seaboard System Railroad. The L&N had always operated efficiently and provided excellent service, being rewarded with the nickname "The Old Reliable." The Louisville & Nashville had been controlled by the Atlantic Coast Line Railroad but operated independently since 1902.

Seaboard Coast Line was a result of the merger between the Atlantic Coast Line and Seaboard Air Line Railroads in 1967. In 1972, Seaboard Coast Line Industries (SCLI) was formed to put all the Seaboard Coast Line entities under a single banner. This included the Piedmont & Northern Railway and Durham Southern Railway, which it had acquired. The L&N, SCL, Clinchfield Railroad, Georgia Railroad, Atlanta & West Point Railroad, and Western Railway of Alabama all began to market themselves as the Family Lines System, controlled by SCLI, but operated independently. Locomotives were eventually painted in a "Family Lines" scheme with the owning railroad's marks stenciled under the cab windows. The Family Lines components consisted of 16,326 miles covering 13 states. The Family Lines lasted until 1982, when all the affiliated railroads were merged into the Seaboard System Railroad and ceased to exist.

In 1980, a holding company named CSX Corporation took control of the Chessie System Railroad and Seaboard Coast Line Industries, which included the Family Lines railroads. The Chessie System was a holding company that owned the Chesapeake & Ohio Railway (C&O), Baltimore & Ohio Railroad (B&O), Western Maryland Railway, and other small carriers. Equipment was owned by the various railroads under the CSX banner but operated independently.

On January 1, 1983, Seaboard System Railroad began operations. The former Family Lines roads began to see changes as C&O and B&O type operations were being practiced. Mars light removal was one of the many changes.

Seaboard acquired the South Carolina Pacific Railway and Louisville, Henderson & St. Louis Railway (which had been leased to L&N since 1929) in 1984, Gainesville Midland in 1985, and Atlanta & West Point and Columbia, Newberry & Laurens in 1986. Seaboard System was renamed CSX Transportation (CSXT) on June 1, 1986, and on July 1, 1986, Chessie System was merged into CSXT. On April 30, 1987, B&O was merged into C&O, and C&O was merged into CSXT on August 30, 1987. The Western Maryland had been merged into the B&O in May 1983. The Western Railway of Alabama eventually was merged into CSXT in December 2002.

Today, CSX Transportation is a giant company that operates more than 21,000 miles all over the eastern and southern United States in 10 divisions. CSX, with its headquarters in Jacksonville, Florida, operates the former L&N Main Line as part of its Louisville Division, Mainline Subdivision. Much of the traffic is related to the automobile industry, but there are also mixed freight trains, a few unit grain, unit steel trains, and the occasional coal train. The former L&N is thriving and even a few freight cars with L&N or Family Lines markings still can be seen on the CSX rails.

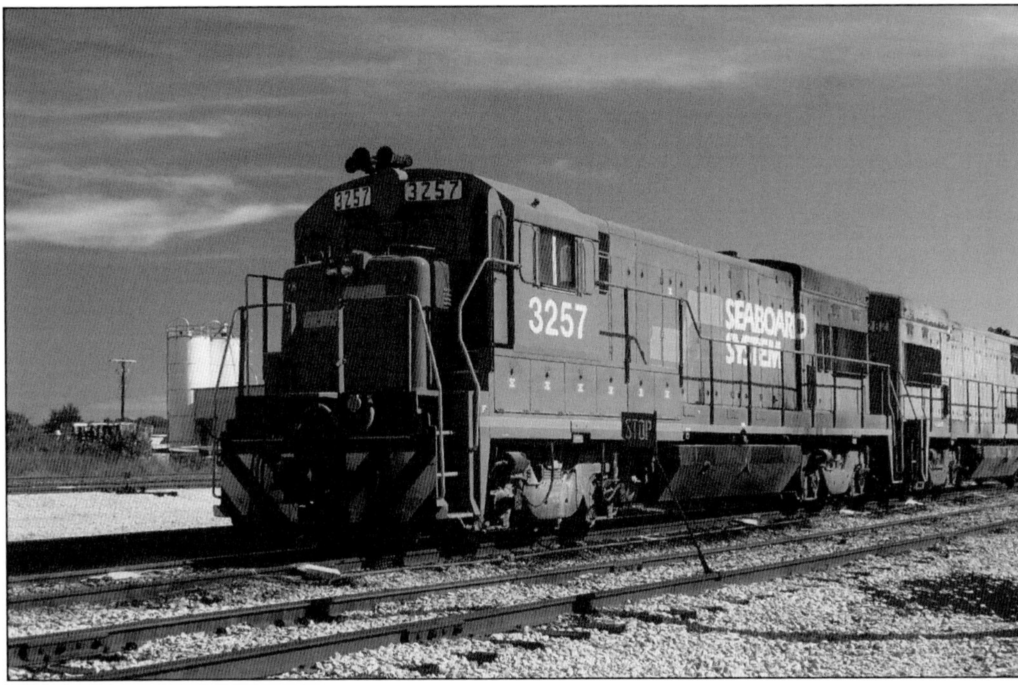

It is August 24, 1986, and Seaboard System U23B 3257 is at Memphis Junction yard in Bowling Green. This is former Louisville & Nashville 2728, which will become CSX 3257 in the not-too-distant future. (Steven D. Johnson photograph.)

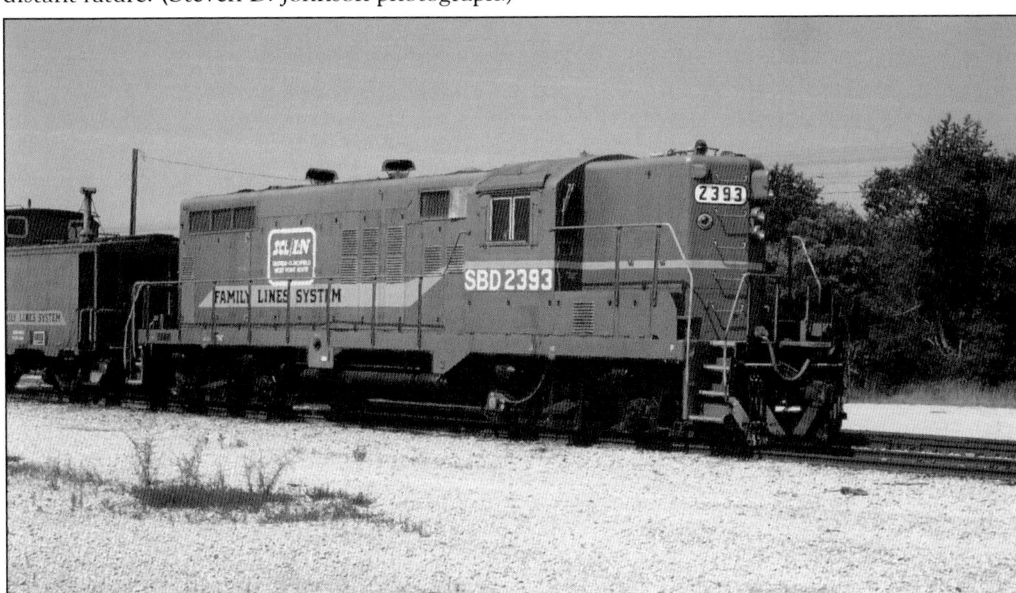

Seaboard GP-9 2393, still in the Family Lines paint scheme, was captured on film on July 14, 1984, at Bowling Green's Memphis Junction yard. The unit is former L&N 2393, one of eight boiler-equipped units purchased by the L&N in 1956 for duel freight or passenger service. By this time, the "torpedo tube" air tanks have been removed from the top and placed underneath, and it is without a steam generator. (Steven D. Johnson photograph.)

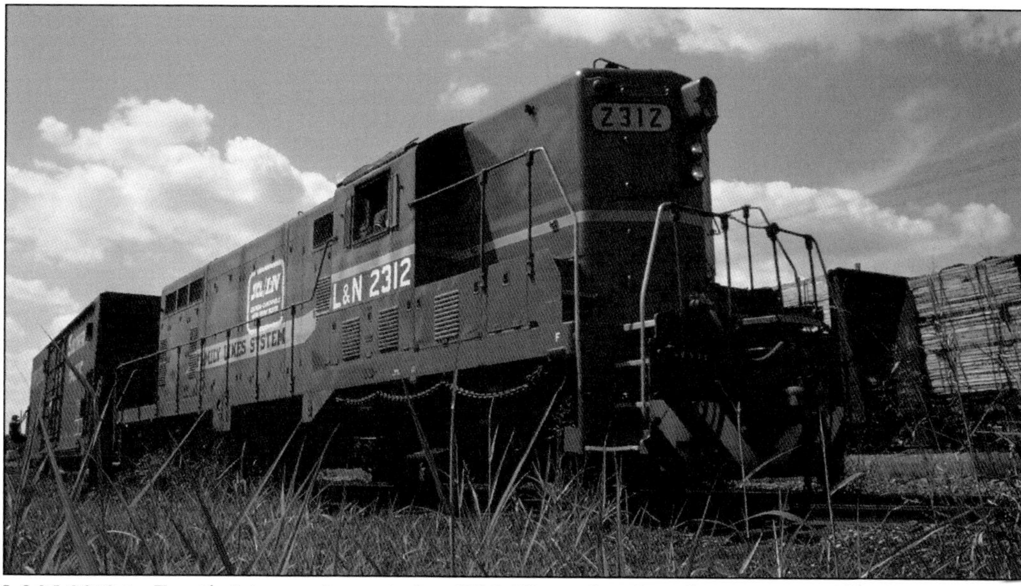

L&N 2312 in Family Lines paint switches E.H. Harris Lumber Company on Clay Street behind the L&N Depot at Bowling Green. In recent years, former rail customers Harris Lumber and Hill-Motley Lumber have had to use truck shipping, as the tracks to reach their facilities have deteriorated, and CSX is not planning to repair them. In 1977, the member railroads of the Family Lines group began to use a gray paint scheme with the initials of the owning railroad painted under the cab windows. (Steven D. Johnson photograph.)

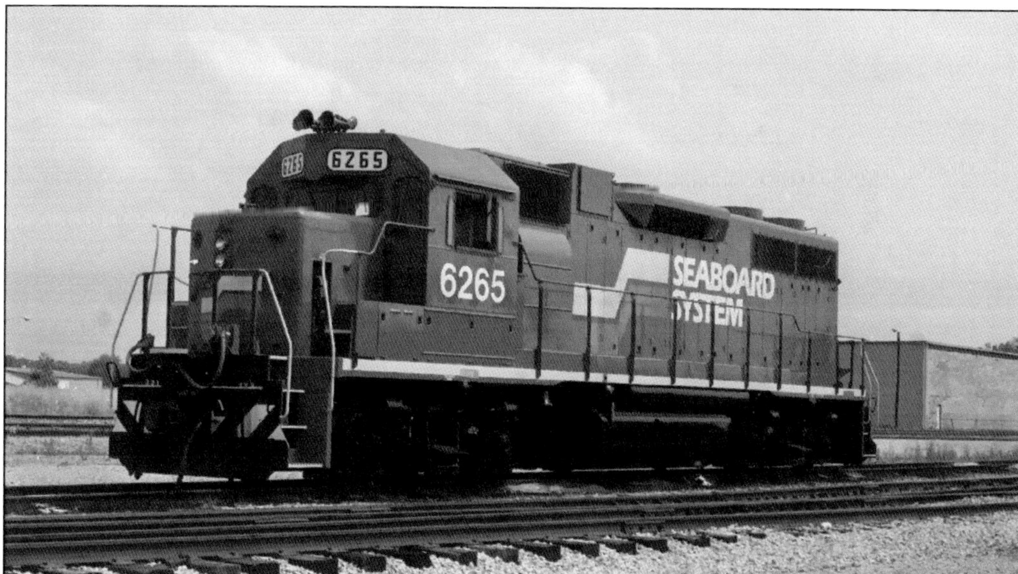

The associated Family Lines of the Louisville & Nashville Railroad, Seaboard Coast Line Railroad (Seaboard Air Line and Atlantic Coast Line formed SCL through a merger), Clinchfield Railroad, Georgia Railroad, and West Point Route were officially merged to form Seaboard System Railroad on January 1, 1983. In 1986, Seaboard and the Chessie System (the merger of the Chesapeake & Ohio and Baltimore & Ohio Railroads) merged to form CSX Transportation. CSX now operates the track through Bowling Green as the Main Line Subdivision. (Steven D. Johnson photograph.)

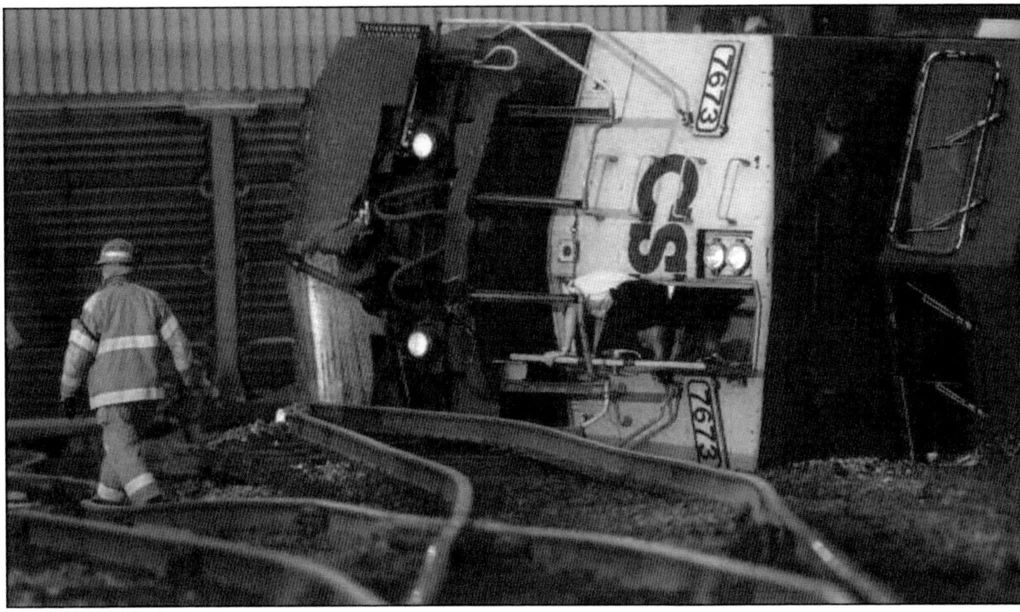

On September 3, 1999, at 5:50 p.m., a Cincinnati-to-Nashville CSX train derailed in downtown Bowling Green near Adams and Main Streets. Three engines and six of the 94 cars toppled over onto their sides, injuring the crew. The FBI determined that debris was placed on the tracks to purposely cause the derailment. Four teenagers were found to have caused $2 million in damages and injuries to two CSX crewmen. This was the first derailment in Bowling Green since the rash of accidents in the 1970s. (Bryan Aldridge.)

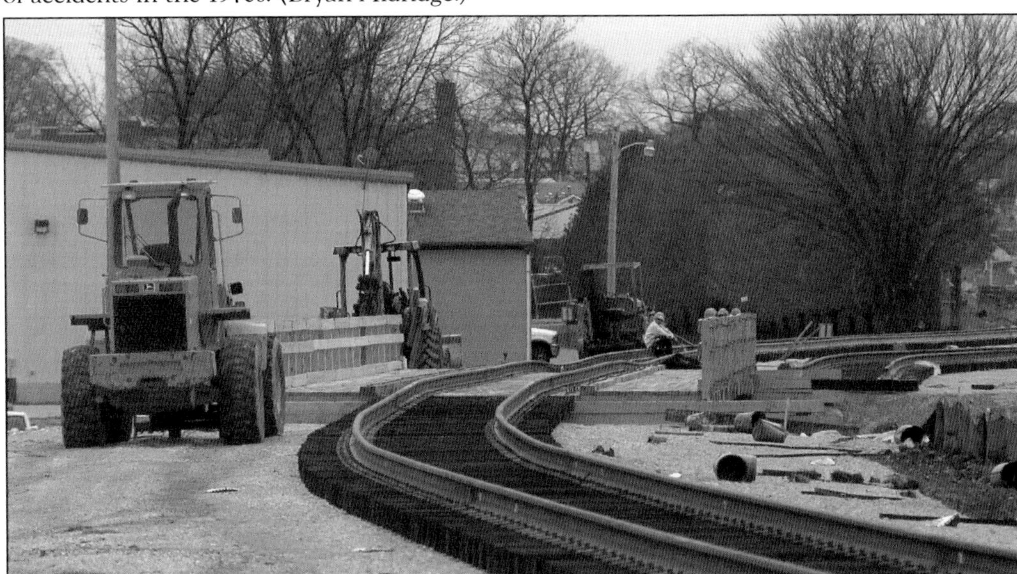

Due to the widening of Bowling Green's Sixth Street underpass, CSX had to construct a temporary shoo-fly track around the construction area. A temporary steel viaduct was erected east of the overpass, and the rails were rerouted during the work. This view shows the almost completed track for the temporary detour. To keep the curve from being too sharp, a few sections were removed from the south end of the old butterfly passenger shed at the L&N Depot. (Chris Gadbois photograph.)

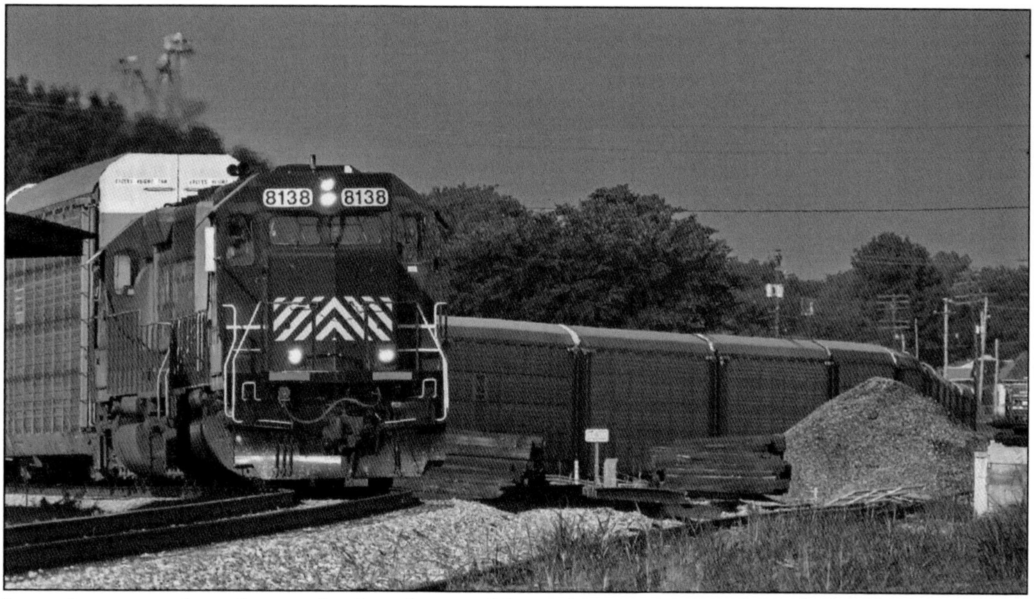

Leased power, such as the unit leading this northbound autorack train through the temporary shoofly track, was in abundance during the expansion of the Sixth Street underpass. The underpass had replaced a much older underpass in 1977. The compressed view makes the curvature of the track seem harsher than it actually was. The last move over the temporary track was the delivery of the L&N Railway Post Office car 1107 to the Historic Railpark. (Chris Gadbois photograph.)

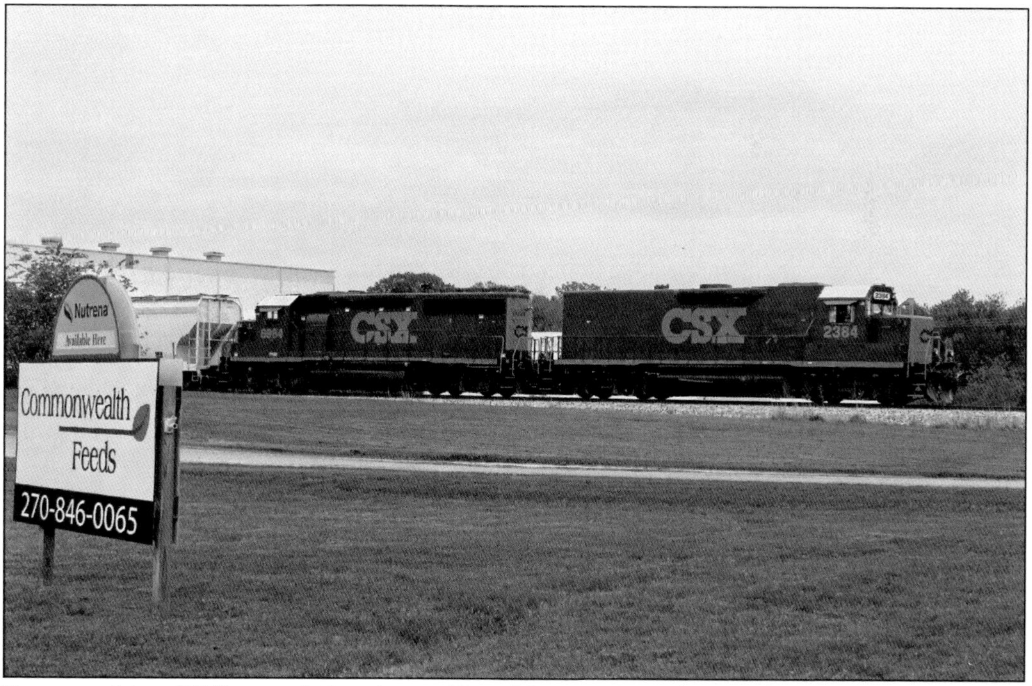

Engineer Matt Walker and Conductor David Long take CSX southbound local J759 past Commonwealth Feeds. The local will work at Sanderson, Salmons, and Franklin in Kentucky before finishing its night at Portland, Tennessee. J759 is one of the busier locals on the Louisville Division. (Kevin Comer photograph.)

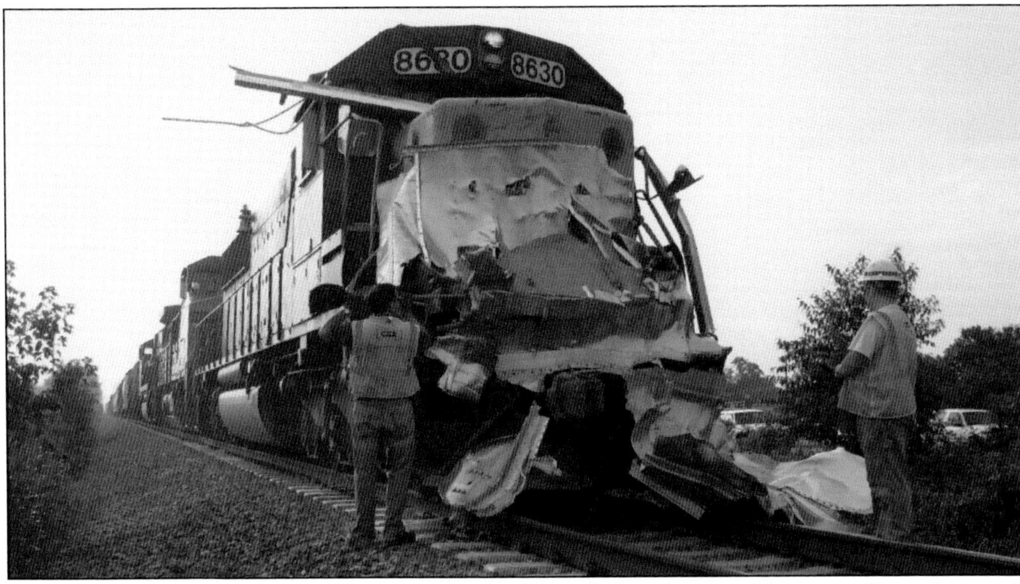

This is what can happen to a tractor-trailer truck loaded with grain when it pulls in front of a moving train at a crossing. This incident occurred at a crossing in north Bowling Green around sunrise on June 4, 2010. The train is stopped about a half mile from the impact. CSX trainmaster Toby Asher attempts to clear debris from the locomotive. There were no injuries to the crew or the truck driver. (Kevin Comer photograph.)

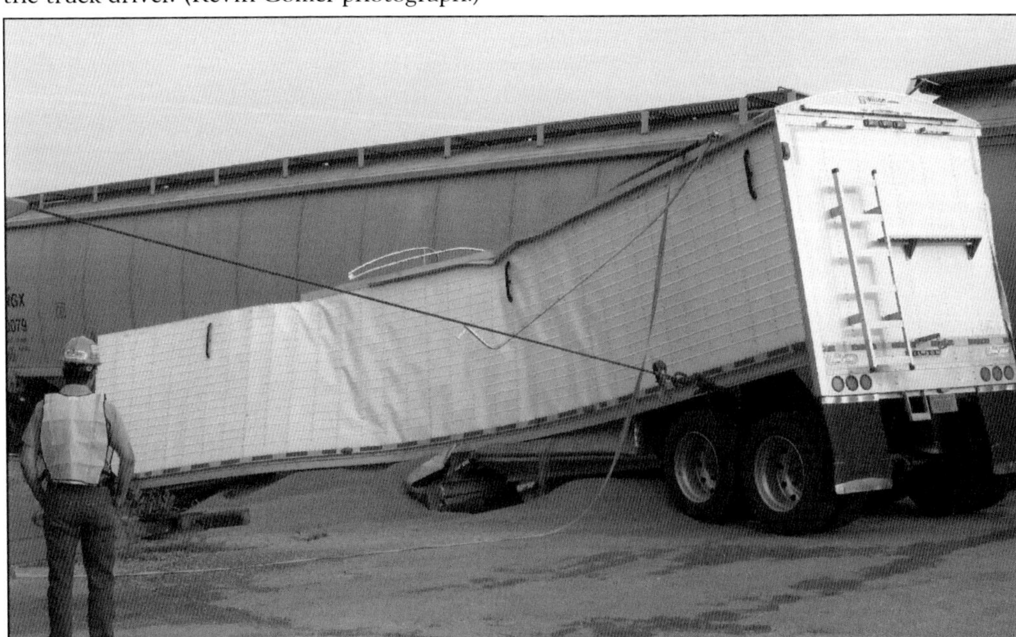

The truck cab and half of the trailer are on the other side of the crossing. Much of the trailer middle is wrapped around the locomotive cab. A train crew is almost helpless to stop when a vehicle pulls into their path. The speed and weight can propel the train several hundred feet even during an emergency braking application. Always stop at railroad crossings and make sure a train is not present before proceeding. (Kevin Comer photograph.)

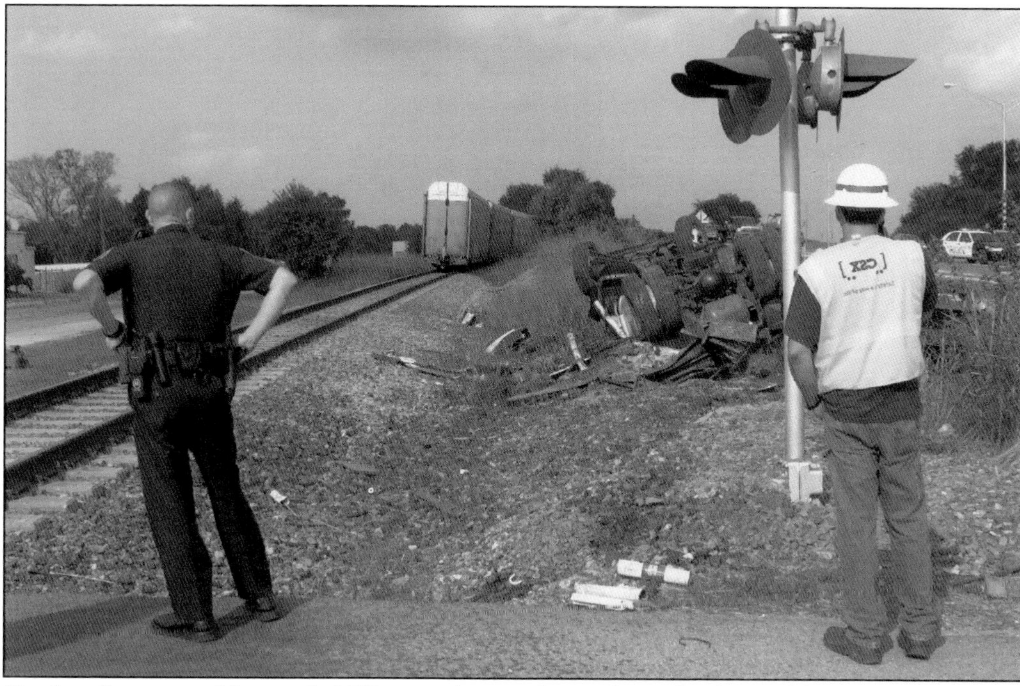

On the afternoon of August 9, 2010, a truck moved into the path of a northbound autorack train at Tobacco Road in north Bowling Green. A crewman from the train came back to the truck to find the driver crawling out of the only space that was not crushed. The lucky man had some bruises and scrapes but was otherwise unhurt. Police and CSX personnel look over the scene in the photograph. (Kevin Comer photograph.)

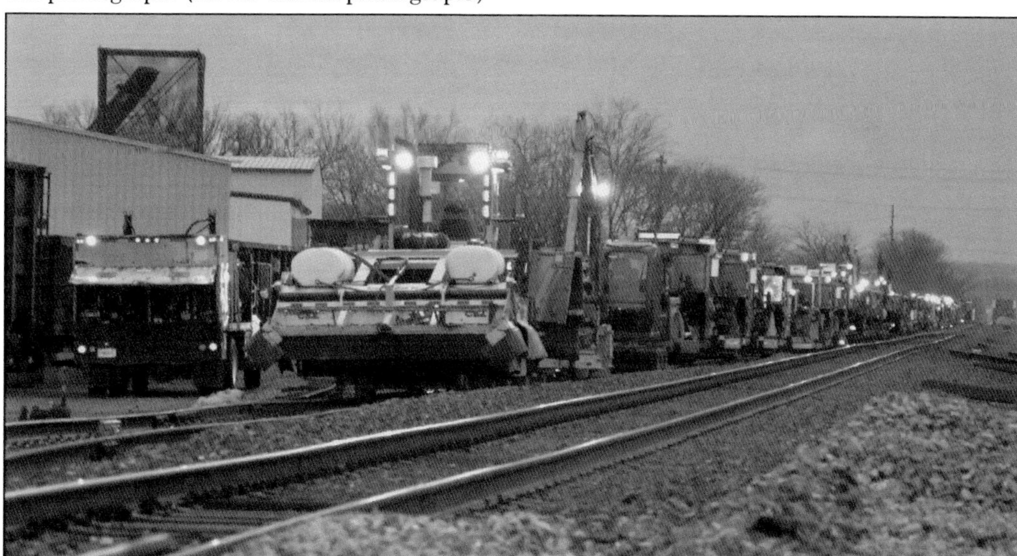

On the morning of March 15, 2011, CSX had a large group of maintenance-of-way equipment lined up along the Harris Lumber spur near the L&N Depot. The equipment arrived via a special train and worked in the area for several days replacing ties along the main line. The equipment stretched from behind the Historic RailPark, over Veterans Memorial Boulevard, to a point near Main Street. (Kevin Comer photograph.)

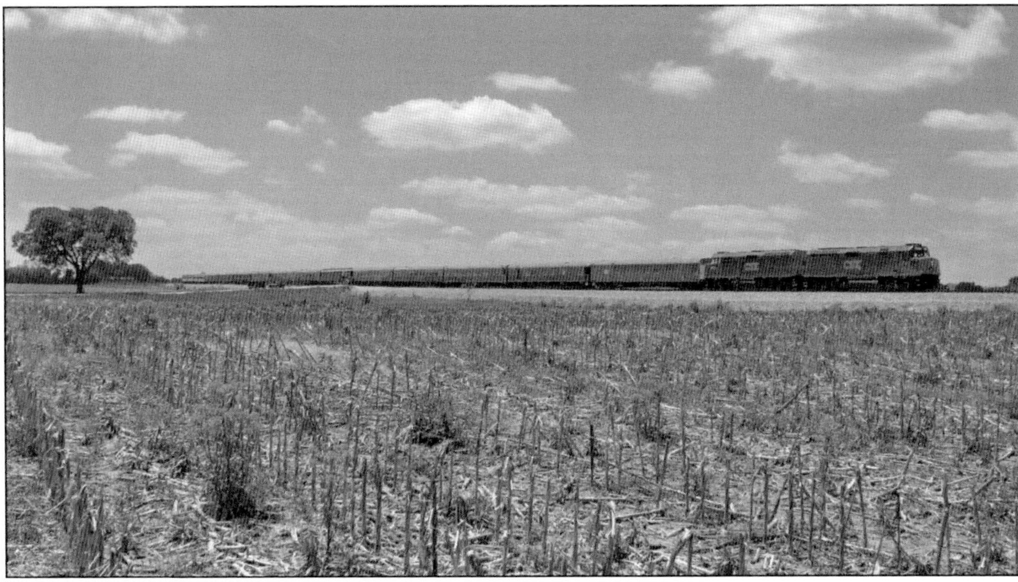

Long ago, several passenger trains converged on Louisville, Kentucky, for the Kentucky Derby. Union Station was a hub of activity with all the extra trains coming in for the Run for the Roses. In recent years, Amtrak, CSX, R.J. Corman Railroad, and Norfolk Southern usually run special passenger trains with vintage cars. Pictured, the 2011 CSX Derby Special leaves Woodburn, Kentucky, as it moves north toward Bowling Green on the way to Louisville. (Kevin Comer photograph.)

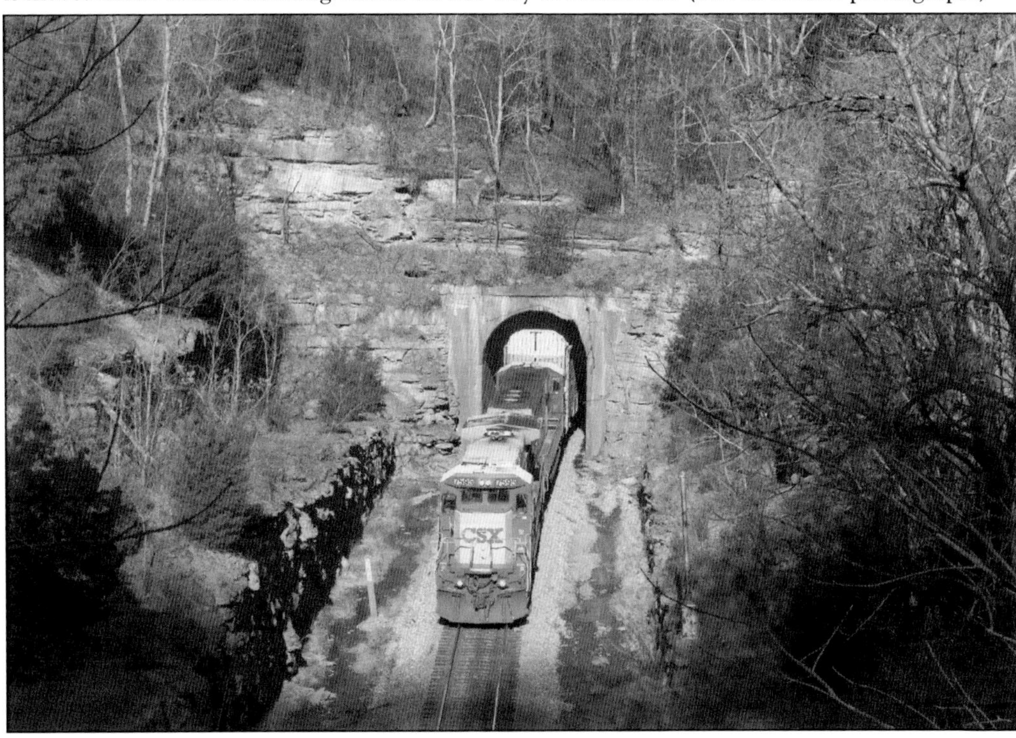

This photograph was taken from above the 1,000-foot-long "Big South," the southernmost tunnel at South Tunnel, Tennessee. CSX 7655 is seen emerging from the northernmost tunnel, Little South. (Doyle Massey photograph.)

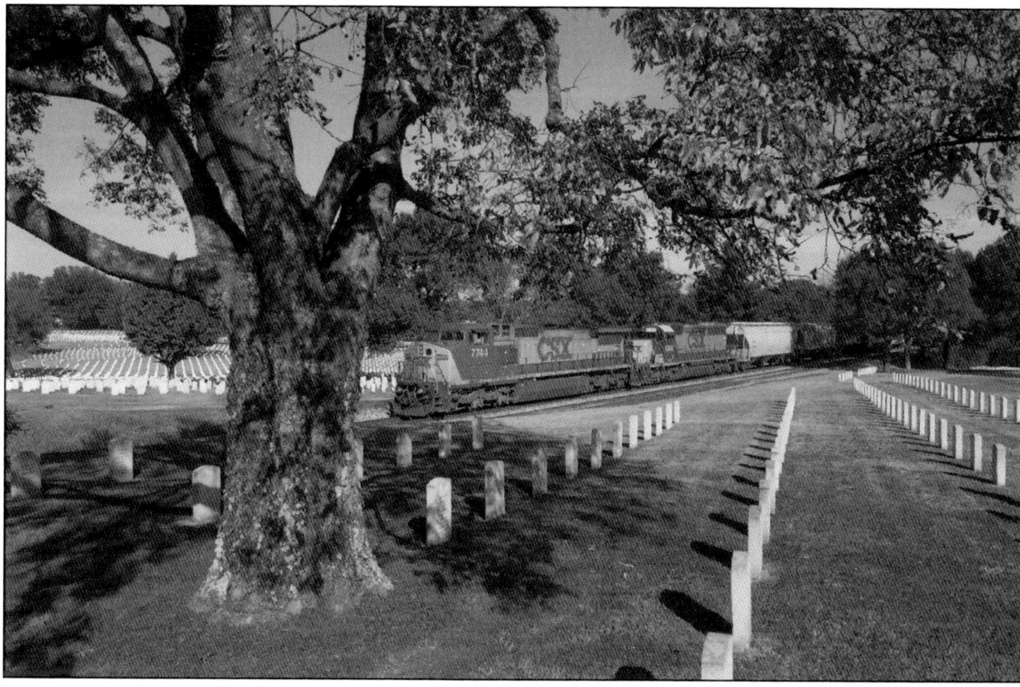

The former Louisville & Nashville Railroad runs through the middle of Nashville National Cemetery, dividing it almost equally in two parts. Established in 1867, the cemetery contains more than 33,000 interments, with over 16,000 of those being Union soldiers from the Civil War. Many of those fallen may have battled over or protected the L&N Railroad. Frequent CSX trains, such as the northbound pictured here, pass among the headstones daily. (Doyle Massey photograph.)

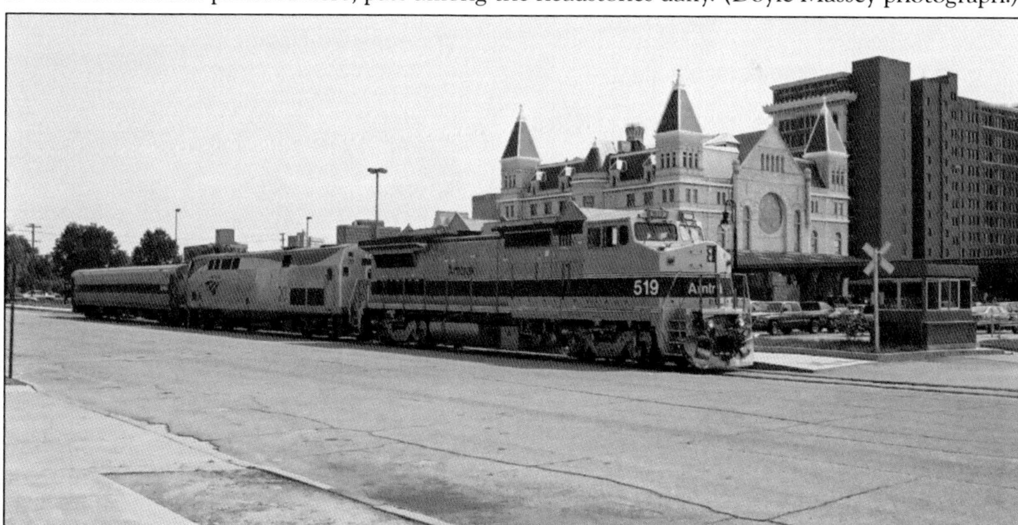

Pictured is the Amtrak train 850, the *Kentucky Cardinal*, at Louisville's Union Station on May 24, 2003. Three days a week, the train ran as a connection to Amtrak's trains 50 and 51, the Chicago-to-Washington, DC, route, via Indianapolis *Cardinal*. The other four days, it ran strictly as a Chicago-Indianapolis-Jeffersonville-Louisville train. Before 2001, it terminated across the river from Louisville in Jeffersonville. The train was discontinued on July 6, 2003. Due to the track conditions involved, this was a notoriously slow train. (Doyle Massey photograph.)

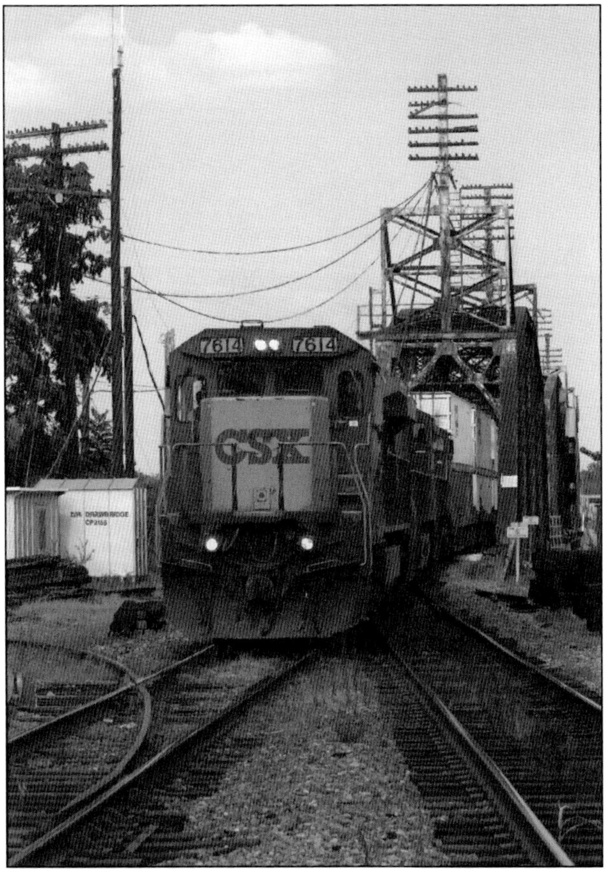

CSX C40-8 7614 exits the Cumberland River Drawbridge at milepost 190.4 in Nashville, Tennessee, with a train of double-stack containers. Built in 1916, "C.R. Drawbridge" is actually a swing bridge, where the center span can be turned to allow boats to pass underneath. When the river is at normal depth, the span is seldom opened but is tended 24 hours a day. The original covered bridge was destroyed during the Battle of Nashville in 1864. (Doyle Massey photograph.)

Nashville, Tennessee's Kayne Avenue Yard is the former site of early Nashville rail operations. Visible is a southbound coal train getting a crew change, and the Nashville yard switchers, former L&N units. Union Station is in the background. This is a favorite spot of photographer Doyle Massey. (Doyle Massey photograph.)

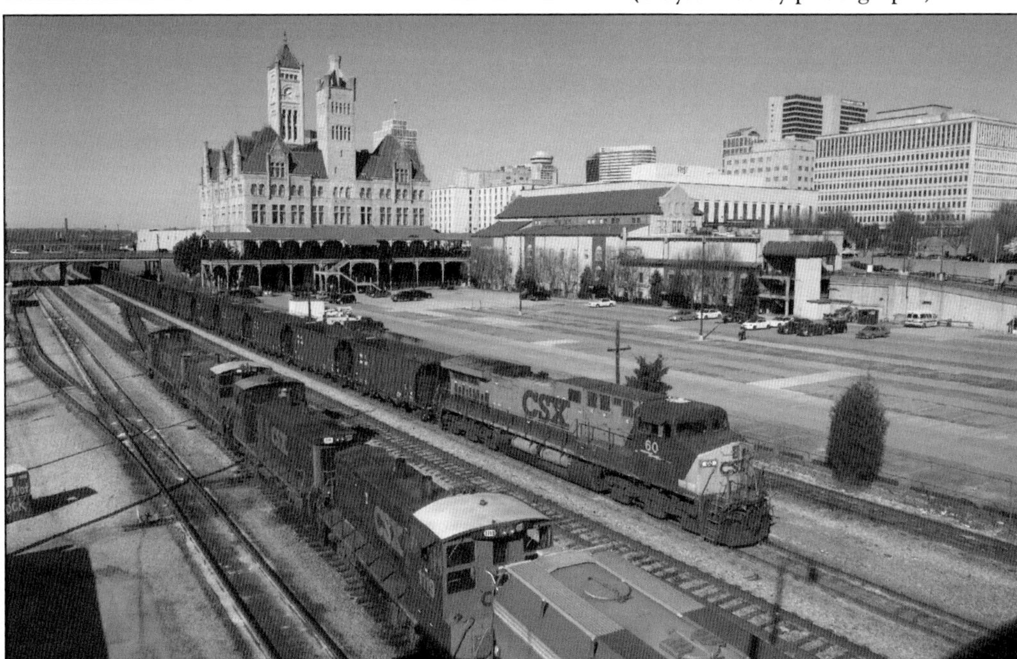

Seven

Historic RailPark and Train Museum

As rail passenger service in Bowling Green came to an end in 1979, the Louisville & Nashville Passenger Station was boarded up and left abandoned. A new freight yard had opened nearly five miles to the south at Memphis Junction, with all operations moved there.

The building was sold by the L&N and went through various owners, eventually ending up in the hands of Bowling Green businessman Mike Clark in 1990. Clark valued the property on the outskirts of downtown and looked to find a good use for the structure. He made improvements to help stabilize the building, repairing roof tiles and replacing stolen copper guttering. When a buyer approached Clark about purchasing the site who did not seem very interested in retaining the structure, concerns grew that the building might be razed.

In 1993, local businessman David Garvin, Operation Pride chairman Dan Cherry, and Bowling Green mayor Johnny Webb organized a group pledging $100,000 to purchase the depot from Clark with restoration in mind. Clark dropped his asking price from $149,000 to meet the offered price because he wanted the depot saved.

With fundraising underway, a new source of funding became available via the Intermodal Surface Transportation Enhancement Act (ISTEA), which meant that money was provided to state highway departments to enhance transportation routes. Some of the money had to be spent on historic preservation. Cherry's successor at Operation Pride, Kathie Curtis, with others, submitted a plan to restore the depot. The ISTEA committee visited the depot in 1994 in order to act on the request for funding. In 1995, Gov. Brereton Jones announced at the depot that the proposal had been funded in the amount of $765,000. The Depot Development Authority (DDA) was created in 1995 to handle the project. HTNB Corporation of Indianapolis was hired in 1996 to renovate the building. As the exterior work progressed, the DDA applied for another grant to complete the restoration. In 1997, Gov. Paul Patton announced another $500,000 would be provided. By April 2001, the interior was ready for tenants, and Kentucky's first digital library moved to the depot as a branch of the Bowling Green Public Library.

During this time, vintage rail cars were acquired by individuals and by the group and restored for display, including a passenger locomotive, L&N railway post office car 1107, a 48-seat diner, L&N sleeping car *Towering Pine*, a caboose, and L&N office car 353. All have been restored and interior tours are part of the museum experience.

Later, after the library moved, the space was divided between office space and space allocated for a museum and gift shop for the Historic RailPark and Train Museum. Today, the two-story museum contains high quality exhibits, and the static display of railcars featuring an L&N passenger consist is second to none. The city-owned property is managed by the Friends of the L&N, a nonprofit volunteer group that continues to acquire and restore railcars for display, while also constantly upgrading the museum. Immediate plans for the group include the restoration of Glasgow Railway Combine No. 109, which had sat deteriorating in Glasgow for more than 50 years. This will be a major project for the RailPark, but once complete will tell the story of segregation and "Jim Crow" laws, small town passenger operations, and wooden car construction techniques. Another restoration project will bring an original World War II hospital car to the RailPark from Louisville, where it was used for storage at a government facility. The group hopes to complete a cosmetic restoration of the exterior, and eventually acquire furnishings to restore the interior. Displays will tell the story of railroads' roles during war, and possibly of military medical professionals. Other projects will include a shed to protect the consist of equipment from the elements, and possibly a very authentic roundhouse structure that could be used for archive/library space, and offices, and house other acquired equipment displays.

Area railroading is celebrated annually at the Historic RailPark the first weekend of December during the Festival of Trains. The historic station also is home to the sHOw Modular Model Railroad Club, which provides operating model train layouts during museum events as well as a permanent operating display featuring modeled elements of Bowling Green rail operations in the 1950s.

For a look back at the Louisville & Nashville Railroad, visit the Historic RailPark and Train Museum in Bowling Green.

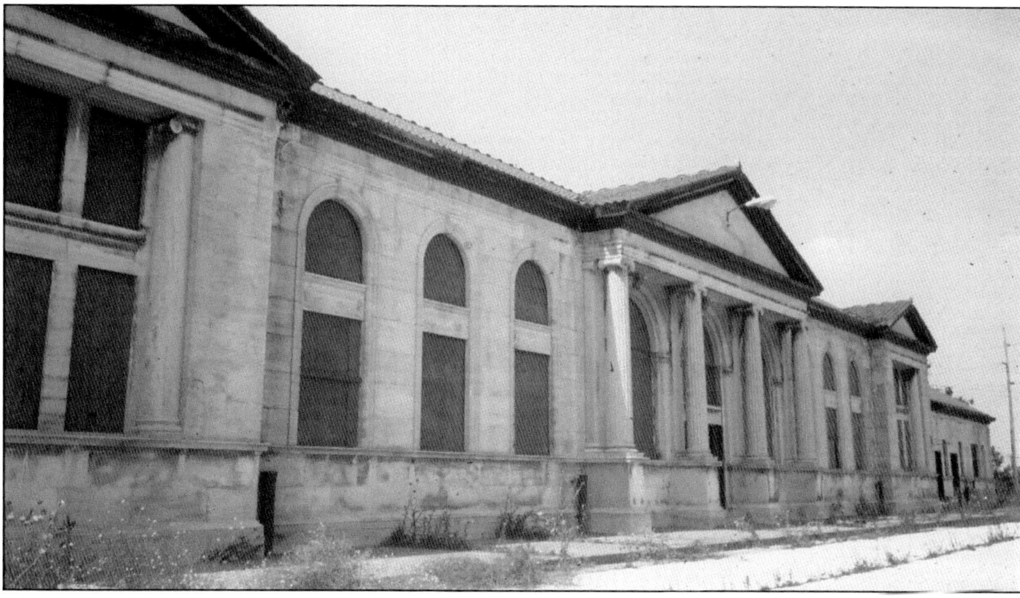

As L&N's passenger station in Bowling Green sat neglected, the deterioration became extreme. Roof leaks damaged floors and ceilings and flooded the basement. What had once been a vibrant hub of activity in Bowling Green was now a depressing sight. Purchased by local businessman Mike Clark, possible uses for the property were explored. It was feared that it would be razed. Shown here, the depot has been boarded up to stave off further deterioration and vandalism. (Historic RailPark Collection.)

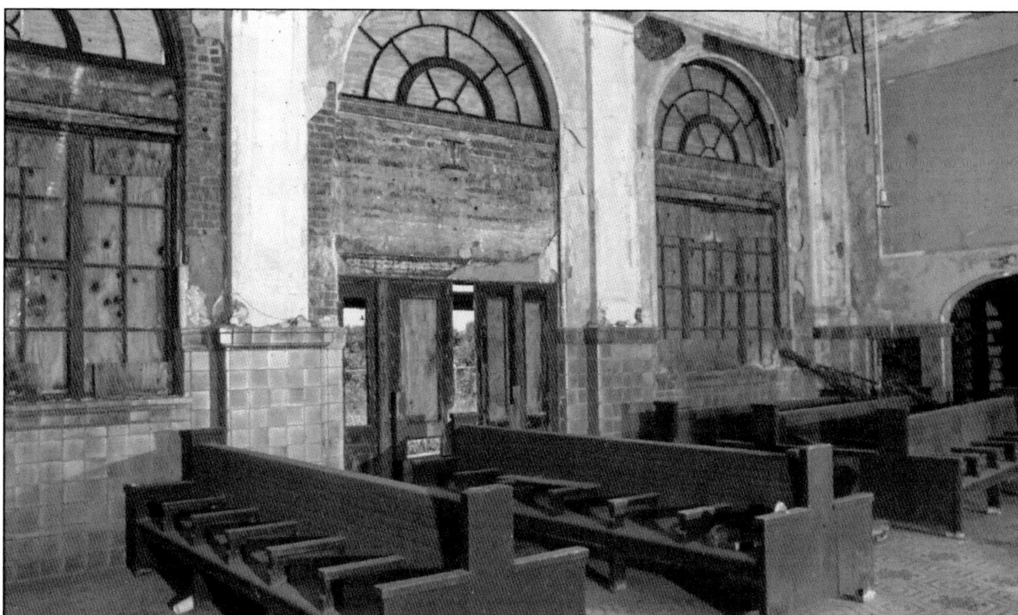

This view of the interior of the main lobby and waiting area of L&N's former passenger station in Bowling Green shows the neglect that the former elegant depot has endured. Wooden benches where travelers waited for trains are grouped together near the back entrance. These benches would undergo restoration by local scouts as an Eagle Scout project for use in the restored depot. (Historic RailPark Collection.)

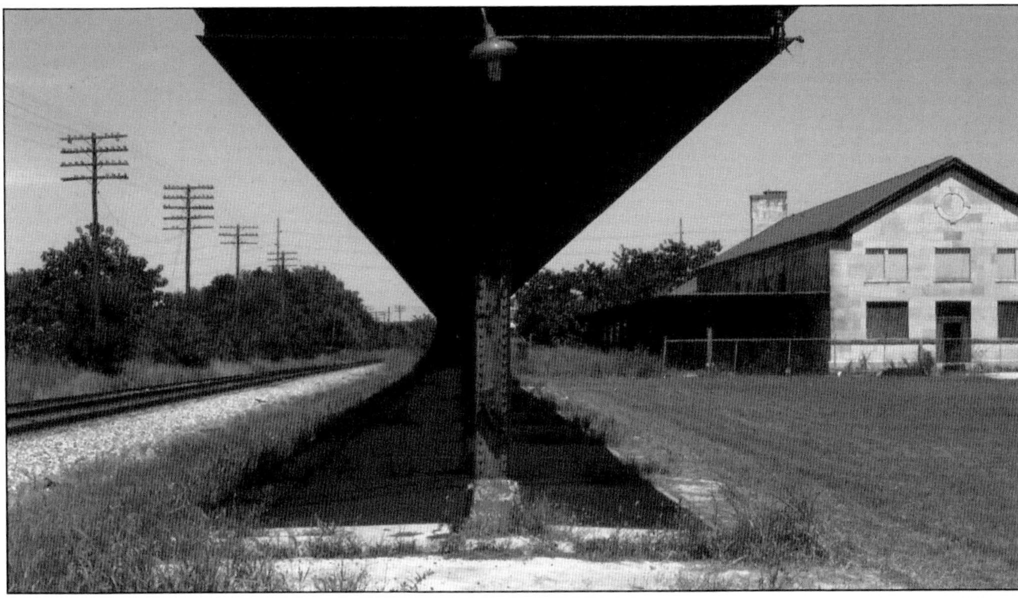

Looking north, this photograph shows L&N's overgrown passenger station in Bowling Green and butterfly platform. At one time, two stub tracks ended at each end of the main building, two passenger tracks ran between the main platform and the butterfly platform, and still another passenger track, main line, and siding were originally on the west side of the butterfly shed. (Historic RailPark Collection.)

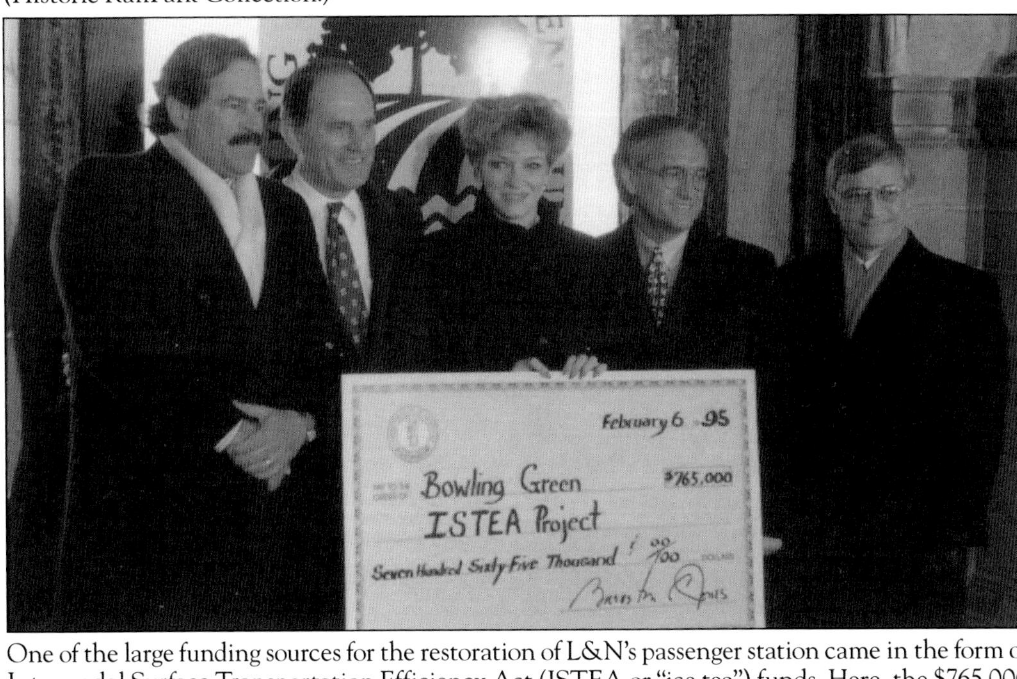

One of the large funding sources for the restoration of L&N's passenger station came in the form of Intermodal Surface Transportation Efficiency Act (ISTEA or "ice tea") funds. Here, the $765,000 funding is announced by Warren County judge executive Mike Buchanon, Gov. Brereton Jones, Operation Pride director Kathie Curtis, Mayor Johnny Webb, and Operation Pride chairman Dan Cherry in the main lobby. This ensured that the 22,000-square-foot station would be restored. (Mike Dowell photograph.)

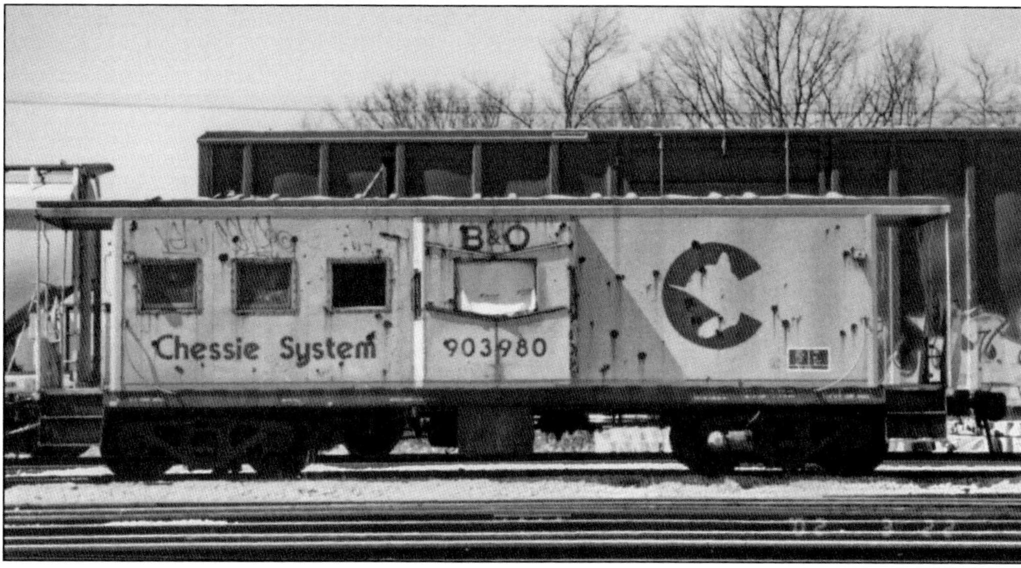

CSX Transportation donated this former B&O caboose to the Historic RailPark. It was later painted in L&N red with yellow trim and numbered as L&N 6497. L&N employee Rayburn Wells had been shot and killed while riding in original L&N caboose 6497. CSX donated track, and R.J. Corman Railroad donated labor to build the 450-foot display track for the Historic RailPark acquisitions. (Historic RailPark Collection.)

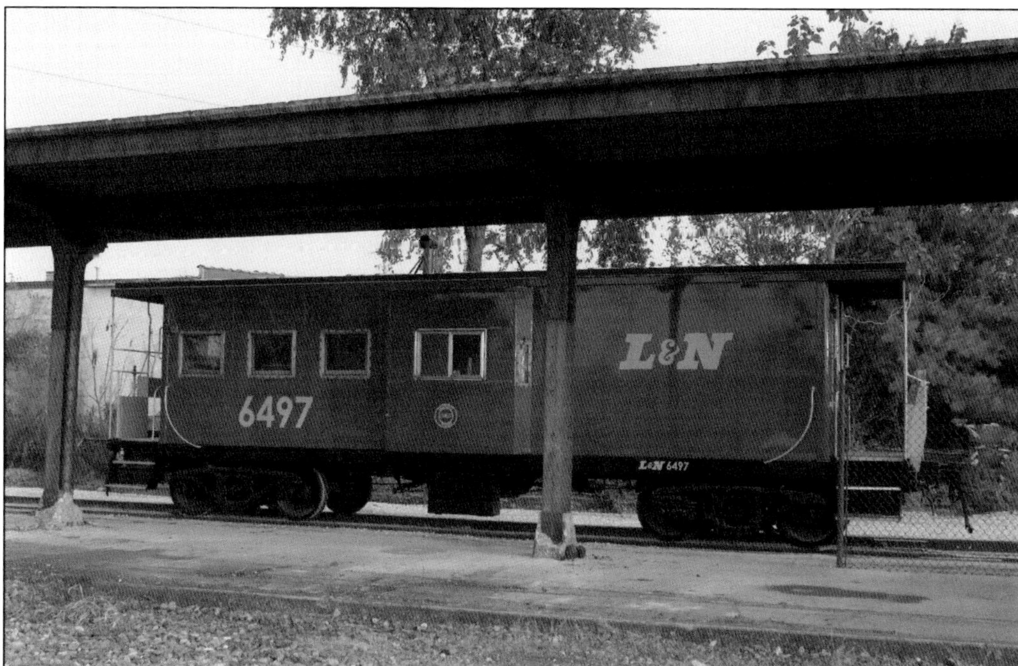

The former B&O-Chessie System caboose at the Historic RailPark has had many interior features removed and now serves as a rental facility for children's parties. Storyboards inside tell the history of cabooses and the functions they served for the railroads. Sometimes part of the railcar tours, the future of the 6497 may hold another restoration and return of interior furnishings. (Kevin Comer photograph.)

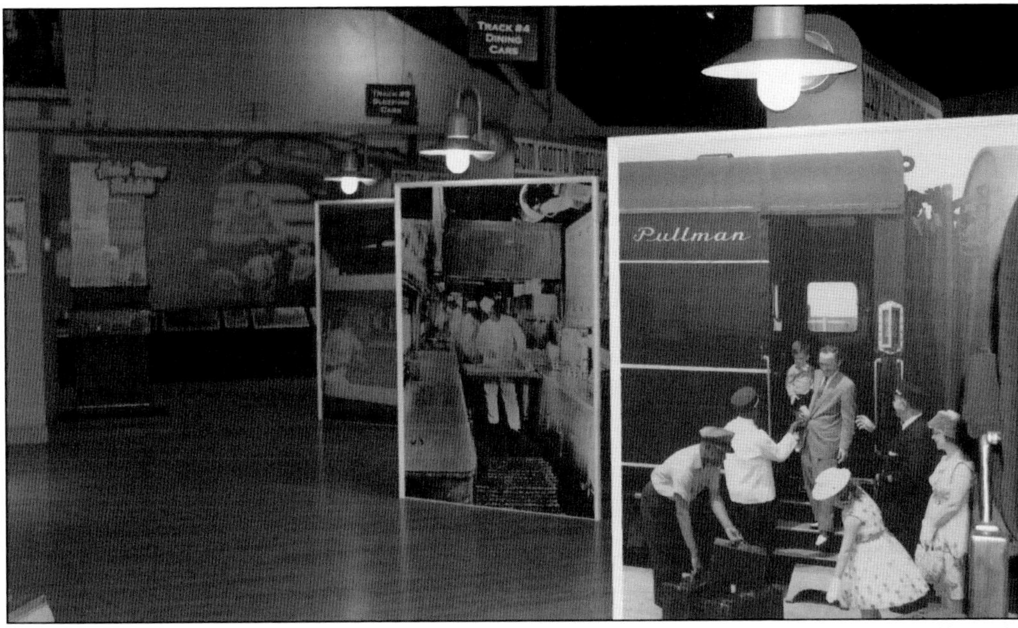

The Historic RailPark and Train Museum contains many fine educational displays telling the stories of the railroads. While the Louisville & Nashville is a primary focus, displays concerning the great locomotive chase, hoboes, dining and passenger cars, railroad business, and military railroad operations are also featured. Artifacts and employee stories are also preserved. A theater on the second floor shows vintage and modern railroad films. (Kevin Comer photograph.)

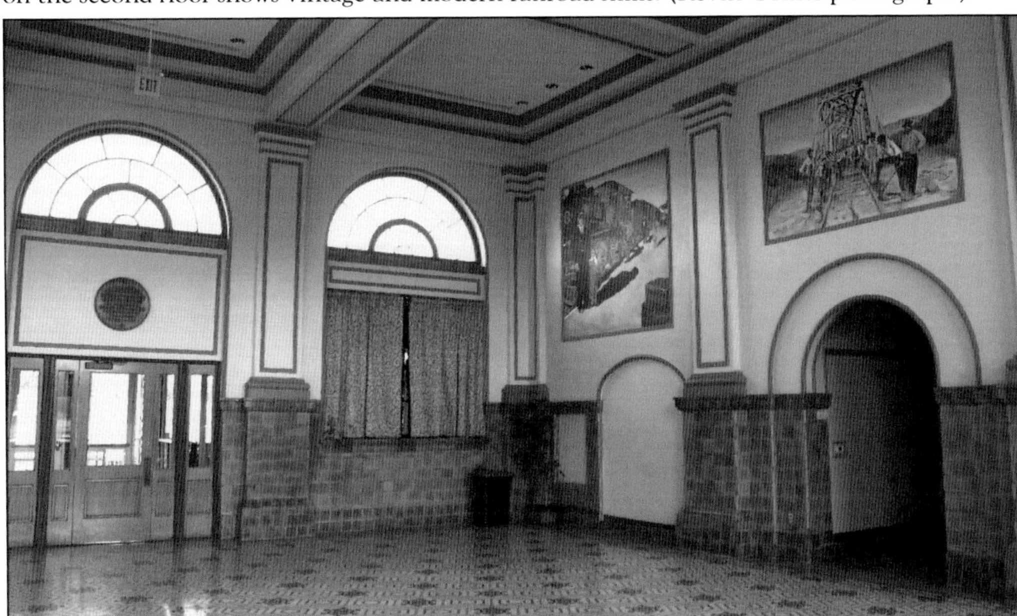

After the restoration of the main passenger lobby, six murals depicting L&N scenes were painted high on the walls. Later, the "colored waiting room" and a previously unfinished area upstairs became the RailPark's museum. The back platform was converted to a digital library and, later, office space and a gift shop. Freight areas and other railroad offices were restored to leased office space. (Kevin Comer photograph.)

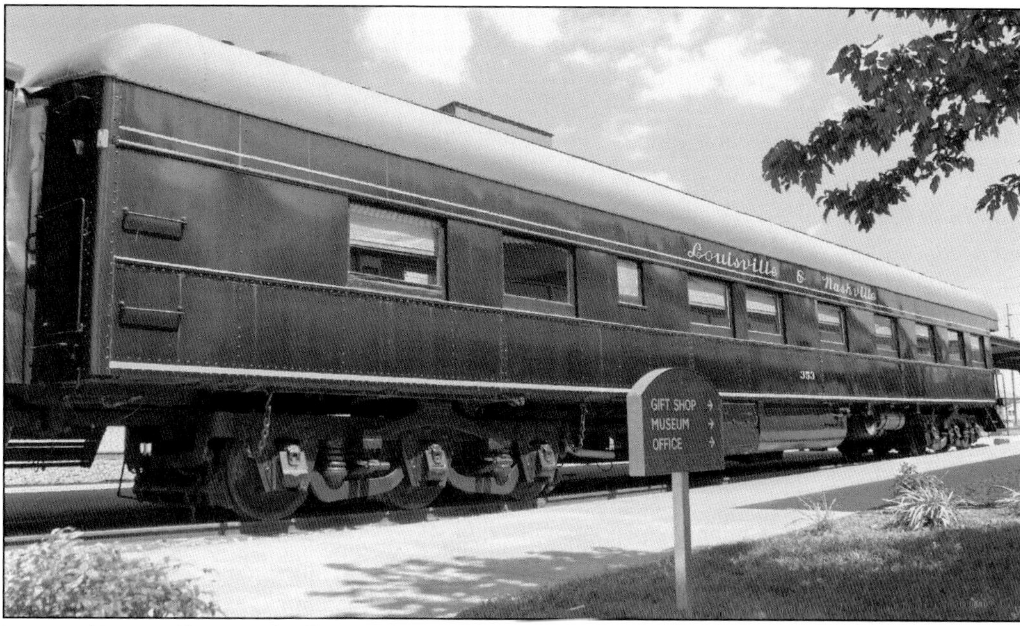

Restored Louisville &Nashville presidential business car 353 is the oldest known surviving car built by the railroad. The 76-foot, 7-inch car was built in 1911 at L&N's South Louisville Shops and was the most elegant car until at least 1922. The car was likely assigned to L&N president Milton H. Smith during those years. The 353 boasts a sitting room with observation platform, two state rooms with shared bath, dining room, kitchen, and steward's quarters. (Kevin Comer photograph.)

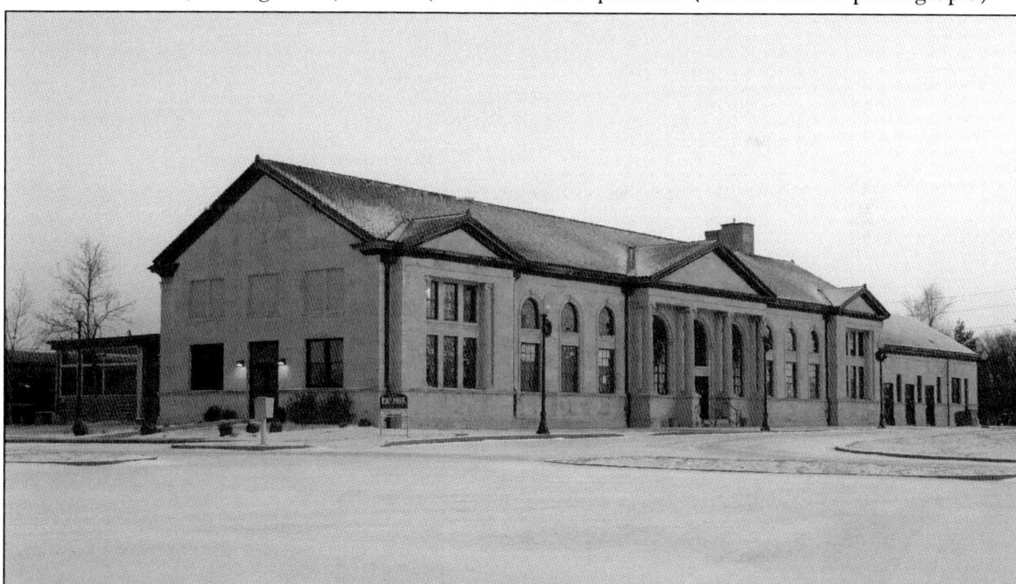

Louisville & Nashville's restored passenger station is one of Bowling Green's treasures. Visiting the old station today, it is hard to imagine that it was almost destroyed. If not for a handful of resourceful people who were intent on preserving the building, it would have been lost. It not only hosts the Historic RailPark and Train Museum, but also houses offices and hosts gala events, weddings, receptions, lectures, meetings and is home to the sHOw Modular Model Railroad Club, which includes a large model train display depicting Bowling Green. (Kevin Comer photograph.)

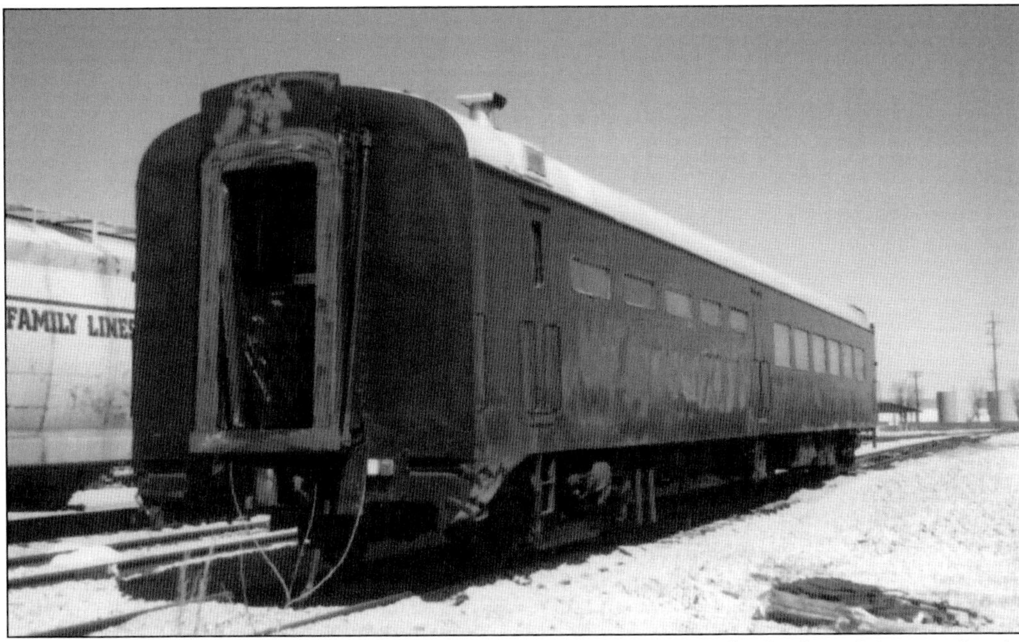

Former Southern Pacific diner 10202 was purchased from Kentucky Railway Museum by the Bowling Green Convention and Visitors Bureau for the Historic RailPark. The 48-seat diner was built by Pullman Standard in 1949 and had served on the Overland Route until derailment damage forced retirement in 1976. KRM had repaired the car and named it *Kentucky Inn*. (Historic RailPark Collection.)

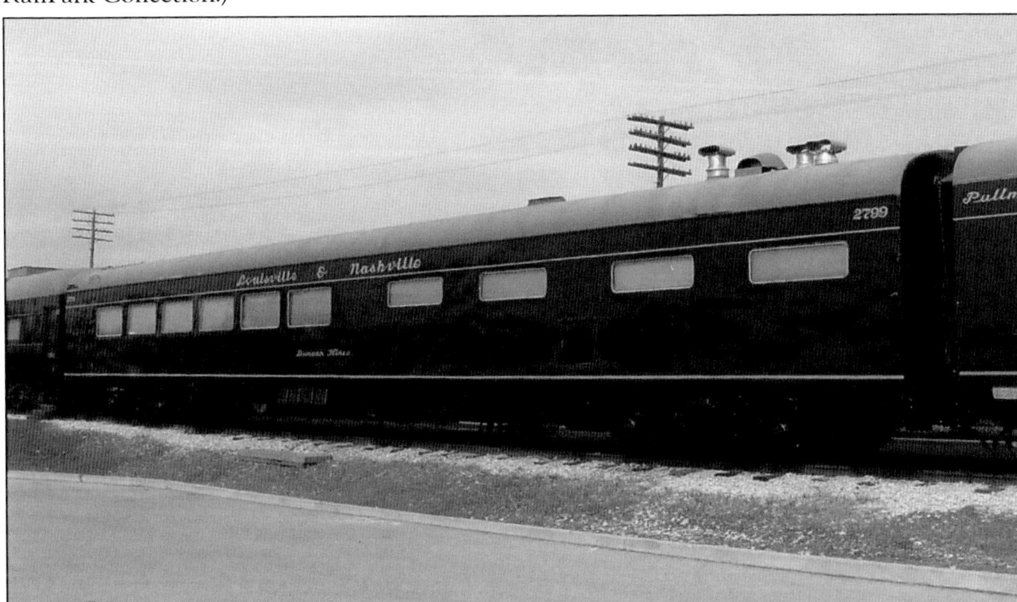

After restoration in Bowling Green, the car was renamed *Duncan Hines* in honor of the famous Bowling Green native. An L&N diner previously had been named *Duncan Hines*, but was destroyed in a derailment. The 48-seat former Southern Pacific diner has a full stainless steel kitchen where meals were prepared. The car is available for meetings, parties, and other events. Murals featuring L&N scenes decorate both ends of the dining area. (Kevin Comer photograph.)

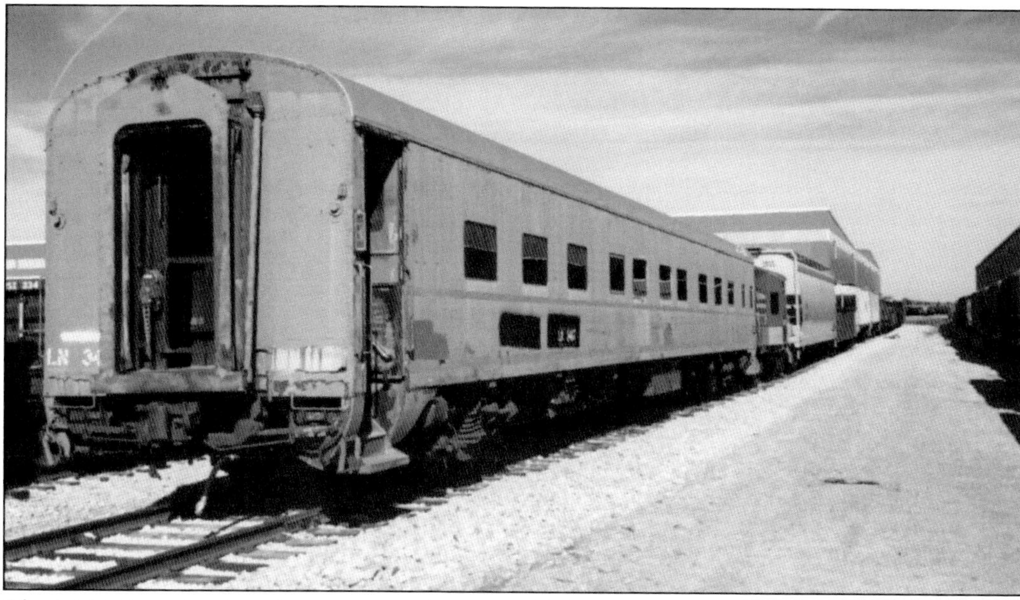

The L&N *Towering Pine* sleeping car is shown at R.J. Corman's South Union Distribution Center prior to arriving at the Historic RailPark. In 1953, the L&N began receiving the first of 22 *Pine* series sleepers. The cars were named for types of trees in the South and featured six open sections, six roomettes, and four double bedrooms. The interior accommodations were designed based on customer suggestions. This car was assigned to such trains as the *Pan American*, *Humming Bird*, *Georgian*, *Gulf Wind*, *Flamingo*, and *Azalean*. (Historic RailPark Collection.)

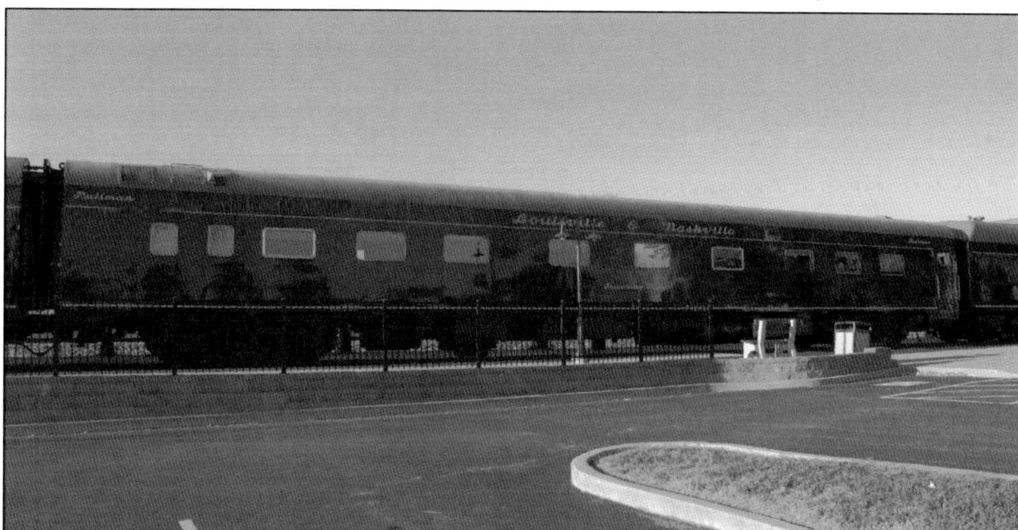

The restored *Towering Pine* sleeper has portions set up to show the different configurations that the car offered for overnight accommodations. The car's interior is completely intact and contains six roomettes, each with a private toilet and sink, six section units that are chair seating but turn into upper and lower berths with curtains for sleeping, and four double bedrooms. The *Towering Pine* was in service from 1953 to 1972. Dorian Walker purchased the *Towering Pine* for the Historic RailPark and Museum and rode as a passenger on the car to Bowling Green from Kansas City. (Kevin Comer photograph.)

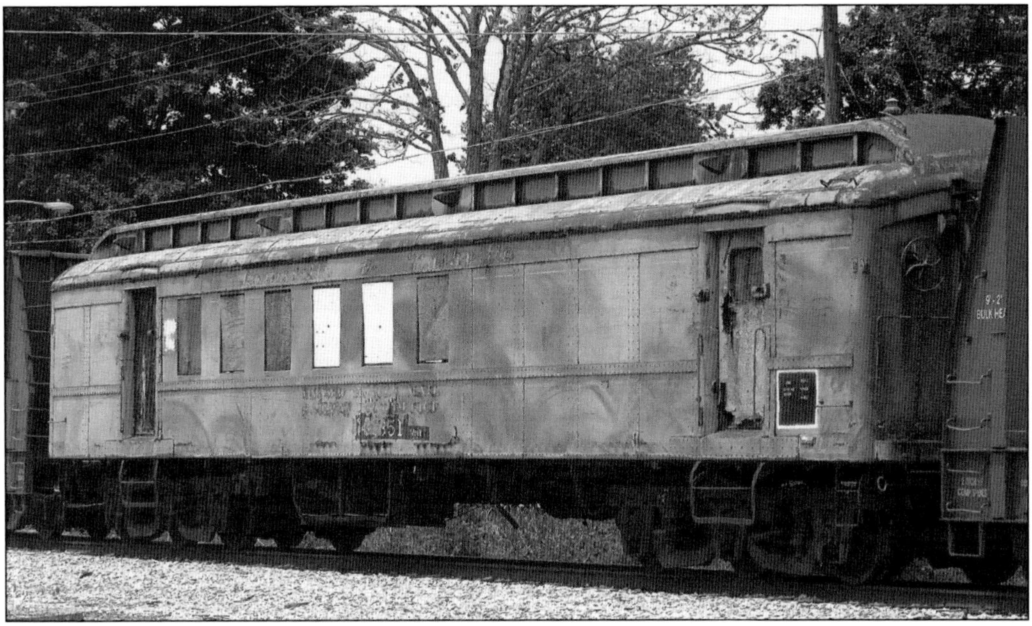

R.J. Corman Railroad brought the L&N Railway Post Office car 1107 from Bluegrass Railroad Museum in Versailles, Kentucky, through Bowling Green on June 11, 2006, and stored it in Auburn, Kentucky, on the Memphis Line. Eventually, the car was returned to Bowling Green for placement on the display track at the Historic Railpark and Train Museum for restoration. The car is pictured here in Auburn, Kentucky. (Chris Gadbois photograph.)

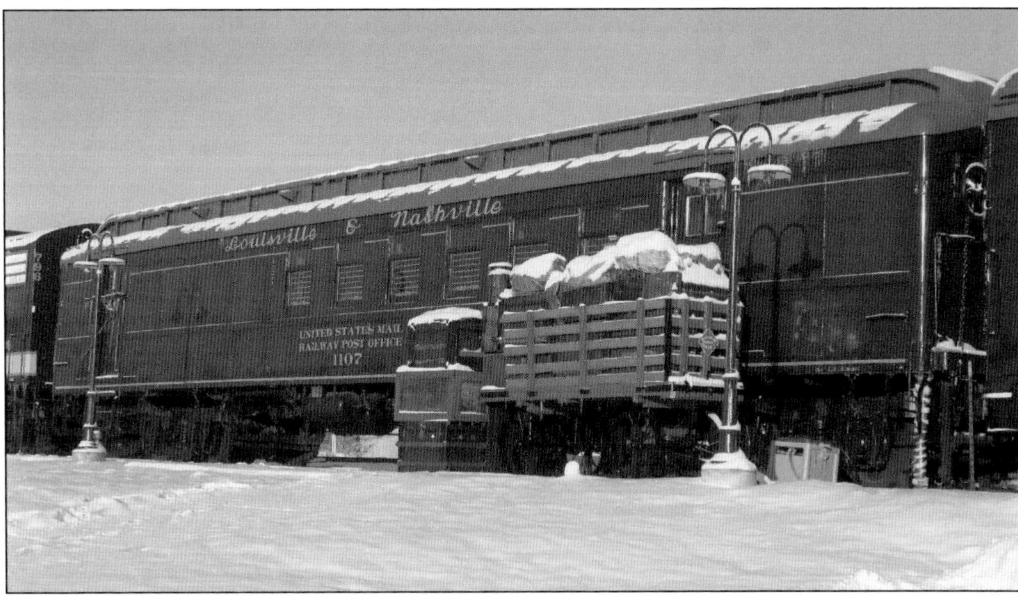

L&N Railway Post Office (RPO) car 1107 was built in 1921 and is one of only two remaining from the L&N's original group. The RPO was purchased from Bluegrass Railroad Museum in Versailles, Kentucky, and restored by Historic RailPark volunteers in Bowling Green. A big assist came when many interior components were located at Pennsylvania Railroad Museum. The remarkable refurbishing of the interior of the car makes it one of the highlights of the RailPark tour. (Kevin Comer photograph.)

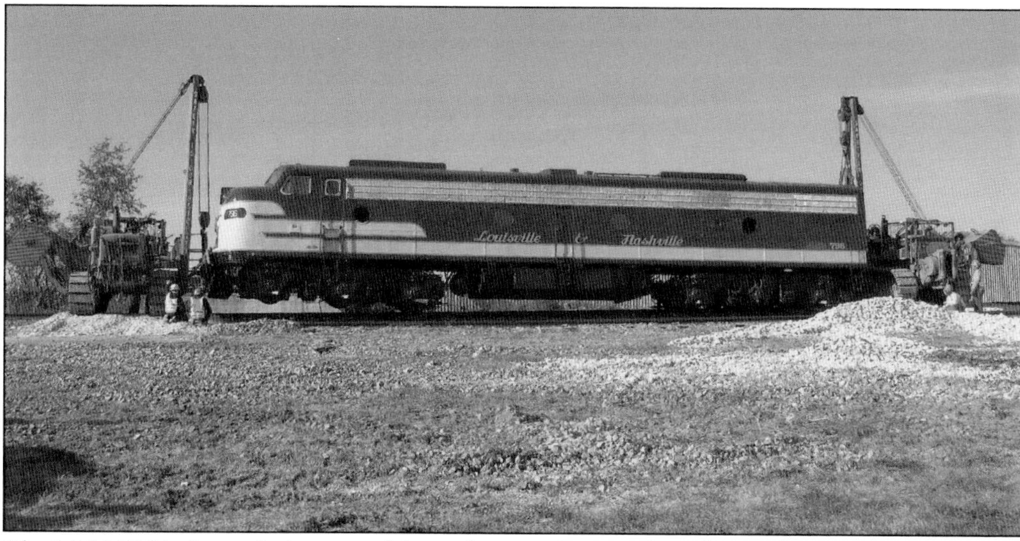

The L&N 796 is shown being moved from the main line track to the display track at the Historic RailPark on October 29, 2008. The locomotive's exterior was cosmetically restored and painted at Evansville, Indiana, during 2007 and 2008. The much anticipated move from Evansville to Guthrie by CSX and from Guthrie to South Union by R.J. Corman Railroad had taken place on October 8. After coming to Memphis Junction yard, CSX finally moved it to its new home. R.J. Corman Derailment Services crews handled the lifting and placement. (Kevin Comer photograph.)

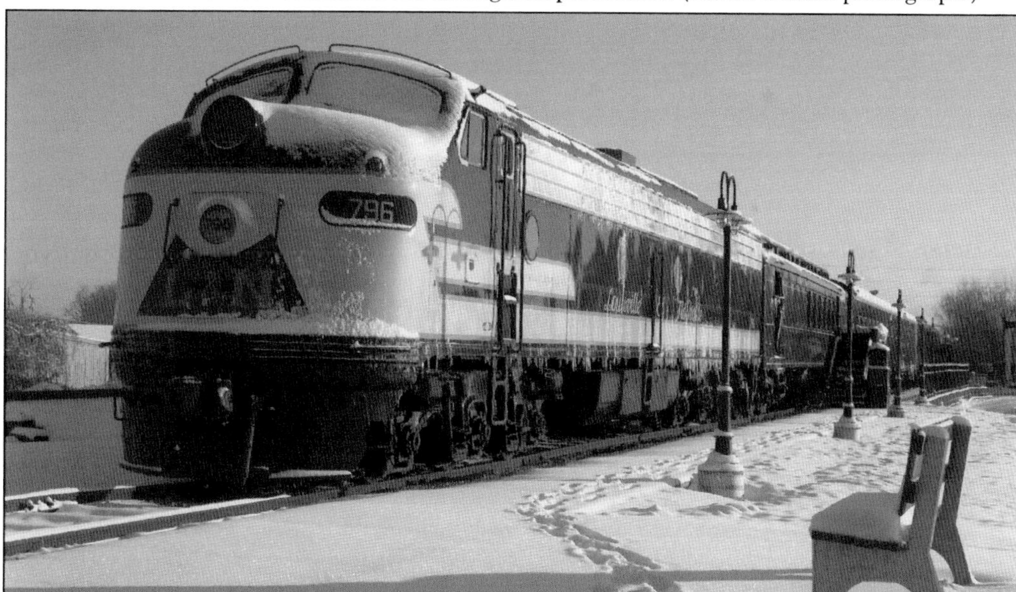

Original L&N E8A 796 was built in May 1951 and, later, traded back to EMD. This replica was originally Chicago & Northwestern E8A No. 5028A built in June 1953. It was renumbered to CNW 513 in 1974 and then sold to Metra in 1977 for commuter train service. In 1991, CNW 513 became Kalamazoo, Lake Shore & Chicago No. 95 and pulled the Michigan Wine Country Dinner Train. After being unable to acquire surviving L&N 770 from Kentucky Railway Museum, the Friends of the L&N Depot settled for this locomotive for restoration and display. (Kevin Comer photograph.)

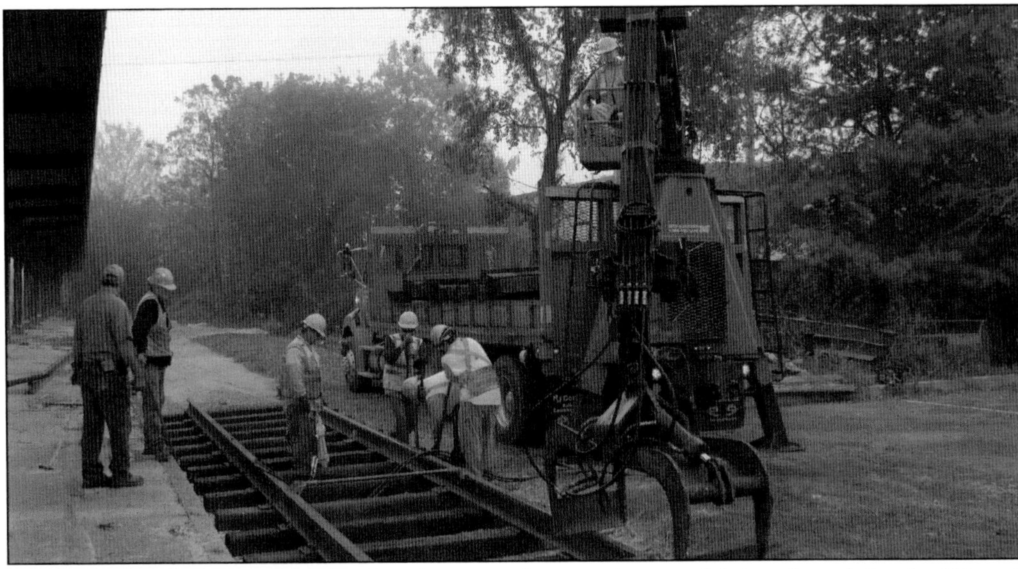

A crew from R.J. Corman Railroad is shown working on laying additional track for the Historic RailPark in October 2011. The new track will allow the addition of hospital car No. 89456 in the following week, plus space for Glasgow Railway (L&N operated) combine No. 109 after restoration, and another future acquisition. CSX assisted with rail and components for the expansion. Both companies have been involved in assisting the Historic RailPark from the beginning of operations. (Kevin Comer photograph.)

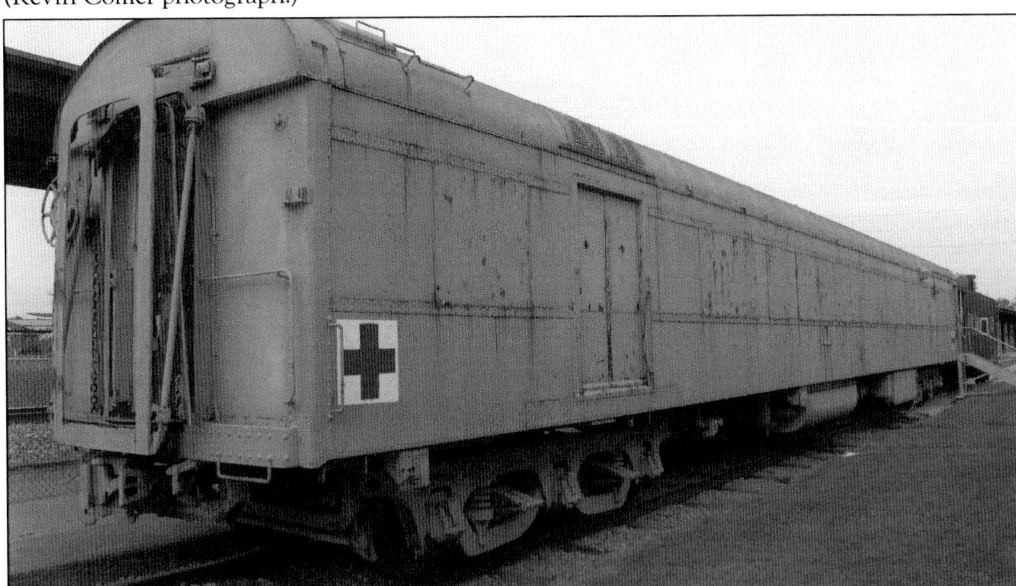

World War II hospital car No. 89456 arrived at the Historic RailPark and Train Museum on October 18, 2011. Two groups of 100 cars each of this type were constructed during World War II. Each car had three-tiered bunks for 36 wounded patients, living quarters for a doctor and nurse, a small kitchen, and receiving/dressing area. The car interior was removed when it was placed at the Naval Ordinance Station in Louisville, Kentucky, in 1970. It had been used for storage prior to being donated to the Historic RailPark, where it will be restored as a museum exhibit. Only a handful of these types of cars still exist. (Kevin Comer photograph.)

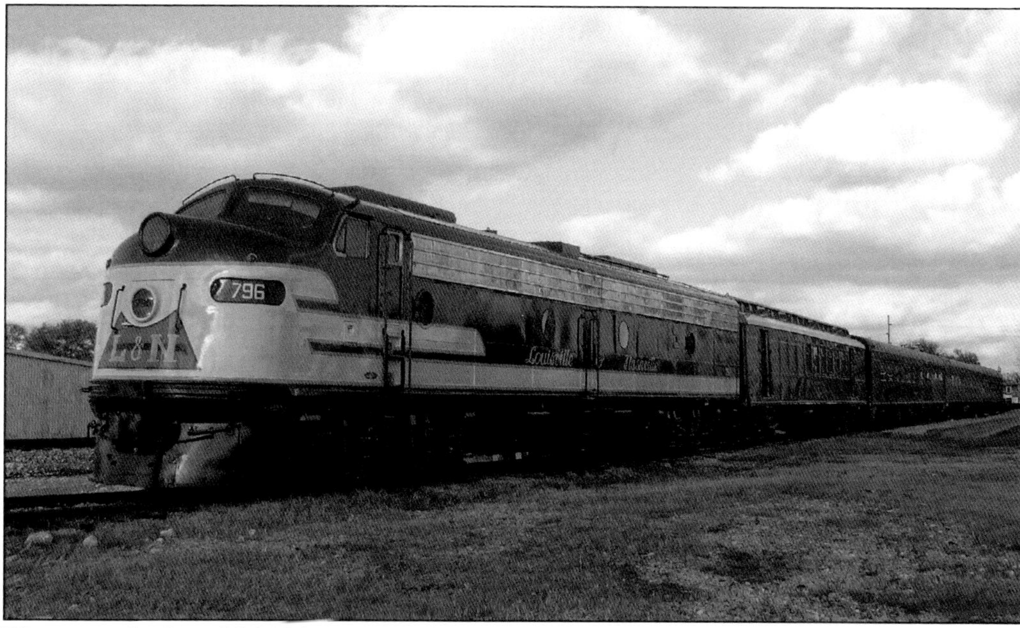

The static display of L&N locomotive 796, L&N Railway Post Office car 1107, L&N *Duncan Hines* dining car, L&N *Towering Pine* sleeping car, and L&N business car 353 are laid out as they would have been on a run down the main line. Following the locomotives, one would have seen "head-end cars" such as baggage cars and post office cars. Next there would be passenger cars such as coaches, sleeping cars, and dining cars. If a business or office car were on the train, it would be the rear car. (Kevin Comer photograph.)

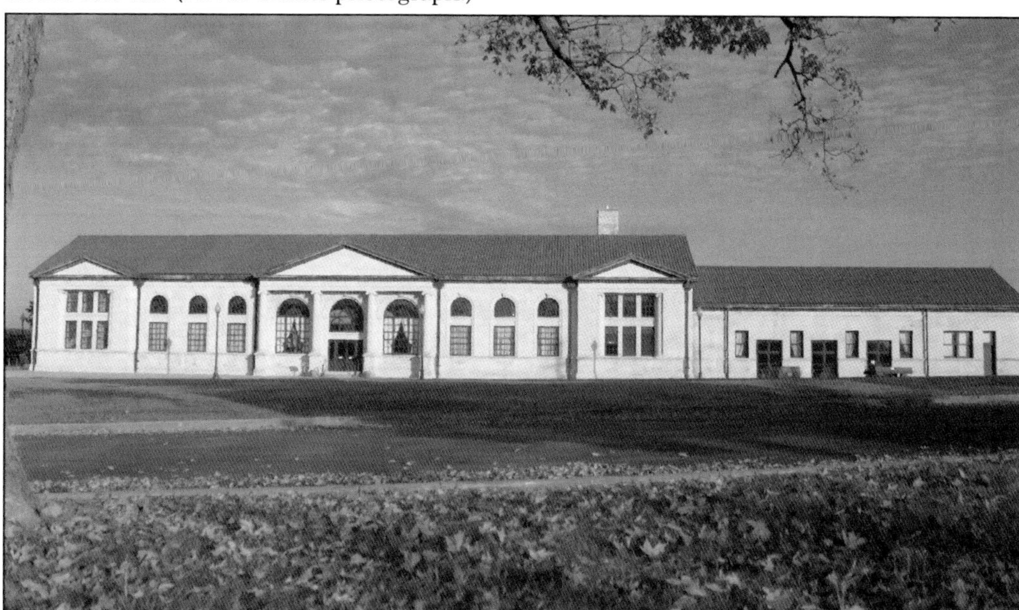

Louisville & Nashville Railroad's passenger station in Bowling Green has become a favorite spot for photographers. On a daily basis, no matter the weather, travelers stop in and spend hours visiting and photographing the classic station, the vintage L&N passenger train consist that looks like it just pulled in for a stop, the old platforms, and even passing trains. (Kevin Comer photograph.)